HOW TO
WIN
CUSTOMERS

HEINZ GOLDMANN

HOW TO WIN CUSTOMERS

HEINZ GOLDMANN

Hawthorn Books, Inc.
Publishers
New York

Contents

It will help to read this first

Please do not read this book like a novel.

Take your time over each chapter and always have a pencil handy so you can mark passages that you consider particularly important. (The ones that are important for you and the ones that are important for someone else may not be the same.)

The examples given in this book have been chosen from many fields. You can translate almost all of them into your problems and your experiences and your line of work. What this book has to tell you is told in these examples from practical life—through them are presented the most important principles of sales technique, tried and tested by practical selling in many countries and many circumstances.

The job of selling is so rich in ever-new variations and ever-new problems, has so many chance happenings, and comes under so many incalculable influences, that situations *may* occur where you can act in contradiction to the proved methods presented in this book and still make the sale. But these exceptions don't prove the principles are not valid for successful selling. Selling is no haphazard game, where you can throw aside principles and experience.

Each chapter in this book begins with four guiding questions and five problems (case studies) from practical sales work. If you can answer the four questions—really answer them—and solve the five problems, you can skip the chapter and go on to the next one. If you feel convinced that you can skip all the chapters in this way, you are either the perfect salesman every firm is looking for or else you are dangerously uncritical of yourself. But you wouldn't even be looking at this book if you thought you knew it all.

After you have read the chapter, you should be able to solve the five problems and to answer the questions—the solutions are either directly in the text or else they emerge from the study of it. The cases are planned to exhibit the practical meaning of the instructions and principles presented in the chapter, and to serve you as a personal check. Make sure, therefore, that you find the solutions.

If you are training salesmen, you can use the problems as themes for discussions, as test questions, and as a basis for role-playing in salesmanship courses and at sales conferences.

The principles and suggestions for successful selling in this book are based on the author's experience of selling and of instructing more than 270,000 salesmen in 16 countries. Since the first issue ten years ago, many new experiences have been added, which has induced us to publish this new and considerably enlarged issue. It should prove helpful also to you.

Geneva, 1973   Heinz M. Goldmann

Dedicated to the creative salesman

Servant of his organisation
friend of his customers
ambassador of his profession

Foreword

Whereas the beginning of the 'technical era' was accompanied by an increasing wide-ranging literature concerning all the individual spheres of production the decisively important question of marketing the ever-growing flood of production was largely left to chance and traditional methods that fell far behind modern developments. This discrepancy has often had very painful results.

That salesmanship can be and must be a fine art in order to keep step with technical production is a fact that has been only recently recognised. It was a long road strewn with obstacles that led from the exclusive reserves of the merchant with 'royal patent' to the star salesman of our days who is familiar with all the possibilities of technical knowledge as well as having a deep understanding of the fascinating psychological inter-reactions between customer and salesman.

It is Heinz Goldmann's great merit that he has presented and illuminated an extensive and many sided complex of topics with excellent clarity in this book, which makes such a valuable contribution to the knowledge and insight of any reader, be he salesman by choice or necessity, be he a beginner or an expert in the field, or occupying the highest position in the industrial orbit.

Professor Dr Ing H. Nordhoff
Managing Director
Volkswagen Ltd, Wolfsburg

What is creative selling?

Is creative selling a kind of magic?

Is it a technique for plumbing the depths of a man's soul?

Has some ingenious brain invented and patented a new set of never-fail selling tricks?

By no means!

Selling is almost as old as mankind. Nothing really new, nothing of outstanding importance has been discovered in this occupation in recent years. Most of what is known has been known for ages. For these reasons, we know only a few principles of fundamental importance in the psychology of selling. All the rules are only variations of these principles. It is the job of all sales education to get across this point properly—much more important and much more correct than looking out new tricks. What are these principles then?

What, then, is creative selling? Here are the 16 areas:

1 *The idea area.* One never sells an article as such—one sells an *idea*. The idea of how it can be used to fulfil the customer's wishes.

2. *The needs area.* Whatever is to be sold must be fitted into certain primary human needs. You can awaken and unfold these needs, but you cannot enforce them.

3 *The feelings area.* Only a few purchases are motivated by reason.

4 *The habit area.* The human resistance to newness and change is the strongest force the salesman meets.

5 *The low-pressure area.* Energetic selling is not the same as high-pressure selling.

6. *The quality area.* No article is bought for its excellent qualities alone.

7 *The price area.* Price, by itself, is rarely the factor that decides whether a sale is made.

8 *The inner conviction area.* Customers generally have only luke-warm feelings about the value of even a good offer. Therefore, the salesman must be convinced that his goods, his firm, and himself are right.

9 *The reasoning area.* Winning an argument with a customer usually means losing a sale. But don't think losing an argument means making a sale, either.

10 *The objection area.* A sales interview in which the prospect doesn't object to any of your points seldom ends in a sale.

11 *The access area.* Many sales efforts never even become sales inter-views.

12 *The selling process area.* The selling process normally takes place in a series of four psychological events that you can recognize, bring about, control, and use. These are Attention, Interest, Desire, and Action : AIDA.

13 *The tactical sequence area.* The salesman can promote the selling process through six tactical sales steps. These accomplish Definition, Identification, Proof, Acceptance, Desire, and Action : DIPADA.

14 *The appeal area.* A slight change of a few words in a single sentence of a sales talk may make or break a sale.

15 *The Conference selling area.* The customer is *not* always right.

16 *The customer relations area.* The traditional dialogue form of the sales conversation is more and more replaced by group confrontation.

One chapter of this book is devoted to each of these areas, one of which, the twelfth, is treated as four sub-areas. In each of these areas, sales are created and sales are lost.

Can *you* become a really good salesman?

Not all those who know something about offering goods to customers—or even about *selling*—can become *real* salesmen: not through training courses, not through books, not through strenuous work. They need these, and more. For they can't become real sales-men unless they have real strength—the strength to face people who don't want to face a salesman, the strength to face and master the demands of a strenuous profession, the strength to find and face their own shortcomings and correct them. Too many people never realise these facts.

Selling is a profession that cannot be learned in the flick of an eyelid. Being tired of some other job doesn't make a man into a salesman; neither does the vague hope of making money in a hurry. Selling demands professional knowledge just as any profession does. It is no job for people who just want to pick up easy money. The selling career is an exacting career and the selling job is hard work.

The salesman's personality is under a pressure that most people can't take. He must feel at ease, cordial and friendly in the presence of people who have little or no wish to see or to listen to him. In the face of their resistance he has to make them aware of needs which they did not realise and on which they quite likely do not want to spend money. He must be tactful and agreeable, yet energetic and firm enough to gain a hearing and to gain it without using methods that will make his prospect regret the interview. This first step to sales success has to be achieved not once but *innumerable* times, day in and day out, month in and month out, year in and year out. These demands on the personality can lead to conflicts that become the real causes of failure for a salesman. But success, not failure, can come to the right kind of man who feels that the selling job has a hold on him, who gives himself up to it gladly, provided he is ready and willing to learn and use the new methods of work that have proved their value. He will know, from his growing experience and satisfaction, how well he is working.

Why does a salesman have less success than he and others expected of him? Why do so many sales managers complain about the ineffectiveness of their salesmen? There are five outstanding reasons:

1 Many salesmen—especially the experienced old-school old-routine men—are dead sure that their 'own method' (which is often very unmethodical) is the only right one. 'Nobody can know any more about selling than I do—I've been selling for blankety-seven years!' On that theory, they ignore the experience and teaching of others—'they know better.'

2 Salesmen can blame every lost sale on something—the customer, the merchandise, the time, the weather, the type of business; they could blame it on themselves, but they rarely do. In consequence they cannot apply analytical self-criticism to find the true cause— they refuse to think of their own mistakes and therefore cannot learn from them.

3 When they escape from an interview without a flat turn-down, some salesmen are happy—so happy they forget that the prospect got rid of them without an order. They hope for the order to-morrow, but tomorrow seldom or never comes.

4 Many salesmen are far worse sales psychologists than they think. They overrate their own insight into human nature, if only because they resist getting any insight into their own personalities. Hence they act from their own over-confidence and use the wrong psychology on their customers and prospects.

5 Many salesmen rely too much on improvising and not enough (or not at all) on planning and system. But experience has shown again and again that systematically planned hard work achieves more in the long run than sparks of genius. Selling is no activity for the merely gifted dabbler. It is a question of gaining factual knowledge and developing abilities as well as achieving a suitable attitude towards your work.

ONE

The idea area: What do you sell?

Can you answer these four questions?

1 What does it mean to 'sell the idea' of an article?
2 Is 'selling ideas' the same as selling intangibles or services?
3 Can you define the task of a salesman in one sentence?
4 Can the 'sale of ideas' principle be used when selling to dealers?

Can you solve the following five problems?

1 Frank Brown sells a line of high-production accounting machines. He is a technical expert, knows his machines thoroughly, presents a good appearance, and inspires confidence. On nearly every call his prospects see him gladly and listen to him attentively. One day, Brown has real news for the controller of a firm that he has visited often—a truly super-efficient machine. 'There's nothing like it on the market,' he says quite truthfully. 'No other machine is as well-designed or as durable as this one.' And he goes on to speak, very informatively as he always does, about the various technical merits of the machine. His prospect doesn't doubt a word Brown says—he even affirms the points Brown is stating. But no sale. Can you see why? What should he do differently?

2 Sheridan Wilkins is a very energetic life-insurance agent. He has been working for fifteen years with up-and-down results. He visits six to eight contacts every day and works on them intensely. As his company sees him, he is somewhat one-sided and on his record he is

no star salesman, but he knows more about insurance than anyone else in the organisation. He can talk for hours about insurance. More and more prospects tell him, however, that they already have their insurance programmes set up and don't want to waste his time discussing them. What's wrong?

3 Howard Robinson, an engineering expert on heavy industrial machinery, has undertaken to represent a big firm manufacturing conveyor belts. Before beginning active selling, he has spent six months in intensive study of his line and compiled a highly illuminating set of comparative specification and performance data. He is now visiting prospects, who are without exception impressed by his compilation of comparative information but cannot be stimulated into any enthusiasm for buying Robinson's conveyor belts. Did Robinson choose the right way?

4 Jerry Pugh, a stock-car race driver when he was younger, lives and breathes cars and motor cycles. He has been an auto salesman several years but has never turned in results to compare with those of his firm's best salesmen; in fact, he is third low on the totem pole and the two below him are pulling up, even though he knows more about cars than any of his colleagues and is vastly more enthusiastic about the cars he sells. Perhaps he is too enthusiastic? Or does he know too much? Could this be an error?

5 Here are four pairs of sales appeals. Which of each pair is the more effective? And why do you think so?

(a) Two travel agencies advertise all-expense tours to Italy, featuring approximately the same places and the same price. The advertising designs and media are both high-grade. The big type in one of them says 'Tour to Italy.' The other suggests: 'Enjoy the Italian Spring.'

(b) Two dishwashers are displayed at a home-appliance show. The poster at one booth says: 'The XYZ Machine—a technical marvel for your kitchen.' At the other booth the poster says: 'Now you can wash dishes with folded arms.'

(c) One electric shaver is offered with the slogan, 'Shave yourself electrically.' Its competitor's slogan is: 'Try shaving in bed!'

(d) The counter card for a face cream announces it as 'The Cosmetic Miracle'—which it is. The counter card for another one assures the ladies: 'You too can have a softer skin.'

(e) A particularly sharp and dented table knife is offered in one Department Store as 'a new extra knife' and in another as 'serve your guests the most tender meat in your home!'

What do people buy?

Anything sold is sold to satisfy some certain need. The article is only a means to an end. Therefore, the salesman should never try to sell the *article* to the customer; his task is to stimulate or create the customer's desire to achieve the objective, with the help of the salesman's goods. The *idea* of the purpose of the article is the primary factor. Not the accounting *machine*, but smooth office work and reliable book-keeping are the selling appeals. Not the insurance *policy*, but the assurance of economic security for the client and his family. Not the *conveyor belt*, but the more efficient handling of materials. Not the *car*, but travel and comfort. Not the *tour*, but fun in the spring. Not the *dishwasher*, but relief from drudgery. Not the *shaver*, but luxury. Not a *face cream*, but beauty. Not the *knife*, but tender meat. The ideas are the real objectives of the purchase.

A customer can be indifferent to accounting machines, insurance, conveyor belts, and cars; but he can hardly be indifferent to the idea of smooth office work, family security, efficient materials handling, or comfortable travel.

How many ideas to each product?

There are as many ideas behind the creation of goods as there are human desires and needs. The goods are inanimate material objects and they can come to life only as they promise to serve the customer and satisfy his desires. The work of a salesman is surely far easier when he sells economy, security, utility, and comfort rather than mere inanimate articles—because the articles are only means to ends and therefore, to the customers, much less important than the ends. Salesmen prove this point every day, for the successful salesman has learned to sell the ideas whereas the also-ran tries to sell goods and forgets about the ideas. What sorts out the successful salesman from the dreary average is the recognition and application of this important fact.

For every object a salesman might try to sell, there are many ideas he can sell. Which idea depends on the customer and the customer's needs. To one man the car idea is investment, to another it is prestige, to still another it is power or fun, to another it is transportation. The salesman must learn to sense and to use the idea appeal which will move the customer.

Sales thinking starts with underlying general appeals, and the salesman should know them. For instance:

You don't sell	*but you sell the idea of—*
Food,	—tasty meals, easily prepared.
Clothes,	—attractive appearance.
Furniture,	—comfort.
Shampoos,	—good looks.
Sweepstake tickets,	—money to spend.
Rakes,	—more fun in gardening.
Corrugated cartons,	—undamaged shipments.
Wallpaper,	—a pleasant room.
Education,	—success in life.
Tour tickets,	—vacation enjoyment.
Sewing Machines,	—fine clothes at lower cost.
Industrial machinery,	—more efficient work.

But how about dealers?

'Sale of ideas' is a fine principle for consumer selling. But salesmen who sell to dealers often object that 'sale of ideas' is not for them. 'My customer buys yard goods and intends to sell them; I can't sell him on looks, security, prestige, or comfort, because he doesn't want to use the stuff himself.'

Is this objection worth anything? No. For the dealer also buys ideas—not dress goods, frying pans, coffee, radios, appliances, soap, or paint. He buys the idea of profit-making. That idea is his primary concern. The more a salesman concentrates on helping the dealer with his sales, the more smoothly and successfully will his own selling go.

Can you stick to the idea?

In the following chapters you will meet several examples of sales in which the capacity to sell the idea of an article as distinct from selling the article is the factor that decides the purchase. Now think of your own work: Do you actually employ the 'sale of ideas' principle in your own day-to-day activity? What do you tell your prospect? What is your chief sales appeal? How do you bring your goods into the selling interview? What are your opening words?

Only very few salesmen completely master the full meaning of this fundamental principle that ideas are what they have to sell. When you master the idea and use the method you will have much better contact with your customers, for the chances are that you are now much like other salesmen in speaking too much about an article and too little about the idea behind it.

Conviction makes the sale

To sell means to *convince* someone of the advantages of the proposition offered to him. The emphasis is on the word *convince*.

Out of this emphasis on conviction and out of the principle of 'sale of ideas' emerges the fact that there is not any significant difference between selling some concrete article and selling an intangible—a service, programme, project contract.

Neither is there any difference between selling a commercial article or intangible on the one hand and 'selling' a non-commercial proposition on the other hand. You promote a club or church picnic, a company dinner, or a holiday activity by stressing the idea of benefit and by making the idea convincing. You do the same things in matters of personal advancement—getting a job, getting a raise or a promotion. In each case, the person who makes the proposition is a salesman who wants to convince someone that his suggestion is worth being accepted. He always sells the idea behind an article or an intangible.

We are all salesmen

If you are a flour-mill owner and push a public campaign to eat more bread—

or if you are a husband who has to persuade his wife that the Bigshots simply must be invited to dinner—

or if you are a boss giving directions to workers—

or a negotiator in a worker-employer settlement—

or a student applying for a fellowship—

—you are a salesman and you have to *convince*.

The ability to convince is one of the most important elements of success in every occupation and in every profession. It is therefore not surprising that top salesmen get on well in life.

In any sphere a project seldom succeeds by itself. It has to be sold. A pre-condition for success anywhere is : selling equals convincing people.

That is why everyone can use sales knowledge. Just think how many good suggestions, projects, intentions, offers and the like have miscarried simply because the person behind them did not possess this selling mentality or could not master it.

The work of the professional salesman demands this attitude to a far greater extent. At the same time he naturally needs to absorb the principle of selling ideas or else he will be unable to produce consistently successful results.

Now, can you answer the four introductory questions and solve the five sales problems?

You don't sell an article—you sell an idea. Every salesman must understand this principle and act accordingly.

The idea area is the first area of creative selling, where sales are made and sales are lost.

TWO

The needs area : Are your goods saleable?

Can you answer these four questions?

1 Do you know the connection between the buyer's needs and his motives for buying?
2 What are 'conditioned needs' and what is the specific place for them in selling technique?
3 Have all buyers the same primary needs?
4 What is the importance of the ego-appeal in selling?

Can you solve the following five problems?

1 An old manufacturing firm launches a new typewriter with a number of important and radical new features intended to inaugurate a new era of typing efficiency. The machine is technically far ahead of any typewriter ever made. But after a determined effort to get it accepted it has to be taken out of production because stenographers and typists object to using it and office managers consequently avoid purchasing it. A real improvement encounters a negative reaction. How can you explain this?
2 An automobile manufacturer offers automatic transmission as standard equipment on his high-priced sports model. Sales fall off as buyers turn to a competitive car with standard gear-shift transmission. Next year, the manufacturer goes back to standard transmission. Do you think this was a wise decision?
3 A restaurant chain takes over an established high-priced

restaurant in a plush winter-sports resort. The place reopens with a big promotion after being refurnished and redecorated in the best modern style, with the finest obtainable food and drinks and a first-class staff at the bar, tables and kitchen. The kind of people who spend money and set fashion come once, then drift off to a nearby place in a converted barn with whitewashed walls and sawbuck tables. Trouble shooters check up and find that the explanation doesn't lie in prices, service or quality of food and drinks. How can you explain the customers' attitude? Does it in any way affect your sales?

4 Morgan Jones sells timekeeping equipment. Several big factories rely on his machines and his recommendations. On the old principle that a happy customer is a good prospect, Jones makes a quiet study of the offices in the factories he serves, and realises that time clocks could help the management tighten up clerical work and improve efficiency. Neither office managers nor company officers dispute the facts of Jones's study, but they don't install his time clocks. One of his colleagues suggests that the difference lies in selling to a businessman rather than an engineer. Is that the problem?

5 George Whitney has called on his entire sales and technical organisation to help him plan his proposal for a turbine replacement needed by a power company. Whitney offers the company one of the best-thought-out plans he has ever proposed, but gets no welcome. Everyone heckles him about some irrelevancy; no fault is found or can be found with the engineering and technical side of the proposal, nor with the price. Whitney eventually realises that being logically right may mean being psychologically wrong. This helps him correct his attitude. Can you draw conclusion from this for your own sales activity?

The salesman and the product

The salesman often has no part in deciding what goods are to be produced, or what is to be the method of manufacture. It is amazing how many companies by-pass the salesmen on this point, and salesmen are quite sure that this practice contributes to the mass of unsold and unsaleable goods that clog the market. They feel that they are often the only people in an organisation who have direct contact with the people who buy the product, the only people who know the customers' needs.

On this point the salesmen may be right. And there is another important strong objection to bypassing the salesmen. For the salesman who has not been consulted has an alibi built into the offer. His test of saleability is simple: 'Do my customers buy it?' If the customers don't buy on the first few selling tries, and if the salesman wasn't consulted, then he says to himself that the product is unsaleable; and he can prove what he says by not selling it. Clearing product design with the salesmen might force them to put more effort into selling and less into excuses.

What do we live for?

For goods to be saleable, the first essential is that they should correspond with these 'primary needs.' Exceptions are goods related to *conditioned needs*—that is, goods that are brought so they can be used in the production, sale, or use of other goods. In this case the salesman offers the goods not to a consumer but to an intermediary with a different set of needs. Even where the goods offered for sale are standard in respect to price, quality, and performance specifications, some needs remain to be gratified by the personality of the salesman, the prestige of the house, the habit of a long-term connection, or the like. (This problem touches on The Feelings Area of Creative Selling, discussed in the next chapter.)

All people, generally speaking, have common aims and desires: for instance, the desires to be rich, to be admired by others, to be successful, to maintain good health. We all strive to achieve the things which give our lives meaning. They are the desires and aims which influence our actions and reactions as individuals and as buyers. We feel needs for the things and the experiences that will satisfy these desires. Those that everyone feels are the ·*primary needs*.

Articles which satisfy the need for greater comfort or convenience (a dishwashing machine, for example), which heighten our attractiveness in the eyes of others (clothes), which save money or labour (a duplicating machine), which promote health (vitamin tablets), which gratify the human play urge (golf clubs)—in fact, all articles which gratify personal desires or needs—always command a ready market. The extent to which this ·essential saleability can be converted into sales depends on the ability of the salesman to master the art of selling the idea behind the goods. To sell the idea he must perceive the key idea that corresponds directly with the primary need of the prospective customer and kindles his desire. He must understand human motivation.

What are our primary needs?

How many primary needs are there?

Theories on this subject are varied. Some people say there are only a few primary needs; others identify a great number. One list names sixty-eight! One names only two! Since scientists disagree, we must employ common sense. Here follows, therefore, a common-sense list of eight more recognisable needs from the point of view of salesmanship.

1 *Self-assertion, ego drive.* This need is served by social status, power, influence, prestige, position, acknowledgement, popularity, competitive success, creative accomplishment, self expression, initiation.

2 *Sex drive.* This need is served by being loved, by good looks, by other kinds of attractiveness, by the sense of being effectively masculine or feminine.

3 *Companionship.* This need is served by having friends, by social contacts, by being likeable, by having and loving a family. It is sometimes called *gregariousness.*

4 *Self-preservation.* The desire for good health and protection against illness is a manifestation of this need.

5 *Acquisitiveness.* Out of this need arise such desires as the collecting urge, the desire to own things, the gambling passion, and the striving for financial success.

6 *Curiosity.* This need gives rise to the thirst for knowledge, the fascination for experiment, and other manifestations that challenge discovery.

7 *Comfort.* Whatever promotes relaxation or permits indolence, gratifies this need.

8 *Security.* Among the security needs are protection against pain, fear, and worry.

The creative salesman learns and understands how to align his selling methods with the primary needs that everyone has. He cannot *create* primary needs—they are called primary because there is no need to create them—but he can arouse them. One of the needs most readily used is the need for social status, and it is almost always possible to arouse the desire for prestige. Almost everything a person buys affects that person's prestige. The manner in which it affects his prestige leads into The Feelings Area of Creative Selling, the subject of the next chapter.

Solution of the five problems

The five problems are now not particularly difficult to solve.

Why was the technically perfect typewriter not an instant success? Because its radical new features called for changes from a familiar system and collided with human inertia. The typists resisted the need for new learning. Moreover, a feared loss of prestige was involved in the almost certain lowering of output during the re-learning period and in the probable increase of errors and blunders during the same period. To some typists, doubtful of their ability to relearn, the new typewriter was a threat to security. Any successful plan to sell the typewriter would have had to anticipate and offset these threats. The best offsets would be convincing demonstrations of ways in which the new typewriter would serve the needs it appeared to threaten.

The automatic transmission in the sports car bucked up against the self-expression, prestige and competitive aspects of the need for self-assertion. The sports-car enthusiast gets prestige out of the speed of his car and his skill in controlling it. The automatic transmission took one whole area of control away from him and thus denied him not only prestige but also self-expression. It also reduced the speed of the car and put the owner down in competition.

The new luxury restaurant was far behind the converted barn in satisfying the need for self-assertion, and it conflicted with the need for comfort. In a resort where everyone could afford the luxury place, there was more social status in the atmosphere of the old barn. The luxury place, if only because of its expensive furniture and decoration, had an uncomfortable tone of dress-up formality in contrast with the informal relaxation of the barn.

The resistance against time clocks in the factory office was based on the employees' attitudes. Management knew, and Morgan Jones eventually learned, that white-collar workers value the fact that they do not punch clocks whereas factory workers do. The time clocks would thus cut into their social status. Selling time control at the office must make allowance for these attitudes.

It is not only the goods which have to fit our primary needs. Obviously the preparation of your sales-talk and the way you put it over does so as well. If you are not careful, his need for self-assertion will cause your customer to put forward logically unimportant objections to your offer and—while you are trying to win him as a customer—treat it with petty, hypercritical arrogance. A suggestion can be *too* good and *too* accomplished and bring out feelings of inferiority in your customer. Feelings of inferiority can take away from customers all pleasure at the idea of an interesting project and induce them to refuse to identify themselves with the proposition.

In all these five cases, the failure had the same cause: the offer hurt or threatened the customer in the area of one (or more than one) primary need. Object of this chapter was to show the importance of a closer and better observation of the motives behind actions and reactions.

The creative salesman will recognise the importance of improving and sharpening his observation of the real motives behind people's actions and reactions. His offer and his presentation have to correspond to our primary needs in order to be successful.

The needs area is the second area of creative selling, where sales are made and sales are lost.

THREE

The feelings area: How does the customer react?

Can you answer these four questions?

1 When do emotional reactions influence the sale of industrial goods?
2 Why are so many emotional reactions interpreted as acts of reason?
3 When two competitors are offering the same merchandise under the same conditions, what factors decide which one gets the order?
4 What help does motivational research provide for day-to-day selling?

Can you solve the following five problems?

1 Two firms are offering corrugated-board cartons to an appliance manufacturer at the same price. Quality is identical. Both carton manufacturers are new to the customer. Both enjoy a good reputatation. Firm B gets the order. What might be the reason?
2 Life-insurance salesmen know that getting a man's signature on a policy application becomes more difficult if the death of the client is mentioned specifically, even though the whole sales interview is an indirect discussion of problems raised by the client's possible death. But if the salesman concentrates on the responsiblities of a family man, on the need for bringing up and educating his children, on his family's need for financial protection and material security in the future, he brings the fountain pen nearer and nearer to the dotted

line. How do you interpret this pattern of reaction and what does it teach you?

3 Toothpaste manufacturers have known for a long time that people do not often buy toothpaste for hygienic or scientific reasons, that all of them and especially women usually choose their toothpaste from other buying motives. Current toothpaste advertising appeals strongly to these other motives. Does this fact suggest any new set of approaches for your own sales efforts?

4 Martin Blake has spent months trying to close a deal for installing fluorescent lighting in a small factory in Ohio. The owner, Abraham Wilson, cannot be brought to the point of decision. He agrees that fluorescent lighting would be more efficient, superior in quality, and less expensive. He doesn't think the price is excessive. He will put it in 'when the time is right.' Blake keeps after him, and Wilson often asks him to come in and talk over some aspect of the project, often an aspect already discussed. Eventually, Wilson suggests 'tomorrow morning.' 'Could we make it next day?' Blake asks. 'I ought to be at Bullister's over in Canton tomorrow morning; he's converting his plant.' 'Did you say Bullister?' 'That's right.' 'His whole plant?' 'The whole plant—no incandescents except fire and emergency lights.' Mr Wilson says, 'Well, I'll be damned,' and asks Blake if he can get in to see him in the afternoon. How should Blake interpret his reaction, and how can he use it to close the sale?

5 A fish-packing firm in Maine is trying to stabilise its business with a foreign customer. The customer buys often but irregularly, and the Main people lose orders quite often to a Norwegian competitor who offers the customer no visible advantages; indeed, the Norwegian's price is a shade higher. The Main firm finally gets its contract for two years ahead by offering the customer a quite simple proposal: 'If you wish we will put your firm's label on our cans, or we will overprint our label to say, "Specially packed in the United States for Blank Fish Import Company".' An offer of this sort is always attractive. Does it suggest a useful approach you might use when you cannot offer the customer any material advantage as against your competitor? Can you further develop this idea? Does one of your competitors use it? If yes, look for another way! If nobody has done it before the idea should be particularly valuable for you. Especially if it is anything but customary in your line of business.

Our reasons and our emotions

It had long been thought that consumers and business men made buying decisions as the result of rational and reasonable thinking. But we now know that buying decisions are linked with our primary needs and that emotions enter strongly into these. Many supposedly rational reactions, closely studied, turn out to be based on acknowledged emotion. Research in motivation gives more and more light in this area. It appears that the reasoning process performs only a censoring, selecting, guiding, interpreting, and hiding function, whereas emotion is the force that drives people to decision. Often, what appears on the surface to be an act of reason is an emotional reaction wrapped up in a 'reasonable' explanation. In interpreting his customer's reactions, the salesman must always be on the alert for such disguises.

Modern Motivational Research, using psychological and psycho-analytical methods, will in future be at least as important to Sales Management as traditional Market Research. The progressive sales-man derives a lot of knowledge from Motivational Research, which often discovers surprising reasons concerning the deeper motives for a buying decision. But quite apart from this, you get a much better perceptive faculty for the reactions of your customers through study of the relevant literature. Many pertinent examples showing the hidden motives for buying habits and buying decisions will train your ability to comprehend irrational currents in the salesman-client relationship.

Sun-ray lamps will improve the health, and that fact is often the stated reason for buying them. The buyer's real reason is often to improve his appearance and give himself greater self-confidence in his associations with others.

Journeys abroad undoubtedly have cultural value and contribute to breadth of experience. People most often make them, however, for the real reason that they want romantic and adventurous experiences.

Quality is said to enter into many buying decisions about clothing, and appearance, style, and fashion enter into quality. But the sales-man who remarks, 'I wish I could wear that suit,' is not appealing to the customer's reason but to his self-esteem—and this appeal often brings on the purchase.

A car is transportation, and may be bought entirely from reasoning based on that fact. But a car is a bright beautiful attract-ive thing that many people want and buy when they could get their transportation at less expense and greater convenience from buses and subways. Moreover, having a car is part of 'keeping up with the neighbours.' A new car impresses people—even if only the owners.

Even factory modernisation, a matter in which sound reasoning should rule the decisions, is sometimes undertaken with motives other than improved technical efficiency. An owner or a board of directors dislikes to fall behind a competitor or even an associate in exemplary modernity. Almost every business man accepts a modernisation operation as evidence of rapid development and growth—which most people want for themselves and for which they envy their neighbours.

We all know how a nationally promoted product may have greater appeal than a similar product not widely publicised. It may have this appeal even though the less-known product is better, especially if the product is exhibited to associates and friends. (But remember also that some people take pride in owning the 'unusual,' or 'rare,' or 'primitive.')

Many people who should own a 17-inch television set, to fit their pocketbooks and their living-rooms, strain their budgets and crowd their homes with a 24-inch or 30-inch behemoth because the big one conveys a greater impression of elegance and wealth. Conversely, women often buy shoes too small for their feet, or wear dainty shoes where they need rugged ones.

Special sales offer an opportunity for reasoned and thrifty buying, but we all know that many people haunt sales and buy things they don't need or even want because they can't resist bargains.

A prospect may get greater emotional satisfaction from turning down a too-aggressive or over-confident salesman than from accepting the sound offer the salesman makes. Sometimes in tough, protacted negotiations it turns out that it was the spark of human contact that was lacking, and many experienced salesmen can tell happy tales of how this was established by some small concession, a surprise phone call from a friend—either of the salesman or of the customer—or a friendly gesture or a sudden discovery of mutual interests, and how this was the turning-point that made the sale.

Rivalry and pride of person and organisation enter into business decisions. Mr Wilson didn't want his factory to be old-fashioned alongside Bullister's. The Blank Fish Import Company gained and enjoyed prestige from having its own name on the canned fish it imported.

An appeal to personal feeling, discreetly introduced, can frequently help the buyer to settle his decision.

The personal element

When a buyer's decision doesn't fit business common sense, as when the appliance firm took the poorer carton offer in the first problem of this chapter, it is usually realistic to look for some personal reason that contributed to the decision—perhaps a reason for the other man, perhaps a reason against yourself. Perhaps the salesman admired the tasteful new decorations in the office and mentioned in passing that he had been to the same business school as the buyer. It would hardly be surprising if in the end they talked more about the school than about business. It follows that the buyer would transfer the good impression he had of his former school friend to Firm B which he unconsciously identified as the more solid of the two contractors. He would also be more inclined to believe in delivery promises from a school friend.

The insurance men learned, before there were any psychologists, that a customer with his mind on his death is indecisive and procrastinating; but a customer with his mind on his family and proud of what he can do for them in spite of any misfortune is easy to talk to and ready to listen.

A salesman can often improve his accomplishment by giving more consideration to human inclinations and weaknesses, watching more alertly for symptoms of the customer's emotions and feelings. In short, he should pay closer attention to the personal element in his selling activities. Devoting personal attention and effort to the customer releases appreciation and interest. It creates, in almost every situation, some friendly disposition and readiness to co-operate on the customer's part. There are many personal matters the salesman can bring up without effusiveness or undue familiarity. He can speak, for instance, of the customer's hobbies, his successes, his interests, his working methods, his views on business matters, the progress of his undertakings, and many other things. These topics are not buttons to push for a sure sale, but they often break the ice. Every good salesman has seen a sulky or preoccupied customer thaw, slowly or suddenly, when he realises the salesman is really interested in some feature of the business organisation that gives the customer pride—how he got it started, what difficulties he licked, where he got the idea.

Getting along with people

A very successful salesman once declared that he could win over the most obstinate prospect if only he could succeed in getting him to speak of himself or his work. Every salesman should read Dale Carnegie's book, *How to Win Friends and Influence People*. It will suggest many good ideas for him and furnish a useful philosophy for a selling career.

Have you, yourself, thought of the many small services that a salesman can perform for his customers? He can keep them up-to-date about many technical developments. He can give them whatever information he has about current business conditions and new ideas for promoting business. He can suggest interesting reading matter, either for business or relaxation. He can always, of course, invite him to a show or ball game or a round of golf, provided there isn't any implication of a cheap bribe. He can, without servility, often attend to an errand for the customer. He can even—with caution —sometimes call the customer's attention to a good buy that may work against the salesman's immediate interest. Such a simple thing as saving foreign stamps for a customer's philatelic son has been known to help build a lifelong business connection. But always remember—such services and attentions must be small and natural, not exaggerated or inappropriate, and above all not unethical efforts to 'buy' an order.

Selling is rendering service. The salesman must want to render service, and he will find opportunities every day. His foremost service, however, is to make sure he and his firm fulfil promises and meet delivery schedules and otherwise see to the customer's business satisfaction. This service attitude, together with a lively interest in other people as people, will create the proper 'climate' without which every sales attempt is a strenuous and unremitting struggle. Only in such a climate is the customer conditioned to let himself be influenced—by a good salesman with a good product. Without these last two requisites, no psychological methods of any kind will help.

But in all selling transactions emotions of one kind or another play a part. Let us look at ourselves, for we salesmen are also customers. Do we not know certain stores and certain sales-people that we find uncongenial and avoid, even if avoiding them costs us time and money?

People react more psychologically than logically. To recognise this requires self-knowledge and empathy. Why do you go to the movies, why do you dance, why do you travel during your vacation, why do you overtake cars when driving, why do you read magazines, why do you enjoy sports, why do you look at yourself in the mirror? Try to discover your own, real, deeper motives. It will help you in your sales activity.

We know, then, that no one can calculate mathematically how a customer will react. Accordingly, the salesman must study closely the individual and his emotions. By doing so he will soon learn that a person is more easily influenced through his emotions than through his intellect. Therefore, seek to discover the human being in your customer.

The feelings area is the third area of creative selling, where sales are made and sales are lost.

FOUR

The habit area: The salesman, innovation and the power of routine

Can you answer these four questions?

1 How should a new product be presented?
2 Is the buying habit a positive or negative factor in selling?
3 When a customer has not responded after several calls, is it a good idea to switch salesmen or perhaps to have two men work together on him?
4 What risks does an aggressive sales campaign create when a new product is being introduced?

Can you solve the following five problems?

1 Stanley Bird represents a steel company that has an excellent grade of steel for razor blades. He has worked long and vainly to interest a razor-blade manufacturer who continues to use a competitor's slightly inferior steel. Bird can give the customer better service, and prices are the same. But Bird's competitor has supplied the customer since way back when, and if he doesn't get the order when he expects it a phone call will bring it in. Bird, trying to dislodge this established supplier, has the toughest task a salesman ever meets. Which?
2 The manufacturer of a high-grade line of kitchenware keeps getting consumer inquiries for its pots and pans from a high-income small town whose only hardware dealer simply won't put the line into his store. Instead, he carries a line that is famous for being out-

right junk. Despite the national advertising and the consumer inquiries, he tells salesman after salesman that he has always stocked the inferior line and sold it profitably for twenty years and sees no reason for changing. This is a lunatic buying policy, but how would you go about influencing the dealer to change it?

3 The E Steel company perfects a new type of deep-hardenable chromium steel so far superior to anything else that selling it to manufacturers should amount to nothing more than writing the orders. But the manufacturers don't see it that way. Throughout the country, the production chiefs of the smaller firms are especially obdurate. When a sales conference gets after the reason for the resistance, it turns out that the salesmen most successful in selling the new steel are those who were least aggressive and played down its revolutionary character when they were introducing it to customers. What's the explanation? What conclusions can you derive from it?

4 The K Company has built up a good business supplying imported perfumes to soap manufacturers. It has also perfected a complete line of domestic perfumes, every bit as good as the imported material and perhaps better, which it offers to a customer who could save thousands of dollars by using it. No response. The K salesman offers to guarantee the costs of a trial batch of soaps using the new perfumes. Nothing doing. The perfume buyer says he would try it, but 'somebody else' opposes it. Even the general manager refers to 'somebody else.' The K top management explores the problem with their opposite numbers in the soap company's brass, and it is still 'somebody else.' What's behind all this stubborn nonsense?

5 From time to time one or another manufacturer launches a new brand of cigarettes, but the new brands seldom go over unless there is some outside helping factor (as when filter brands got a big play from people frightened about cancer). A manufacturer who found the public tiring of his established line had the problem studied carefully and turned up the fact that a fairly large number of people are always meaning to try the new brand when they buy their next pack. But more than half of these people forget all about it when they step up to the counter, and automatically ask for their old brand. What can the cigarette manufacturer's salesmen do about this?

The force of habit

There are countless examples of how the force of habit wrecks sales efforts. There are also many examples of enterprises that survive through the force of customer habit although they have a poor sales force or practically none. Their customers are used to buying from a familiar supplier, and the suppliers make more money than they deserve to—but not for ever.

In some lines of business (particularly in the tradition-bound heavy industry) the knowledge of the habit-factor leads to the standstill of any real selling effort. The supplier of a regular customer trusts his 'faithfulness'—and his competitor gives up. 'There's no sense in trying—they buy from B for the last twenty years!' Fortunately, sooner or later another energetic salesman will prove how wrong it is to speculate on the continuous numbness of customer reactions. In this connection, of course, the risk of a wrong purchase plays a role too.

Routine buying undoubtedly has some advantages to the customer. It saves a lot of trouble and avoids the risks that are always associated with any kind of rearrangement. By setting on one supplier, one kind of material, and one practice of ordering and receiving, a purchasing agent does indeed reduce some risk and much effort. But unless he reviews and revises his routines from time to time, he misses opportunities. He is in obvious trouble if his routine was fixed on a poor decision at the beginning. But even if it was a good decision five years back it isn't necessarily a good practice today—new and better suppliers turn up, market conditions change, old suppliers often fail to keep up standards. Nevertheless, we all need routines, and our routines and our customers' routines often lag behind new developments and modern needs. For this reason if no others, salesmen will always be encountering habit-conditioned sales resistance. And because this kind of sales resistance can be very strong, manufacturers and producers often do not dare to risk introducing valuable new ideas and new products. Habit-conditioned sales resistance must be taken into account whenever a manufacturer plans to invest money in a radical innovation.

Resistance to change can be due to the following reasons:
1 Risk
2 Habit
3 Satisfaction with present conditions
4 Cost
5 Criticism

People are afraid of risk; avoid effort; do not wish an improvement of present conditions; are opposed to the direct and/or indirect costs connected with the change; have a dislike for self-criticism or criticism by the surroundings or by the old supplier which may set in after the change.

The salesman must consider these reactions, he must recognise and influence them in order to sell novelties or items which are new to one particular customer successfully.

How innovations should be presented

Innovations, as a rule, can break into the market only in two situations. The salesman has no difficulties when innovation is the very idea behind what he is selling—as in women's fashions or in articles that people buy because they are novelties. But technical and similar innovations must be portrayed as *simplifications* or *developments* that will fit existing use habits, rather than as radical new departures. The less a habit must be changed, the better the chance of winning customers. Some people, of course, like innovation, and salesmen tend to hope that novelty or innovation contributes strongly to the buying motive; but in many instances it is the salesman who likes the novelty because it gives him something new to talk about. The customer may not want to hear about it.

You, the salesman, should therefore show the customer that the new article fits directly or indirectly into an existing habit. You must convince the customer that you are in no way using him as a guinea pig. He will welcome every detail you can offer to show that the testing period is over, that the new product or idea is practicable. He is likely to be favourably impressed if you can tell him that leaders in his line of business are using or have accepted the new item. But above all you should be ready to make it clear to the customer that adopting the innovation demands no special effort, not even during the transition or re-education period. You must be in a position to offer the customer and his personnel every imaginable help—instructions, directions, service, both initial and continuing—in the introduction and early use of the innovation. And in offering the innovation you cannot be too careful to avoid any remark or any sales point that the customer could take as a criticism of his previous methods or purchasing arrangements, or as a hint that he is old-fashioned. Customers are more sensitive in such matters than many salesmen realise—especially old-fashioned customers.

Another problem arises when the cost of adopting the innovation is likely to be high. In such situations the salesman wants, and should have, authority to arrange for old equipment or old merchandise to be taken off the customer's hands, either by trade-in or by arrangements to sell it elsewhere. A purchasing agent is naturally reluctant to take responsibility for initiating a red-ink entry on his firm's books; even if the intention is to achieve future benefits, it's hard to start off with what looks like a loss.

Trying to force people

Don't try to force people to change their habits. You can't force them. If you could, you might be rendering a useful service to society; but you can't, and if you try, you won't make sales.

The typical customer of habit, such as the razor-blade firm that wouldn't listen to Stanley Bird, just lets the orders go on and on to the established supplier while the outsider breaks his heart and gets nowhere. This kind of problem is hard for even the most experienced salesmen to lick. But it can be licked—if the salesman has the patience of an angel and the persistence of a gold prospector. In such a situation, time and your competitor's habits are on your side. Sooner or later, the insider slips up and neglects his customer on some important occasion. Meantime, you can be making ready by studying the problem to find what exceptional advantage or special service you can offer the customer. You must offer something—maybe price, maybe quality, service, prestige, technical assistance; one or more of the scores of buying appeals must be presented to show where and how your offer is a better one than your competitor's. Using these, you can at some time induce the customer to give you at least one trial order.

Even if the competitor doesn't slip up and hand you your opportunity, you may be able to suggest that it isn't good policy to be dependent on one single supplier. Even if the buyer-supplier bond is old friendship you may be able to establish yourself also as the buyer's friend, although that process is a long and strenuous one in most cases. But the customer should never be asked to do anyone a favour or give anyone a break, except himself.

When should salesmen be switched?

It would be a good idea for the salesman in Problem 3 to make suggestions to the customer for improvements in his production or sales. If after a number of visits to a customer it is apparent that a salesman is making no progress a change of salesman is something that can have good results. The salesman should have help from his company's technical people, and indeed, in more and more companies, he is getting it today. Properly trained and directed, the technical man can help open and keep open many doors that would be closed to the unassisted salesman.

Long familiarity may create a poor selling situation. After years of contact, the customer and the salesman may come to know each other too well. They have nothing new to exchange, no more to learn about each other; nothing exciting happens when they meet. Perhaps they bore each other. Even worse, perhaps they are too friendly; for a buyer can and sometimes does turn down a good friend, being sure he will 'understand,' in a situation where a businesslike and relatively detached competitor presses for the order and gets it.

Sometimes the sales manager can usefully come into the picture; the mere fact that he *is* the sales manager may impress the customer enough to loosen up his habit of refusing to buy. Certainly the sales manager should have some greater experience than the salesman he is managing. And the manager (or even some other salesman) may have just the right personal manner to appeal to just this customer. No salesman, however capable he may be, can be the right contact for *all* customers. In the case in question the sales manager happened to be an engineer and was able to put his special knowledge to the service of his grateful customer.

The kitchenware manufacturer switched salesmen until finally one of them got through to the stubborn small-town hardware man. This man started off by commenting on the dealer's new delivery truck, which was indeed something special in the community. This led the dealer into exhibiting his pride in the store's modern and up-to-date layout, equpiment, and stock. The dealer was pulling customers away from other retailers in near-by towns, and was proud of doing it not by price cutting but by offering good service and good merchandise. That opened up the situation! The salesman suggested tactfully and indirectly that his firm also offered good service and high-grade kitchen-ware, and that dealers could switch as reasonably as dealers' customers. Before long he was talking about advertising allowances and demonstrating the advantage of his line to the dealer's store clerks—and writing up the first order.

The delicate touch in influencing others

When a sales force has the job of introducing new goods that do inevitably alter existing habits or methods of working, the too-aggressive selling techniques may be dangerous. The salesman who can offer something that is a genuinely revolutionary advance finds it hard to state his good sales points without directly or indirectly bringing attention to the shortcomings of the customer's hitherto excellent methods and practices. They may not even have been excellent, but the customer has found them workable and very likely has been proud of them. At the beginning of the sales interview, he doesn't want to be convinced that his methods are inferior to the new methods and practices the salesman's proposition will require. Nothing is more difficult than convincing a person about something when he doesn't want to be convinced about it—or when he does want not to be convinced about it.

In such a situation, you cannot hurry your customer. You must take your time and develop the new idea step by step and very carefully and tactfully. Before your customer can make a decision in favour of anything revolutionary, he must compare his old methods with your new methods, must see the need for a change and the advantage of making the change, and must above all, want to make the change. It is your job, as a salesman, to bring about this want. If, therefore, your customer is satisfied with what he has, you must lead him to feel he will be even better satisfied with what you offer.

The delicate touch might succeed in getting the new perfumes a trial. The 'somebody else' who has to be convinced is more than likely an old and experienced perfume expert, the kind of man the soap company might find harder to replace than the chairman of the board. Neither top management nor anybody else wants to force an issue with such a key technical specialist. So the perfume company needs to get him on to their side. In the situation described, where the two company managements are in contact, the perfume people could arrange to have the perfume expert sent to the perfume plant to 'investigate' the new line (always provided the salesman hasn't got himself too hoplessly cornered). His investigation might include a study of the production methods, and he might even turn up some suggestions the perfume company could well use. In any case the perfume expert would be participating in the approach to the revolutionary change, and could regard the new perfumes as a line on which he himself had worked and as something in a sense his own.

Through such an approach, the customer is made a 'spiritual partner' in the seller's proposition. In this good relationship climate, he can allow himself to be convinced because he wants to be convinced.

The cigarette-brand situation provides a massive proof of the difficulty of changing buying habits, even when the customer is somewhat ready to make a change and has decided to make it. Combating this kind of relapse into habit is an almost impossible job for the salesman of the cigarette manufacturer if only because he doesn't come face to face with the habit-chained customer. The customer must be kept to his new decision by reminders and selling appeals at the point of sale. The retailer can't be asked to present these orally; he can scarcely discriminate between the old and new cigarette brands. So the reminders need to be advertising displays and other things that will help the buyer *not* to say automatically, 'Gimme a pack of the Old Brand.'

To summarise: Do everything you can to reduce the customer's risk, assume the hardship of change for him (your customer's service). Show him how—through your proposal—he can become even more satisfied than in the past (or make him dissatisfied with the present situation—but carefully). Calculate with him the cost involved, and protect him from criticism from his surroundings.

One more practical experience: it is often easier to hold the sales conversation in a 'neutral' place, or in your office, where the importance of the change is not so apparent to the customer as in his own surroundings. Factory visits, clients courses and expositions can favour a productive sales climate.

Habit is a strong sales blocker. Don't crash into it head-on. When you are introducing an innovation, plan your sales interview carefully. Try not to make the new idea sound 'too new.' Don't find fault with what your customer is currently doing or using. Make it evident that you recognise the sound judgement that guided him. Make him your partner. Make him feel good in your company. Only in these ways can you help him to get out of old habits. Don't try to play the saviour—let him be the 'smart' one.

The habit area is the fourth area of creative selling, where sales are made and sales are lost.

FIVE

The low pressure area: Avoid high-pressure selling

Can you answer these four questions?

1 Do you know the difference between forceful selling and high-pressure selling?
2 Is all high-pressure selling harmful?
3 What connection is there between high-pressure selling and salesmen's earnings?
4 Is truth alone enough to have your customer believe you?

Can you solve the following five problems?

1 A lumber dealer's salesman, Mike Brewster, has been talking to a residential contractor about a shipload deal in framing and siding for a new subdivision. Mike realises that his customer is also talking to a competitor, and his ulcers start to gnaw. Price and terms are pretty well fixed by trade custom, so the decision pivots on delivery time. 'Is May 15 okay?' The prospect frowns. 'Well, would May 1 help?' The order is placed for May 1 delivery, and now Mike really has something to worry about because he had his neck out even with May 15. When he wires the order to the mill, he knows he's in trouble—the mill can't ship till June! Order cancelled, and customer soured for keeps. Could this contact have been kept alive?
2 Martin Miller has been trying to close a deal with his customer for a heavy sheet-metal press to replace one that is near wearing out. The customer puts off the decision and doesn't seem much impressed

by Miller's proposition in any case. Miller pushes harder; he has warned the customer that delivery will take about six months; now he says the plant is getting backlogged with orders and he soon can't offer delivery in less than twelve months. The customer says he can't decide now—come back next month. By next month, Miller has forgotten his story. When can he deliver? In six months, he says. The customer hasn't forgotten the twelve-month scare talk, and pauses a moment to think about it. Miller goes into a panic and comes up with a dodge from an old book on selling tips. ('Make a special offer in the final stage of your selling talk if it's the only way to save the sale.') So he proposes : 'How about winding this thing up? If you place the order right now, we'll take five per cent off the quoted price.' Now the customer says he'll have to have time to think about it and suggests Miller leave—but he doesn't invite him to phone back for a decision. Miller figures the order is lost, but he doesn't know whether this is worse than another similar situation, when he did phone the prospect back and was told that a competitor had made a better proposition and did Miller want to offer a little more off the quoted price? What conclusion do you derive from this example?

3 Claud Johnson has brought in an order from a small cigar dealer for the biggest and most complex cash register his firm makes. His sales manager wants to know how this little one-man shop can use this expensive and big-capacity unit. Why didn't Johnson sell him a medium-size model that would do everything he needed? 'He asked for this one!' Johnson explodes. 'I'm a salesman, not a guardian!' Is Johnson right or wrong?

4 The VV Chemical Company makes the best varnish on the market for office-building floors. 'I buy it in truckload lots,' says a purchasing agent. 'And they treat me like a beggar. I don't want a letter from the chairman of their board, but by golly they're not doing me any favour, even if they act like it. I'm going to try a drum of X's varnish, and I'll use it if it's half as good as VV.' All very successful companies are liable to such an attitude. What is your situation?

5 An auto salesman listened helplessly to a cold and polite voice on the telephone: 'No, thank you. I'm not in the market for a new car. When I want one I'll study the specifications and get in touch with the dealer I choose. I had a call like this last year and I am sorry I let myself in for a very poor deal. So I've made up my mind not to talk to salesmen. Sorry.' A person who has been injured as this man was doesn't forget it. Now, another salesman and another dealer must suffer for the bad selling of a competitor. This case of

high-pressure selling illustrates the consequences that can follow the irresponsible or incompetent activity of one salesman. A customer's single negative experience can outweigh a dozen positive ones. For this reason all selling organisations should be concerned to see that their competitors as well as themselves train their sales personnel properly and apply decent sales methods. How would you answer this disgruntled buyer?

How high-pressure selling started

The heyday of high-pressure selling was around the time of the First World War. Something about the times or the business atmosphere built up the belief that the ideal salesman was the one who could *break down* any resistance, *overcome* any buyer, sell anything to anybody. The customer? Let him look out for himself. Sales managers coached their salesmen in aggressive, high-pressure selling. They were to *sweep away* all forms of sales resistance, by hook or crook, even if it meant employing extreme methods—extremely dirty, that meant, in many cases. The system resembled a psychological prize fight, with the customer the opponent to be *knocked out*. The idea was to *fight* for the order and that the end justified the means. If the customer eventually got satisfactory goods, he would soon forget or forgive the way they were sold to him. If he didn't forget or wouldn't forgive, never mind—the salesman might never see him again, or another salesman could be assigned to him, or competitors X and Y would interchange each other's disgruntled customers.

This kind of reasoning blew up in the sales managers' faces. Customers developed guards no one could get through. Some refused to see any salesmen. Others blacklisted certain people or companies. Buyers let themselves be caught once, but not much oftener.

This damage to confidence between salesman and customer has greatly injured the professional reputation of salesmen and has made the selling task extremely difficult. There was only one way to re-establish confidence and that was to shift to low-pressure selling. Low-pressure selling is consistent with the business ethics to be expected from a decent salesman who knows that all his activities must benefit his customer and his business community if they are to benefit himself. Sales organisations in increasing numbers have accepted this professional and ethical outlook and reputable organisations have planned their sales training to guide their salesmen towards sales morality. Today's buyer is not seen as a fool to be victimised, and every salesman must realise the fact—if not for ethical reasons then because the buyers are nowadays trained for their function and are intelligent and realistic individuals.

Some sales instruction—too much of it, for any at all is too much —aims even today at the concept of the old-fashioned customer who was the salesman's proper prey. Salesmen who embrace this concept not only underrate but invariably offend any buyer who is exposed to the trade tricks they have learned through this approach. This kind of sales method is aimed at a kind of backward individual who no longer exists. Increasingly, today's buyer is smarter than today's salesmen.

Sales morality plus forceful selling

The Number One principle of sales morality is : *a sale which does not benefit the customer harms the salesman.*

This principle does not forbid the salesman to engage in forceful selling. Forceful selling and high-pressure selling are not the same thing. Selling is not easy, and the salesman must be forceful and tough. He should apply all his skill to the selling job, and use all honest means to induce the customer to buy from him. He cannot give up even though he finds all doors closed against him on his first approach. With all this forcefulness and toughness, however, he must realise and never forget that it is his proper function to serve the customer. He has enduring success only if he translates this principle into practice in a way that satisfies the real needs of the customer. 'One-time business' is bad business. Selling is the art of 'how to win customers'—not how to overpower the customer.

If the salesman should discover, in the course of conversation, that his offer can be of no benefit to the customer, he should not push the offer. He should most particularly not push it if the customer is inclined to place an order because he trusts the salesman and is well disposed towards him. Orders of this kind are in fact akin to high-pressure selling in that they do not benefit the customer. They can have heavy repercussions, such as bad debts, cancellations before delivery, complaints that cannot be adjusted, costly return allowances. The salesman should always conduct his selling interviews so that he can meet the customer again and again with completely good conscience. This is the best way for him to judge whether he has used high-pressure selling or not.

A red light for sales executives

High-pressure selling methods kick back on the seller, as was shown in the introductory examples of this chapter. But the harm they do is not always evident at the time it is done. For instance, a high-pressure salesman who covers a large area can turn in a whacking big volume of orders for a long time—until he starts around his territory again. Striking and unnaturally big orders from any salesman, especially any new salesman, should flash a red light for the sales manager, and bring on an inquiry to see whether they have been obtained through high-pressure methods.

The sales manager, however, should seek to prevent or discourage high-pressure methods, not merely to discover and get rid of the salesmen who use them. First in this connection, he should avoid using high-pressure methods on his crew or else his salesmen will use high-pressure methods on their customers. Again, he should plan the salesmen's compensation so that they are not tempted to resort to high pressure. For the salesman in a money pinch is tempted to get the sale and never mind the future. The pinch may be felt because he is on a straight commission or on an inadequate salary-plus-commission basis. Or it may be felt because he is rushed into the field without adequate training or introduction. Or it may be felt because he is expected to turn in orders before he has time to make a decent acquaintance with the customers in his territory.

As a rule, good sales work begins to show only after a certain period of working in. The efforts and value of a salesman should therefore be judged, always, on a long-term basis. Customers who re-order regularly over a long period are valuable to the house and the salesman's pay should contain a recognition of this fact, perhaps in the form of bonus over and above commission or salary on business from such customers. Salesmen should also be encouraged to call on customers within a reasonable time after getting an order, first because there is always a reasonable chance for repeat business and second because salesmen aren't likely to try high-pressuring a man they know they must see again in the near future.

Rate your salesman, and pay him, according to how well he does his two jobs: to win customers and to keep customers.

Twenty suggestions on avoiding high-pressure selling

1 *Think honestly of your customer's needs.* Resist the temptation to sell him the most expensive article you have, or he will learn that

your recommendations are made in your interest, to get your sales figures up as high as you can, without reference to his needs. If you are going to make an assortment of offers, don't start with the most expensive; the high price may kill the sale for good. But when the expensive article is the one the customer really needs, be candid and tell him so.

2 *Pay attention to the little fellow.* Don't grow indifferent or contemptuous towards small customers. Business firms may spend large sums telling the public about their service policy and other public-relations attitudes (even though they may not be quite sure what 'service' they mean). Help your firm to get value for its public-relations money. Identify yourself with the idea of service to the customer. When you serve him you help yourself; after all, *your* salary or commission depends on what *he* can buy, and small customers become big customers as they prosper. In many cases, service can pinpoint sales opportunities. For instance, consider the commuter who stops at the suburban garage for a few gallons of gas to fuel his station jalopy—there's little profit in a year's business of this sort, but when the jalopy is about to break down the garage that does the servicing is first in line for the repair job or for the sale of another car.

Never forget that small customers are often sensitive. They are quick to suspect indifference and they are bitterly wary of high-pressure selling methods.

Do not forget, either, that the customer who places a small order may be testing you. He may have a big order in the offing. Smart purchasing agents often test a new supplier with a small order, and very likely some of your best accounts started off with a string of small orders.

The customer is the reason, object and goal of all your efforts. It is his attitude which decides about success or failure of a salesman. Not your Company—your customers pay your income!

'Sell' this mentality to the non-selling Departments too. You will help in creating a 'sales-positive' atmosphere which serves the interests of everybody. Have you ever made an effort in this direction?

3 *Be fair to your customer.* Don't misuse a monopoly or any other strong market position. If in times of scarcity or great demand you conduct your selling activity as a distribution of favours, time will bring its revenge. Your monopoly may be broken, a seller's market can change into a buyer's market abruptly, restrictions on goods may be lifted, the market must change sooner or later, and if it doesn't change then substitute products are bound to appear. No

salesman and no establishment can live long without the good will of his customers. Whether a buyer is begging you for goods or you have to sell hard to get an order, always let him have the feeling that he is your valued customer. This obvious principle is violated all too often. But it enforces itself. The time and trouble expended to keep on good terms with customers are an investment that will pay handsome dividends in the long run.

4 *Stick to the truth.* Avoid making promises that you can't make good, in the effort to induce the customer to buy. Promise less than you can do, rather than more; then any surprise you give the customer will be pleasant and he will be grateful. If you agree to a delivery schedule you cannot keep, you may get an order but you may never get another one. In selling industrial goods especially, you must be scrupulous and precise in your undertakings regarding delivery, for your customer bases his arrangements and his promises on yours. If he must remind you of your words, they will sound much more firm in his mouth than you may have intended when you said them. He may have put the words in your mouth—so don't be trapped by the customer who wants to understand more than you intended to promise. If a customer interprets what you have said as meaning more than you meant, restate your proposition to prevent misunderstanding and disappointment. If he deceives himself, he will be angry at you—not at himself. Remember that you don't make a sale on the basis of what you say but on the basis of what the customer believes. So don't stand quiet while he lets his hopes lie to him.

Whatever the immediate situation, it is never your statement but rather your customer's trust in you that decides whether you get the order. So be trustworthy. If you can't promise delivery when he wants it, give him a promise he can rely on and sell the idea of dependability. If you are sure it's a date you can't miss, maybe your firm can improve on it, and perhaps you can tell the customer of this possibility. Perhaps you can suggest that the slow delivery date is the result of your product's being supremely good and therefore in demand; an automobile ad campaign was once built around the slogan, 'The car worth waiting for!'

5 *Stick to the point.* Plan your sales interview and the logical line of your sales talk, and stick to it. You need to be flexible, but don't wander or ad lib. Improvised sales talks nearly always lead to high-pressure selling. Unplanned sales talks are forgotten. Protect yourself and free your mind from memory details by making careful notes of every selling interview and the points that were discussed. Include in these notes any special resistances and any sales appeals

that particularly aroused the interest of your customer. With the aid of such records you can aim your future sales interviews to hit the target. Unfortunately, most salesmen either make no notes, or incomplete notes, or irrelevant notes. But professional buyers invariably makes notes—complete, full, and relevant. Their notes put them on top of salesmen who don't take notes.

6 *Allow your customer his freedom.* Avoid tie-in selling. A customer never likes being told that he can have the merchandise he wants only if he takes a stipulated quantity of something else that he doesn't want. Tie-in sales may move some merchandise, for a little while, but they don't win customers.

7 *Be a gentleman.* Avoid acting like a 'supersalesman.' The storybook supersalesman is a Go Getter (he doesn't care a damn about anybody); he's Good and He Knows It (he's a bluffer) : he has A Smooth Line of Talk (a mishmash of wheedling nonsense). All this is supposed to impress colleagues and customers, and some green salesmen actually try the act. In one way, it does impress customers—the wrong way. A good salesman should talk well and to the point, not ramble or chatter. If he really knows what he's selling and talking about, he can express all the essentials in a few words. If he does, what he says carries weight and increases his chance to influence the customer and make the sale.

The salesman should study the needs of his customer, with the customer's help. Thus he is in an essentially advisory position, and can propose a solution. The proposal is more likely to be satisfactory if the salesman has kept clear of forming any preconceived opinion as to what the customer should do. By listening to the customer and asking sensible questions the salesman gets into contact with him and gains his trust. It is very dangerous to exhibit a headlong attitude of 'decisiveness' and make the customer feel that his role is to submit to a fate the salesman has planned for him. Never give your customer the idea that you are firmly resolved to subdue him whatever may happen. An overly confident salesman gives the customer the possibility to show off, to oppose, to criticise, to defend another opinion, to prove that he cannot be influenced. Do you sometimes see this reaction in your customers? If yes, you ought to hold your temperament back in a hurry!

The customer should always have the happy feeling that he is buying and not the uneasy feeling that the salesman is selling. When a customer says, 'You're quite a salesman,' he isn't necessarily offering a compliment. One successful Swedish exporter goes to extremes to put his prospects at ease on this matter. He always remarks that Swedes are *such* poor salesmen and implies that he's thinking of

himself. In the face of this, people feel that they're· doing the
buying.

Similarly the sales boss of one big outfit has never accepted the
title of sales manager. As chief engineer, he makes his contact with
the customer in the role of technical expert rather than supersalesman. It often happens that 'non-salesmen' such as specialists,
engineers, assemblers, etc. are more successful in influencing customers than the 'professional salesman.' What do you conclude from
this?

The customer should feel at ease in your company. Does he?

8 *Protect your ·customer.* Don't spring price increases on your
customer without warning. As soon as you know a price increase is
coming, give your customer a chance to place orders at the old price
before the increase takes effect. If you can't do this, then as a minimum principle never take an order and raise the price before
delivery. That is the kind of high pressure that really makes a
customer blow up. Don't accept any order unless you are sure your
customer knows what he will be charged—he won't be assuaged
even if you can point out that he has your price list and should have
known the price.

9 *Fulfil your responsibility.* There will always be mistakes; when
they are clearly not your customer's, you must accept them. So accept
them cheerfully and cordially, even though they may not be strictly
yours, without troubling your customer about third parties such as
your suppliers, your plant, your accounting department, or your
boss. Only by thus facing responsibility can you get your customer's
complete confidence. And if your firm won't stand behind you in
this matter, you had perhaps better shift to a firm that will.

10 *Fulfil your guarantees.* You should expect your customers to take
your guarantees seriously, and you should take them seriously. It is
your inviolable duty to make every aspect of a guarantee clear to the
customer before he calls you to make good on it. A genuine guarantee is a powerful sales point, and your customer knows it is genuine
if you live up to it without quibbling. Don't let the customer deceive
himself by reading more into a printed 'guarantee' than the fine
print contains.

11 *Save your customer from his own mistakes.* Be sufficiently far-
sighted to talk your customer out of a tempting order when it won't
benefit him. Sometimes a customer is heading straight into a bad
buying blunder that you can prevent only by talking him out of it.
Tell him so. The order you lose for this kind of reason will win you a
lifetime customer and that is better than one order. In the industrial
field, this readiness to give up a sale is absolutely necessary for a

continuous successful sales activity. The salesman who cannot do this will, as a rule, soon be 'out'!

12 *Keep competition out of the conversation.* The sales interview will be more comfortable for you and the customer if you refrain from discussing competitors or even from mentioning them. When the salesman talks about his competitor, every knock is a boost and every boost is a boost—so how can you win? It may even be wise, if the customer should make an erroneous statement about the competition, to leave him uncorrected, rather than get into a line of talk that wastes time and may become embarrassing. Note also that selling by denigrating another's goods is illegal. If a competitor must be discussed, make sure your attitude is objective, fair, even generous; in that way you will make the best possible impression on your customer. On the other hand, the more you are attacked by a competitor, the more exclusively you concentrate your efforts on your offer.

A very successful car manufacturer forbids its dealers to so much as pronounce a competitive make's name. Every mention, whatever it is, is free publicity for the other company.

But even if you don't talk about your competitor, you should most assuredly know about him and his merchandise, in order to plan your selling interview intelligently. You don't really know your own merchandise until you know your competitor's and until you know every difference between the two and every advantage that the differences give you. Much of the art of selling consists in knowing differences and using them, in being different from your competitor, and often in being a little different from what your customer expects.

13 *Keep price in its place.* Try to nip in the bud any attempt to bargain over price. Convince the customer that your price policy is stable because it is equitable and fair. He should know that if you cut a price you acknowledge that you were trying to overcharge him or else you are letting him chisel you and your firm. You should know the advantages, to both parties, of a stable and fair price system and you should be able to sell your customer on these advantages. To get an order by cutting prices is a cheap trick, and the order is usually not worth while. Worse, the cut price deal breaks up your whole price structure and fixes the future relation with the customer on a price-shaving basis so you can never do profitable business with him. There is more on this point in the chapter on The price Area.

14 *Know your goods.* Be familiar with your product in every respect. When you know everything there is to know you won't be tempted to bluff or guess if the customer asks you a question you

ought to be able to answer. You may know all the so-called 'salesmanship' in the world, but it's no use if you don't know your product.

15 *Make the truth convincing.* Don't be lazy about your sales talk just because it's truthful; it must also be effective, convincing, believeable. Help your customer to verify every statement you make, especially if the statement sounds too good to be true. If anything about your product is too good to be true, maybe you'd better not say it. How would you, yourself, react to being told that Incredible Safety Razor Blades are good for three months' shaving? If you were selling them, you would be more convincing if you gave the customer one blade and asked him to try it and let you know how it lasts when you see him in a week or two. Always prove your statements; many salesmen fall down on this detail and lose orders because they do not realise that very few customers want to admit that they accept unsupported statements from salesmen.

16 *Be modest.* Tell the truth about your goods but do not let your sales talk become a hymn of lavish praise, consisting entirely of meaningless superlative adjectives: 'unrivalled,' 'fantastic,' 'the best in the world,' 'highest class,' 'unique.' Creative selling avoids such meaningless jargon. Use facts. When you stick to facts you can say very complimentary things about your product and still maintain the kind of modesty that convinces the customer. Great quantities of praiseful adjectives especially tend to gag the customer and make your sales talk sound like a pedlar's pitch. You need not, and should never, restrict your sales talk to the kind of dry recital of facts that bores a listener. You can be factual and also interesting if you mention the experience of other uses of your product—but if you merely string a lot of adjectives together the customer will not feel that you are either factual or interesting. Watch your intonation and rhythm; it is easy to fall into a kind of chant after you have gone over the same points in many sales talks. Spoken in the right way, the adjective 'good' sounds more convincing than 'fabulous' or 'superlative'. Above all, avoid 'very', 'very much'. You seldom get the reinforcing effect you want when you use them.

Always remember, as you choose your language and your way of speaking, what has been said often before now: the deciding element in a sale is not what the salesman says but what the customer believes. Hence a forceful expression, a convincing attitude, and a persuasive voice may impress the customer more than any selection of words.

17 *Be specific.* Let your customer have something that he can pin down; otherwise, you're not in touch with him. If you say, 'All the

biggest factories use our metal cleaner,' or 'Our metal-cleaning solution protects metals against everything,' you fairly goad him into challenging you. But how can he challenge you if you say, 'Smith & Brown buy our metal cleaner in tank-car shipments,' or if you say, 'Our solution protects carbon steel sheet against salt spray'? The latter type of statement is specific; the former, general and vague. You can be even more specific if you can give an example or a demonstration: 'Here's a sheet of carbon steel that's been forty-eight hours under a salt-spray test; the uncorroded part was treated with our solution.'

If you are selling for resale, it is vague and irritating to tell a wholesaler, 'Our line of weed killer is a best seller everywhere.' But it is specific and direct to tell him, 'Dealers in this country reordered our weed killer an average of four times each during the 1965 season.'

18 *Follow through on the order.* The salesman's job isn't over when he has taken the order. The sale isn't complete when the customer has accepted delivery and paid his bill. The salesman should stay in touch with the customer and also follow up on his own firm's handling of the order—shipping date, delivery instructions, all specifications, prices, terms, and the like. When the order has reached the customer, the salesman should be alert to help get the purchase properly used—or properly sold. If your customer doesn't use your product properly or sell it properly, you and the product get a black eye. So you should be ready to help.

Business firms have differing ideas about how much responsibility a salesman has for an order after he gets it. They may have specialists for expediting orders and servicing customers. If so, good. But the salesman won't abandon his customer even then; he may be useful in following up the service department. And above all, a good salesman never drops the order and leaves it to be kicked around. Even if he has no formal responsibility after the sale, he always has considerable interest in the contact with his customer. His future orders depend on it. Also, he will suffer from each error, whether he wants it or not.

19 *Admit shortcomings when they exist.* Don't try to get around a valid objection to your product by denying it is valid. To do so is a very bad kind of high-pressure selling. It is, in addition, rarely effective. Worse it makes your whole sales presentation ineffective, because if you won't admit the truth your customer will easily come to suspect that you don't tell the truth.

Salesmen tend to go into a panic when the sales interview takes a turn that endangers the sale. Thus when the customer mentions a feature of the product that isn't exactly right for him, the salesman is tempted to insist that the feature is right and that the fault doesn't exist. But he should remember that very few buyers expect perfection—they make a purchase when the advantages of a purchase outweigh the disadvantages. They know that every product has some disadvantages and they can't feel much respect for the salesman who doesn't know this simple fact or pretends not to know it. Nevertheless, salesmen repeatedly argue against valid objections—and lose sales. An arguing salesman can't win against an arguing customer, and he inevitably gets one. The argumentative attitude is a disease—occupational disease No. 1 of salesmen everywhere—and it is a pity to be infected with it and lose orders. For more on this subject, see chapters 17 and 18.

20 *Be businesslike.* Buffoonery and begging are not salesmanship. A salesman is not a travelling storyteller or a wandering minstrel. To amuse a customer may do no harm, but the customer isn't buying and the salesman isn't selling while one of them is telling a story he hopes is funny. Indeed, the salesman who is an effective clown is quite possibly just that in the customer's view—a clown. And who wants advice on business from a clown? So humour should be kept in its place and not allowed to crowd out sound product information and sales presentation.

And finally, the salesman should never become a 'tear salesman' or a 'mendicant friar.' Never 'please do me a favour' or 'I've been after you long enough,' or 'you can't say no to me,' or 'we'd so like to make a deal with you,' or 'your order would be a particular pleasure for us,' nor 'me as an old friend, classmate, neighbour...' etc. To beg for an order and expose the customer to an unjustified petition is the most unworthy form of high-pressure selling.

One more word of caution: should you take the foregoing for granted and place yourself above such presumption, please consider that only very seldom does anyone feel concerned by these points, except if he has a good portion of true self-criticism—and herewith the possibility to really better himself.

You can get occasional orders by means of high-pressure selling— but at the cost of lost customers. Creative selling works first to win customers and next to win orders.

The low-pressure area is the fifth area of creative selling where sales are made and sales are lost.

SIX

The quality area : How important is quality?

Can you answer these four questions?

1 Which is the more effective as a selling appeal—quality or utility?
2 What is the practical meaning of the principle that the quality appeal is a reinforcing appeal?
3 How many sales points should be developed in a sales presentation?
4 If the customer is uninterested in your offer, can you arouse his desire by using the quality appeal?

Can you solve the following five problems?

1 David Newman sells electrical appliances to retailers. His line is a good one, and Newman can readily demonstrate several advantages to users. His interest, however, is in the clearly superior quality of his goods—the good design, the fine materials, the finish and workmanship. Newman can always lead his customers to agree that his appliances are better in these respects than his competitors' articles. He works on this point: Do they know of any better articles? (They do not.) Can they recommend anything more confidently to their customers? (Naturally not—Newman's stuff is the best.) Are the appliances worth their price, to dealer and to user? (Unquestionably—they are bargains; there's nothing wrong with the price.) Knowing that his customer genuinely admires the appliances, Newman asks for the order : How many do you want right now?

And the sales interview fizzles—right now, the customer doesn't think he'll order any. They are good appliances, but ... Why this negative reaction? Has Newman used the wrong approach?

2 Two truck salesmen are after a fleet order from the same building firm. Henry Smith, a good salesman with a first class truck to sell, is confident that he can get the order because his truck is the better of the two, looks better, and drives faster. Smith works up a sales talk with thirteen specific appeals to points of quality, and he presents them skilfully and clearly so the customers understand them readily. Smith has no doubt of the outcome after his talk, even though it doesn't bring the order on the spot, for on a big deal like this one the buying decision is not usually made in the salesman's presence. But in a few days the purchasing agent phones that the order has gone to the competitor. What went wrong?

3 Sterling Franklin, who represents an insurance company, has a long series of conferences with a manufacturer on the subject of plans for group insurance and retirement pensions. The manufacturer initiated the matter, and Franklin lays before him, thoroughly and systematically, all the advantages of the project he recommends. He produces convincing case histories to show how well the plans work in practice and a full and detailed summing-up of payments, savings, and benefits to both employees and employer. The information Franklin has presented exhibits sound thought and expert skill, and the manufacturer has followed it with attention and apparent interest. When Franklin has finished his story, however, the manufacturer says he will have to think it over. Whatever he thinks, he doesn't buy the project. Franklin, after accepting the defeat, reflects that the same thing happens with too many prospects —they all seem interested but far too many of them turn him down. Does this frequently happen to you too? How does this client reaction show itself? How do *you* react?

4 The women's-coats buyer in the department store is sorry he can't reorder. 'We can't find anything wrong with your coats,' he tells the salesman. 'Their quality is good—better than the stuff that's selling, but your numbers stay on the racks. I don't know—maybe you might tinker up the styling a little.' The salesman reports the story back to his management, but the firm stands pat. The reasons: The coats were not designed to cash in on a fad, and they have sold well up to mid season. The drop in sales, the management believes, is a minor matter, and not enough to call for restyling this article of high quality and proven fundamental value. The salesman is told to keep selling, and soon the orders should pick up. How do you judge the management's position? Would you change it? If yes, how?

5 The men's-wear buyer breaks into the salesman description of his neckties: 'So they're high-grade! So what? High grade doesn't do me any good—they don't sell.' Even a buyer can be sorry about being rude, so he goes on to explain: 'Our customers don't want them. This is a town where people wear old-fashioned ties and don't wear them very often. How can I sell your ties? I can't even wear one without being kidded.' Do you agree with the buyer? If yes, what would you do? If not, how would you try to change it?

The person who is making a buying decision takes quality into account, quite naturally and usually. But he rarely makes the decision on quality alone. Hence salesmen who let the quality appeal dominate their sales talks are making a particularly serious mistake. Furthermore, they often use the quality appeal in the wrong way as well as too much.

Ten rules of creative selling in the quality area

1 *Quality and utility.* The quality and the utility of an article are two different things which should not be confused in a sales talk. Utility comes first in the eyes of the customer—he is concerned about the use he can make of the article he may buy. Quality is the innate value of an article; it may make an article better than another article of equal usefulness. The utility or usefulness of an article is its suitability for a specific use or application. Quality is an objective matter; in most cases a salesman or a customer can point to a detail and say that its quality is superior or inferior to the same detail in another article. People can agree readily that a thing is red, or strong, or heavy, or light, and that one article is more so than another. Matters of quality can usually be measured and proved with fair ease, and quality therefore is tempting to the salesman as a selling appeal. Utility, on the contrary, is subjective and may be hard to pin down in a sales talk. It is often not measurable, and often it cannot be proved—we all know that what is useful to one man is quite possibly useless to another. Salesmen can feel they are standing on very slippery rugs when the sales interview turns to utility. These differences between quality and utility lead to faulty use of both as sales appeals.

If you are to sell goods, the goods must match as closely as possible the specific purposes or uses of your customers or of their customers in turn. In certain cases a high quality is demanded, or wanted; in others, medium or even low quality may be sufficient. It often happens that a manufacturer puts out an article of unnecessarily high quality when a simpler or rougher article would give the customer satisfactory service at less expense. Better quality or best quality does not present additional attraction when it is not required. The design and finish of an article can make it too costly and unsaleable, as when they make for rapid wear or troublesome maintenance. We all know that superfine wool and supersheer nylons are fragile and expensive. Most of us do not want and will not pay for fine hand tailoring or Paris *couture* in the gardening dungarees or the housework aprons. Even when the consumer needs a high-quality article, he often wants educating before he feels the need. The educating job is usually assigned to the advertising people, but sometimes the salesman must perform it. In either case, the quality aspect of the merchandise becomes a selling appeal only when the customer has accepted the idea of need for quality.

2 *The proper use of the quality appeal.* Your object in the sales interview is to sell the idea of the article the customer is to buy. Your task is to convince him that the article you offer is appropriate, suited to his purpose, and as good as he needs. In all logic, sometimes, he ought to be convinced when you simply demonstrate the quality of your merchandise. But customers want more than quality; they put utility first, as has already been said. Hence the appeal of quality should not be over-estimated by the salesman nor stressed unduly in the sales talk. It is better to sell the idea, sell the utility, and put forth the quality appeal to reinforce the other appeals when they begin to take effect. In all the examples at the beginning of this chapter the quality appeals were put forward too soon, too strongly, and sometimes in disregard to other appeals.

The quality appeal, even when it is strong, is not permanently effective against other appeals. Quality could not hold the market for the coats in Problem Four, for example. Even the best articles can become unfashionable. And in this situation, if the fashion fault is not corrected, the pressure on the salesman to sell the outmoded article almost forces him to use high-pressure methods on his customers.

And even though quality is an objective matter, people's preferences in quality are not objective. There is no single concept of quality; the concept differs from market to market, as the situation in Problem Five exemplified. People flatter themselves that they like 'high-quality' things; then they go around to the other side of the circle and decide that the things they like are high-quality things. The appeal to quality in such a situation is aimed at something very shifty.

3 *Overdoing the quality appeal.* When you use quality as a reinforcing appeal, it is vital to choose the points you plan to present and to hold them to a reasonable number that the customer can grasp and retain. It is only rarely good to work on all the favourable points, for a customer's interest doesn't extend to the last details. The essentials interest him—and anything much more than the essentials is likely to suffocate his interest. Selling would be oh so simple if it consisted of reeling off a list of quality features. But a big part of the art of selling is to select the right quality features for emphasis—the ones that specially interest the customer. On that selection, probably, Henry Smith went wrong. While he worked over the thirteen quality points that he had compiled, his rival worked on one utility point— the big one. For building materials are heavy and builder's trucks must carry heavy loads. If the rival's truck could reliably haul a heavier load than Smith's truck, then the firm naturally bought the rival's truck. Worse for Smith—if the rival salesman brought up the point and Smith failed to, it may not have mattered which truck had the greater load capacity; the order went to the man who talked about this essential point.

David Newman made a similar mistake, working a string of quality points democratically, uniformally, and equally to death. He never mentioned the quality the dealer was really interested in— saleability. Dealers know that quality alone doesn't cause people to buy. They may concur with the salesman who harps on quality, but they buy from the salesman who just mentions saleability. Therefore remember: 'less' can be 'more'! Have you on occasion made the same mistake? Then you have certainly spread your arguments, but not achieved any conclusiveness!

4 *Quality and the customer's desire to buy.* If the customer is uninterested from the beginning, you cannot as a rule arouse the desire to buy through the use of quality appeals. If a customer doesn't want an article he doesn't want it any more if it happens to be high-grade.

Newman and Smith, in their efforts to sell electrical appliances and trucks, began presenting their quality points before they had completed the first essential step—arousing the customer's desire. Newman in particular was far off the track, for the quality of the electrical appliances was of interest to the dealer only insofar as it would help sales directly by moving the goods and indirectly by making the customers satisfied. Until the salesman has aroused his customers desire for increased sales, or for efficient trucks, or for financial protection for his family, the soundest and strongest appeal to quality will not move the customer towards accepting the offer. You may be the salesman with the best toaster in the world to sell, or the finest car, or a prize piece of seaside land, or a perfect fire extinguisher; but you won't sell any of these articles unless you arouse the customer's desire for better toast, for a shore home, for luxurious driving, or for protection against fire. Many salesmen fail to grasp this fundamental fact, though they should have found their way to it after a long series of unsuccessful sales talks.

A quality appeal launched too early is a missile wasted in empty space.

5 *What the quality appeal leads to.* The quality appeal is often a shining light far above the earthly level of business. It stays up there unless the salesman brings it down to earth by pointing out to the customer what quality implies *to the customer.*

Women are not the only people who don't know what the auto salesman means when he talks about such quality points as four-barrel carburettors, high compression, and short stroke. The salesman is just talking, not selling, unless he tells what these quality features mean to the customer. (Maybe he doesn't know—ask an auto salesman the next time you hear this kind of pitch.)

People in such a situation let the salesman talk but they do not listen unless the salesman carries on after citing his quality point: 'The high compression means you get more power and mileage out of your gasoline' is something the customer can tie up to himself and his own interests and his own desire to buy.

There is a special reason to be careful about using technical language (or advertising jargon, for that matter) in presenting quality points. The customer who doesn't know what they mean is often unwilling to ask for fear of seeming ignorant. The fear of seeming ignorant grows quickly into the fear of making a purchase. The wise salesman therefore avoids technical terms, or explains them unassertively, or chooses technical terms from the world of the customer's ideas rather than his own.

You might usefully ask yourself how many good-sounding words you have gotten into the habit of hearing without understanding. Do you know, or does your wife, what homogenised milk is? Bond paper? A whole-life insurance policy? Then you might consider whether any customer of yours has grown indifferent to a lot of words you like to use in talking up the quality of the things you sell.

You might get more of his attention if you tell him what your language means when you are dropping the impressive words about quality features.

6 *Quality and performance.* The most important thing about an article is not what it is but what it does. For this reason the salesman who rushes into technical talk about the high-quality construction of a vacuum cleaner or a dishwasher is wasting time for himself and for his housewife prospect. What she cares about is what the article will do for her. She may not know that this or that technical quality feature means good performance, but when she hears a lot of technical language she is very likely to think it means a complex machine that will demand more skill than she has for running it. If she can't understand the sales talk it is natural for her to feel she may not understand the machine.

There is no objection to technical language when the customer understands it. Selling industrial machinery, for example, requires the salesman to be ready with expert presentation of technical details. But in this situation especially the salesman must guard himself against irrelevant statements praising his article's high quality. The technical purchaser, above all others, must buy an article for what it does rather than for what it is. Hence he, more than any other buyer, will freeze up on the salesman who tries to exploit his interest in construction details before convincing him of the usefulness and advantage of the article for his, the buyer's, specific purpose. If you are selling in this market, don't try to impress the customer with your knowledge—let him impress you with his.

7 *Quality and qualities.* When you use the quality appeal in selling you must be specific. Avoid phrases like 'high quality,' 'excellent quality,' 'best quality.' These are general and worn out and dirt cheap. They can't be livened up by splicing in a different set of adjectives. Would you, for instance, be more impressed if you heard about 'stratospheric quality,' 'stupendous quality,' or 'colossal quality'? 'Quality' can refer to almost anything about an article: novelty, durability, stability, flexibility, hardness, solidity, lightness, reliability, fitness for purpose, excellence of construction, and many others. These are *specific qualities*, and when you speak about them you are being specific

8 *Objective and subjective quality.* Even quality is perceived objectively and subjectively. Motivation research has discovered many cases where identical products or products with the same inherent value are judged very differently by the customer, or where

better products are thought to be inferior, and *vice versa*. If the psychological image of a Company and its salesmen are right, this positive judgement is extended to the quality of the product.

How does your customer 'see' your Company, how does he see you and your performance, how does he see your products? The resulting opinion will also be transferred to the quality of your products.

9 *The customer's viewpoint on quality.* The customer stands at the centre of his own world, as do all of us. The salesman is missing this centre if he talks about the article—how modern, effective, or economical it is. He is on the centre if he talks about how the customer will be modern, effective, and thrifty as the result of owning the article. This approach wins the customer's attention for the salesman and for the article.

10 *The quality of sales talk.* The salesman can sometimes accomplish more by giving attention to the quality of his own voice and speaking manner than to the quality of the article he is offering to the buyer. You can verify this fact if you can listen to two salesmen in their selling talks. They may have the same article, and they may present the same selling points. They may even have the same rehearsed speech if their sales manager goes in for that sort of thing. But the two sales talks sound as totally different as the two men because of their different voices and speech manners. The customer forms strong opinions about the salesman and the merchandise from voices and speech manners. Thus the voice can be an important instrument in selling. Do not underestimate the value of the colour and sound of the spoken word, and make the effort to have your spoken word do you and your goods honest justice.

11 *Quality and the buying decision.* Whenever anyone thinks or says that an article sells itself he is wrong. No matter how valuable or high-grade the article is, in a buyer's market the value and quality of an article are taken as matters of course. The creative selling goes on from there, and creative selling is always needed, particularly when a new article is being introduced to the market. You must help everyone in your organisation to appreciate this fact; the men who aren't up against the actual selling situations may fasten firmly to the 'sells itself' illusion. Try to get your firm to send them out with you to meet your customers. It can be done. Many firms do it.

No article is bought solely because of its superb quality as such, but only because it can satisfy some specific need of the buyer or of the person he buys it for. Creative selling demands that you sell the idea above all, then utility, and that the effort to sell quality must come after and be subordinated to these two other efforts.

The quality area is the sixth area of creative selling where sales are made and sales are lost.

SEVEN

The price area : Is high price an insurmountable sales obstacle?

Can you answer these four questions?

1 What connection is there between buying power and buying interest?

2 Can you suggest ten approaches which will make your price seem low?

3 Why is it wrong to emphasise the price of an article at the beginning of a sales interview?

4 What circumstances influence our opinions as to whether an article is expensive or cheap?

Can you solve the following five problems?

1 Two magazines are competing for a place in the advertising programme of an organisation selling agricultural machinery. The price per insertion for Magazine A is £1,100, its circulation 100,000 per monthly issue. The competing Magazine B charges £1,300 per insertion and circulates 80,000 copies each month. Magazine B gets the contract. How can it be the better buy?

2 A large insurance firm has bought its printing for many years from the S Stationery Company. A new printer, the Y Company, seeks the business with a price scale that runs about 15 per cent under the established prices of the S Company. The S Company agrees to meet the lower price quotations and keeps the business.

Before the next big printing order is to be placed, the Y Company offers a still lower price, and again the S Company offers to meet the price cut. But this time the order goes to the Y Company. Can you understand the customer? If you were the owner of the S Company, what would you have done?

3 Gerald Robbins, who sells dictating machines, gets an interview with the office manager of a large textile firm. It is plain that the manager is not warmly interested in dictating machines, but he has been exploring their advantages over stenographer dictation. He has the advertising literature of a competing line of dictating machines, and remarks that the price Robbins offers is far above the competitor's. Robbins knows better—in fact, his price for a strictly comparable machine is about 5 per cent less, and the customer accepts the explanation. But he will 'have to think the matter over.' Whatever he thinks does not bring him to any buying decision, and long afterwards Robbins realises where he made a mistake in going into the price question.

4 A distributor of canned foods works out a plan with a well-known supplier that will enable him to cut the prices of the line by 25 per cent. He announces it with an energetic advertising campaign and stocks up in expectation of a rush of orders that never comes through: the unit volume of sales hardly exceeds the unit volume before the price cut. What went wrong? Must one look at the price psychology from another angle?

5 At a meeting of salesmen of an office furniture firm the sales manager discusses the sales appeals that will best sell the line. He stresses especially the effective presentation of the furniture, the imaginative use of the quality appeal, and careful attention to the specific needs of the different kinds of customers. One salesman starts a heated argument by objecting that the manager's approach would make the selling interview much too complicated. He urges concentrating on the advantageous price; price, he insists, is the overriding factor in selling. His own sales are about average in the organisation. Is he right? What is the attitude of your Company towards the question of price? When is a high price an insurmountable obstacle? In the foregoing problem, how would you answer the salesman if you were the sales manager?

Nobody can deny that high price can be a serious sales obstacle. There is certainly no general method for making a sale when the *only* difference between two offers is a striking difference of price. But price is rarely the only difference. Moreover, from the buyer's viewpoint, price has various meanings. When he is buying raw materials of standard quality the difference of a fraction of a cent per unit can swing his decision. When he is buying a luxury product, even a much higher price may not be a sales obstacle. The salesman who knows how to sell can, as a rule, do a great deal to prevent his customer from being disturbed over a high price if the higher price is justified.

Buying power and buying desire

It is important to clarify the point that buying *power* and buying *desire* are not identical. All sales planning should be done with this distinction well in mind. Many sales campaigns are planned in terms of the prospects' incomes alone, a high-price product being offered exclusively to a high-income group. How much people can buy depends to some extent on what they can *afford* to buy, but how much and what they *want* to buy are another matter. A stamp collector may spend half his pay on stamps; a day labourer with chronic headaches will buy more aspirin than a carefree millionaire. People who have a social inferiority feeling are apt to live on a scale of luxury that bears no relation to their income. An industrial firm whose business management has a highly developed sense of social responsibility can spend disproportionately vast sums on welfare. A super-modern office manager can be readily interested in almost any innovation in office furniture and office mechanisation. A craftsman with deep pride in his skill may buy tools much more expensive than he needs for the work he will do with them. In these instances and in many others, the buying and spending desires are out of proportion to the buying power.

What is the meaning of being able to afford something?

The question about how well an establishment, or an individual, is 'able to afford' a certain article can generally be formulated by the salesman in these words: 'To what extent is the customer willing to make an economic sacrifice, to give up something else he wants or could have?' The question may present itself in even simpler form: 'Can the customer find the money that he needs for the purchase?' The salesman who is to sell the customer then has his task reduced to this : make it clear to the customer that he cannot afford to do without the article offered.

Price-positive and price-negative

A salesman should never forget that the ideas of 'cheapness' and 'expensiveness' are extremely loose. They differ from person to person according to his means and his feelings. The more closely an article matches the predominating desire of the customer, the cheaper it will be to him. Contrariwise, the more nearly an article has the character of a 'necessary evil,' the more expensive it will be —in the customer's mind. A £3 laundry bill can seem more expensive to a housewife than a £4 down payment on an automatic washing machine. A dentist's bill for £8 will certainly seem more expensive than a party for twice that amount, a cabinet for £15 more expensive than a radio set for £18. The first are 'price-negative,' the second 'price-positive' items.

To the person who is buying a desired (price-positive) article, the price is likely to be a minor matter. People don't haggle about price when they are buying sporting equipment, or impressive furniture for an executive office, or a modern building front, or a vacation trip, or party clothes, or labour-saving gadgets, or beauty preparations, or cameras, or television sets—or the like.

Many things can be made to appeal to a customer more strongly than a low price. Customers, for instance, find it annoying to spend money for repairs or correcting faults in something they have purchased. The salesman who can promise freedom from trouble of this sort need not worry unduly if his product is priced a little higher than his competitor's. But if the salesman is selling the repair service, he then needs to convince the customer that the repair job will be successful and give him an article as satisfactory as a possible new one.

Do you sell price-positive or price-negative goods? (They may be price-positive to one customer and price-negative to another!) If they are price-negative, can you single out price-positive aspects to emphasise? Or can you add price-positive features? The answers may decide your success in selling.

What seems costly to one buyer may seem cheap to another. A purchasing agent is more conscious of the cost of a machine tool than is the production chief or the machine operator (hence the salesman often finds himself more comfortable talking to these latter gentlemen).

If a customer has an urgent need for an article, or can think he has, he is likely to care relatively little about its price. If an article is scarce, as when people are hoarding, its price matters almost not at all. The more an article has the character of a 'bargain' or a 'find,' the more readily, as a rule, will any misgivings about the price disappear.

Wanted articles are therefore described as 'price-positive'; 'necessary evil' articles are 'price-negative.'

Dealers and price

For the retailer and in some degree for the wholesaler, price is of secondary interest. First and foremost, for either, is the profit potential. Hence low price is of interest only if it increases sales and profits. A dealer may even dislike to handle low-priced goods since the unit profit is bound to be low. Such big price reductions as those exemplified in Problem Four can also be big profit reductions. Moreover, sudden drastic price cuts excite suspicion. Smaller price reductions are less likely to have these effects. When a price reduction is too generous to be believable, it is as hard to justify as a price increase might be, and may have to be supported by samples and guarantees.

Four basic rules for leading attention away from price

In practical selling work, the question of price is dealt with according to four rules:

First: Offer the article at a fair price, by holding down production and selling costs and sharing the savings with your customers. Impress them with the fact that you are doing so. Then you will have the 'right' price.

Second: Present the article so it will seem to the customer as desirable as you can possibly make it seem.

Third: Get the customer to concentrate his attention on the value he receives for his money when he makes the purchase.

Fourth: Use the proper psychological techniques and timing in discussing price. The remainder of this chapter will deal extensively with the application of this principle.

Price policy

The price policy of the seller is an application of the first of the rules just mentioned. Price policy rarely comes into the province of the salesman. Nevertheless, the salesman can, thanks to his profound knowledge of his customers, usefully point out details which increase cost unnecessarily. Price reductions can also be achieved through standardisation of the product design or the range. In many types of business, premiums have been introduced for regular big orders which help in the planning, buying and production stages.

A good salesman therefore can emphasise the benefits to the customer, of quantity buying and quality features. He can know the discount schedule, bring advantageous break points to his customer's notice, and secure for his customer every possible advantage of the firm's price policy. And he can constantly report back to his organisation the customer's wishes in price policy and their suggestions for distribution economics that can be shared between seller and buyer.

Salesmen and sales management can contribute two especially useful services to the formation of price policy: (1) they can ascertain where sales effort pays best; (2) they can ascertain how much sales effort is wise.

The salesmen and the head office should both make themselves aware of what class of customers is responsible for the largest and most profitable part of the total sales volume. It is common to find that a third of the customers account for two-thirds of the sales, or more. If, at the other end of such a pattern, a third of the customers account for only a tiny fraction of the sales, it may prove wise to quit calling on the small-buying customers, service them by phone or mail, and go after more of the kind of customers that make up the top-buying third.

The head office and the salesmen should also co-operate in a policy concerning prospects who are slow to become customers. There is a time beyond which unrewarded repeat visits are not good business. Some insurance people think it is a good idea to drop a prospect if they aren't getting anywhere after three visits; others stick on to the prospect much longer. A wise decision depends in part on whether the time might be better invested in a visit to a new prospect.

A sewing machine manufacturer discovered that out of a dozen orders, five were placed during the first call, four during the second call, and one each during the third, fourth and fifth visits. In dropping the repeat visits five to three, time was made available for six more sales, with a corresponding reduction in sales costs. Other companies have made a contrary experience. This depends on the type of business. In some cases, the number of repeat visits may almost be unlimited, in others it may hardly be worth visiting at all.

Telephone selling is one way to keep a contact alive when it isn't promising enough to be worth a long personal visit. Are you free to switch to phones rather than personal visits?

Statistical research is valuable to the organisation as a whole but it is in many ways still more valuable, and more directly valuable, to the salesman.

What is the cost of a sales visit?

What is your break-even point? Have you enough salesmen to sell in depth? Do you pay enough attention to your profitable customers? Which uneconomic visits could be avoided?

Do you provide your salesmen with a saleable proposition and a reasonable chance to make a sale?

It is a good idea to break down your customer list into A B C D E groups (e.g. A = your best customers, B = good customers, C = average, D = insignificant, E = unprofitable). But you must review the position carefully, and include the customer's potential growth rate in your evaluation.

Price and desirability

Both the design of a product and the method by which the salesman offers it can stress the aspect of desirability. The choice of a selling appeal can move a product from the necessary-evil and price-negative class into the desired and price-positive class. Once upon a time, for example, the advertising appeal for tooth-paste was necessity—daily dental hygiene; more recently, it has been desirability—'lovely teeth, lovely smile.' Bright colours, attractive design, and being-newer-than-the-neighbours' sell more automobiles because they stir up stronger desire than reliable engines and tough frames. Comfort and reduced effort ('just turn one knob') sell more radios and TV sets than pages of proof that this or that set is technically superior. 'Win a summer-house' sells more lottery-tickets than 'buy a ticket'. It may bring more satisfaction to be the first factory to use the newest type of machine than to simply increase efficiency.

Whatever will raise the buyer's desire for an article is what the salesman should emphasise. If he does emphasise it successfully, the customer's attention is taken off the price and focused on the positive merits of the article and the idea of owning it.

The relative cost

Although the price of an article has been set by sound policy and although the article is desirable, it costs money. The customer will not ignore this cost, and the salesman will not sell very much if he attempts to ignore it. But the cost to be kept in mind is the *relative* cost, the *value* the customer gets in exchange for his purchase money. A sensible customer will not be dismayed about any outlay if he is getting fair value in exchange for it. The salesman should always keep the subject of value in his selling talk.

Let the customer see what he gets for his money. This practice got the advertising contract for Magazine B in the first example. Magazine B's salesman showed the advertiser that his magazine's smaller readership was a better target for the advertising than the larger readership of his lower-priced competitor.

Getting the customer to think of the value he receives (the relative price) instead of the outlay he makes (the absolute price) is frequently decisive in the struggle for the order.

The price-fearful salesman

An essential requisite for keeping price to its proper place in the selling interview is that the salesman himself must not be over-conscious of price. He must rid himself of the price neurosis that grips so many salesmen; otherwise he will tend to refer constantly to the theme of 'low price' and thus lead the customer's thoughts too often and too soon to the matter of price. Salesmen often complain that customers worry too much about dollars and cents, not realising that it is they themselves who can't get their minds off prices and thus bring the customers' minds to the same subject. A more positive approach consists in stressing the *profitable and money-saving* qualities of the article. The salesman of raw materials or industrial equipment can improve his chances of success by this approach, particularly if he supports his points with sound evidence.

Reducing price-consciousness—price-positive appeals

The salesman's collection of selling appeals includes a great many points through which he can stress the profit-earning and cost-saving potentialities of the article he is selling. In addition to these appeals and the approaches that keep attention off price, already mentioned, and the thirty suggestions contained in Chapter 17, all salesmen should be fully aware of the principles that help to keep price from becoming the most important thing in the customers' mind. These principles are:

1 *The method of payment and billing influences the customer's feeling about price.*
(a) Favourable conditions of payment.
(b) Buying on credit and paying later.
(c) Instalment-plan buying.
(d) Non-cash payment plans (Cheque; postal order etc. It is easier to spend money from an account than to take banknotes from your wallet).
(e) Bills that state in full detail the reason for all charges help the customer to think of what he has received as well as what he is expected to pay. A garage bill that says 'Service £7' can seem high; a garage bill that lists lubrication, tyre rotation, a wash job, new brake fluid and other items, each with its price, can make £7 seem like a small total for many values received.
(f) Suitable timing in the presentation of invoices and statements of accounts may be of more value to the customer than a reduction in price could be. It has become common practice not to send bills to charge-account customers until January for purchases made in November or December. This is a special holiday-season situation. Normally it is good business to send bills promptly, before the customer has lost his first awareness of the benefits of what he has purchased.
2 *Routine or habitual purchases are made without much thought of price.*
The more frequently an article is bought in the same circumstances the less the customer thinks about price. If only for this reason a salesman should never neglect his regular customers.
3 *Small extra charges can be as objectionable as a really high price; omitting them can please a customer as much as a real price cut.*
It is a nuisance to the seller and a nuisance to the customer to bill and account for small charges. Laundries long ago discovered that it is not worth the trouble to charge for sewing on lost buttons and making minor mends in clothing; the ones that do these services and make no charge have satisfied customers who cheerfully pay at a higher price schedule than no-service laundries can charge. Appliance dealers, machinery firms, auto dealers and the like have

long known that it can cost more to prepare and submit and collect a bill for a small item than the item itself costs. In such situations it is better for economy and good will to treat small services as services, free of charge. If your company is annoying your customers with puny charges, it is handicapping you as a salesman. 'Each invoice costs us one dollar' maintains a manufacturer of electro-technical equipment, and therefore no longer asks for payment of small amounts, whereas a big garage gives away spare parts which cost less than ten cents and repair work taking less than half-an-hour. Where is your break-even point at which you can make a gift at no cost and win grateful customers?

Additional services are perceived as price-reducing elements.

4 *The right treatment of customers favourably influences their attitude towards prices.*

A customer thinks only casually about cost when he likes to buy from the organisation concerned. He is normally quite willing to pay a little more than rock-bottom prices in order to deal with a concern that makes the buying process comfortable and pleasant.

5 *The importance of price depends on its influence on final costs.*

In selling raw materials or semi-finished goods for use in further manufacture, an important point is the relation between the cost of these components and the cost of the finished article. A manufacturer who sells shoes at £8 a pair is not likely to worry about the difference of 10p in the price of a gross of shoelaces.

6 *The more complex and individual an article is, the less important is the price.*

Raw materials are difficult bargaining objects, complicated machinery easy ones for the salesman. Specially made products strengthen the salesman's position, standardised ones weaken his price position.

7 *The salesman who initiates the selling relationship has a better chance to manage the price question than the mere order taker.*

If the customer knows what he wants, drafts the specifications, and invites bids, price is the big element in the decision and the customer is on top of it. But if the salesman has figured out what his customer needs or can use advantageously, and brings the idea to the customer, the relationship is entirely different. This difference emphasises the importance of truly creative selling. It also emphasises the fact that the less competitive your offer, the more important it is to initiate your sales contacts and not to let the customer initiate them.

8 *The greater the customer's need for an article, the less important is its price.*

When a man is buying what he must get, especially when it is scarce, he does not make his buying decision on the price. This urgency factor begins to apply when his stock is low, even though replenishing it may offer no special difficulty. It will pay you to keep track of your customer's stock situation; making your offer at the right time may be more important and effective than any refinement of sales technique. When a customer buys delivery, his price position is weak.

9 *A stable value (and the possibility of a resale) is perceived as a reduction in cost (e.g. the expense for real values or real estate, the resale value of a car, etc.).*

10 The prestige of the item or the sales locale (a tie bought in New York's 5th Avenue may seem less expensive than a similar tie bought in a supermarket, even if it actually costs more).

11 And then, of course, the performance and advantages of your proposition. More on this in the next chapter.

Now to repeat: A salesman must be familiar with all the various price-minimising situations in order to recognise them and take advantage of them.

Correct Timing—first value, then price

During sales negotiations the first rule on the question of price is to avoid naming it too soon. The price measures the expense to the customer, the sacrifice he must be or become willing to make if he buys your article. For that reason you should deal with the price only after the customer has at least begun to warm to the idea of your proposition. Mentioning the price before this time either scares him off or cools him off. Talking about the price of your article does not arouse the customer's desire for it, may even kill his desire if it exists. That was where the salesman in Problem five went wrong. The stronger the customer's desire for an article, the less important the price. When the customer comes to buy something, therefore, it is usually a mistake to ask what price he has in mind; if you can get him to wanting an article he may buy it even though it is more expensive than the one he originally meant to buy.

Some hints on price

1 *When is the best time to mention price? When the customer asks about it.* When a customer asks about a price, the question usually

means that he has begun to think about having the article concerned. You must always remember this positive factor when the customer asks you about price, even though you may feel that he has brought up the subject too soon. If you want to make some more points before talking price, you can sometimes 'not hear' the question. This device will work when the customer is not yet really serious about wanting to know the price. But it may be better to ask permission, candidly, to postpone the answer ('Would you mind if I hold off on that for a minute?'). Sometimes you need more information about the customer's needs before you can give the answer. If so, by all means ask for it, and get to talking about the customer's problem. You can sometimes start the customer moving in your direction by replying, 'That depends on the model you pick out' (or 'the colour,' or 'the size,' or many other variations). There are many ways of regaining the initiative when the customer introduces price prematurely. But premature or not, if he repeats his question, or otherwise presses for an answer, you must answer directly and responsively. Even so, you can make the answer positive; you can say, for instance, 'Only £98 and it's guaranteed for two years. Besides, you have to see the price in relation to the anticipated lifetime of this equipment, which is ... years. Also, please consider that you can gain ... working hours each day. In your Company, the price of £98 will be more than paid off in a few months.' After answering, you should not pause unless the customer plainly wishes to offer some remark or question—just go ahead with your sales talk. Then come back to the subject of price when you are ready for it or when the customer reopens it.

2 *The effort to control the introduction of price into the sales interview must not be allowed to look like evasion or stalling.* If your customer begins to wonder why you don't mention price, he may guess at some nasty answers. If he thinks you are ashamed of your price, or thinks you are feeling him out for what he will stand, he may grow stubborn or hostile. He is likely to question your price when you name it, and may haggle or even reject your offer. Just as you should avoid mentioning price prematurely, you should likewise avoid putting it off too long.

3 *Whenever price is mentioned, value must also be mentioned.* Never be content merely to state the price. Make it a practice to follow up price statements with a statement about the value of the article priced. Perhaps better, get the value statement ahead of the price statement. Perhaps still better, talk value before and after mentioning price. A good sequence to remember is : *First* value or values, *then* price, *then* value or values *again.*

4 Any customer may react to your price information with a more or less frank statement that your article costs too much. When you hear this objection, you need to find out what he really means before you square off to correct his opinion.

You need to know, and you may have to ask directly, 'Costs too much in relation to what?' Some variant of this simple-seeming question can rescue many orders. 'Costs too much' can mean almost everything or almost anything. The cost may be too great, to name a few possibilities, in relation to:

1 The customer's general financial position.
2 The customer's financial position at the moment.
3 The amount the customer has allocated for your article or for articles in its class.
4 The amount the customer is prepared to spend for your article.
5 What the customer thinks your article ought to cost.
6 The prices your competitors ask for comparable articles.
7 The prices of imitation, alternative, or substitute articles.
8 What the customer thinks you ought to charge him, in the light of other business he has given you or may give you.

The price you offer may be entirely fair, may even be better than the market, yet the customer may object that it is too high. In that situation his objection may mean that:

9 He would object to any price you named, out of sheer routine.
10 He wants to manoeuvre you into quoting a lower price, if there is a lower price.
11 He doesn't want to buy just now, but can't offer a good reason, so he challenges your price.
12 He doesn't want to buy at all, but can't give any reason except price that seems sensible to him, let alone you.
13 He doesn't want to buy, but doesn't want to tell you the true reason.
14 He needs your article and realises that you know it, and suspects you of squeezing him in a tight market.

When a customer says merely that your article costs too much you must obviously find out which of these 14 objections he is making. You can't deal with his objection unless you know what his objection is.

Now you can recognise Gerald Robbins's mistake in his effort to sell dictaphones. The customer stated objection six above; if Robbins had taken a few seconds to think before leaping to answer, he might have suspected objection 12 and not driven his sales interview up the wrong street.

But specifically, how can a salesman deal with these 14 kinds of price objections?

Fourteen answers to price objections

Objection 1 This objection is rarely genuine. As a rule the customer means case 2, 3 or 4 or even 13. The customer's general financial position is rarely too weak to make a purchase that will benefit him. If it were, it would either be public knowledge or the customer would be trying hard to keep it from becoming public knowledge and would manoeuvre to keep you from suspecting it. So if a customer explains a price challenge by alleging that his financial condition is poor, you just don't believe him. If you do believe him, you certainly don't want the order. More likely, his buying desire has not been awakened, perhaps because you haven't warmed up to selling the idea behind your article. If however there is real evidence that the customer cannot in fact afford to make the purchase it is advisable to withdraw the offer temporarily and return to it when the situation has changed.

Objection 2 If you suspect the customer is short of cash for the moment, find out what kind of terms he needs and you can probably work out the deal for him. Help him to understand how badly he needs your article. If a farmer requires a new tractor badly, he may have to borrow from the bank, if necessary, in order to buy it. Or he should sell some less productive property.

Objection 3 Purchasing agents often have a top limit on the price of some article they are instructed to buy. Or business executives have a stated budget that is too nearly used up to leave room for buying your article. These people are not embarrassed by mention of the fact. If you encounter this situation your task is to find convincing reasons for upping the arbitrary top figure or for reopening the budget. Sometimes the problem can be licked by timing the invoice to fall in the next budget period; taking the order for future delivery is the obvious method here, but sometimes you can work out immediate delivery and deferred billing. Maybe you can check the customer's needs for some other purchase (maybe of your own line) and find that he can postpone that one in order to buy the article you offer now. These dealings must often be concluded with other people of the buyer's company (decision makers).

Objection 4 This wishful price objection is very commonly encountered. It means that the salesman has not succeeded in arousing a strong enough buying desire.

Objection 5 Be able to sell the price.   When the customer has a considered opinion about the proper price for your article you can change his opinion only by the unsparing use of concrete factual explanations. Customers underestimate, often fantastically, the costs of simple raw materials and of mass-produced articles. It is hard to correct such misconceptions without getting into wrangles, but it is possible to succeed by selling the idea of the quality of the article. And if many customers come up with this kind of price resistance it is time for the head· office to put forth a factual advertising campaign to stimulate value-consciousness among customers and potential customers.

Objection 6 When the customer thinks your competitor's price is fair and yours is too high, you must know the reason for the difference and be ready to explain it so the customer sees where his real benefit lies. If the benefit lies with your article, you have probably made the sale. If it lies with your competitor—well, you know better than to stick a good customer and have him lose confidence in you. Quite likely, you will need some time to find out what is behind the price difference, and you can tell the customer so; during this visit, you continue to present the advantages of your own article. Keep the discussion concentrated on the greater value you offer (*if* you offer one). The value isn't necessarily in the article you sell as such, but is in the· totality—the package of terms, assurance of reliable supply, service, technical assistance, sustained trade-in value, or what not else. You aren't licked just because your competitor's article is priced a little below yours, if you remember that you are selling more than the article itself. You can lick yourself, however, if you look unhappy and say of course the competing company is a big outfit and can work on lower production costs—or of course it's a little outfit and can cut corners now and then. For in those lines of talk you are selling the rival offer and also confirming the customer's suspicion that your price is out of line—not only for now but for often. Bluntly: If your competitor's price is lower and all other features of the sale are equal, you and your firm must cut the price to meet his, or offer added benefits, or else be sensible and get out of the picture till you can.

Objection 7 If the customer wants to buy a cheap substitute for your article, or try to get by with something that doesn't fit his needs, or make do with a secondhand or worn-out article, your task is to stimulate his desire for the advantages of your proposal. You must know them and help your customer to see them and want them. Compare the two possibilities in their most extreme effects (to make the contrast evident) and underline thereby the advantages of your proposals.

Objection 8 You are being asked for favours. This is simply an attempt to get you to reduce your price and is asking you to do favours, not business. The salesman can either restate the advantages of his proposition and stress its benefits to the customer or he can offer the customer other advantages. Free service, speedy delivery etc. Do not allow yourself to be manoeuvred into a position where the customer establishes how grateful *you* should be to *him* for bringing off the sale. Instead, prove to him that it is entirely to his advantage to make the purchase. Point out the relationship between conditions, price and advantages of the offer.

Objection 9 Customers who routinely object to prices are easy to recognise. Their very attitude indicates that they want the sales interview to continue: If you were to say 'Sorry' and pick up your hat, such people would ask you a question to keep the talk going. So the best selling method is to go on with the talk, concentrating the discussion as always on the advantages of the article you are offering. If you are offering articles at a range of prices, you may find it good tactics to offer something surely too expensive, let the customer challenge the price, and then work into the offer of something in a price range that fits his needs. In applying this tactic it is necessary to avoid two mistakes: (*a*) arguing with the customer about his price objection, and (*b*) giving the impression that you are offering a second-rate substitute at the lower price.

Objection 10 The customer who wants to manoeuvre you into quoting a lower price may be chiselling (as in objection 8) or he may quite truly believe that your first quoted price isn't your bottom figure. If this is your first contact with him, it is your opportunity to maintain a polite but firm attitude that will prevent him from having the same suspicion in the future. To get away from price, lead the conversation around to the advantages the proposition offers the customer *at the price* to which he objects. You are not likely to meet this kind of bargaining if you are selling standard goods from an established price list. It turns up far more often in the case of special goods and articles 'made to order.' In this kind of business the salesman often has to compute the price from a list of elements, or even to use some degree of judgement and perhaps stipulate confirmation from his home office. In such situations the salesman is tempted to make concessions if the customer indicates that he wants them. Such concessions become precedents. If you must bargain on price, it is equitable and reasonable to link a lower price to a bigger order, or to a firm commitment for a series of orders. Such proposals can be developed quite naturally and smoothly out of a well-planned price policy that provides a sliding scale of prices for larger orders. Many firms share with their customers, in various ways, the benefits of larger unit transactions.

Even if the lower price for a bigger or better order does not fit a published price scale, it does not become a precedent; the total of conditions has been changed, not merely the price. The same device—changing the total conditions—can be applied to avoid setting a precedent or getting into future trouble when you must meet a competitor's lower price.

Even though he may have tried to talk the price down primarily for the pleasure of using his bargaining skill, the customer will not necessarily be happy even if you do make an outright price concession. On one hand, it is sometimes true that a customer was contented with an insignificant price concession. In fact, there are customers for whom not the amount of the reduction is important, but the satisfaction of having bargained. Many buyers judge their own skill by their success in price negotiations.

On the other hand, the customer may soon begin to wonder whether he got all the concessions he might have extracted or extorted. After he dribbles that one along for a few more bounces he begins to feel that he's been a sucker. He could have got it cheaper. And what the hell!—He surely paid too much last time if he could screw you down on price this time! And if you cut a price for him, by golly, you surely cut it deeper still for some other guy! You think you gave him a price concession? What you gave him was a lasting and growing grievance.

There are companies which never give in, not even in the hardest fight against competition. From time to time they lose an order, but on the whole they assert themselves successfully and customers respect them for their performance. The explanation for their success lies in the previous paragraph.

Without a firm price policy, no Company can get along in the long run. It stumbles from one problem into the other.

Many a salesman has come to wish he had been tough when the pressure started. Some salesmen wish they were tough; some think they are tough. They aren't tough if they flip into a panic whenever a tough price-bickering buyer goes to work on them. If they wilt in the feeling that 'Everybody just buys prices,' they become defeatist and they just sell prices. In that frame of mind and emotion, they don't sell much merchandise and don't earn much money. It is the job of a good Sales Manager to encounter this defeatist attitude energetically and convincingly (if necessary by his own example).

Train your salesmen to be tough—otherwise they are more touchy on price than their customers and can never win.

If price discussions are serious and frequent, look for the customer's hidden real reason. By questioning hundreds of salesmen, the following 12 motives were discovered:

1 The customer wants to buy at a lower price (most natural reason);
2 he wants to buy at a lower price than his competitor or other customers;
3 he wants to win the argument with the salesman and prove his efficiency;
4 he uses it as a tactical point in order to achieve other advantages;
5 he wants to show off his efficiency to his superiors;
6 he is afraid of being cheated;
7 he considers a concession a sign of esteem (ego symbol);
8 he knows that bargaining pays;
9 he does not recognise the value of the proposal ('isn't worth that much!');
10 he would like to discover the genuine (true) price;
11 he would like to buy cheaper from another supplier (a means to exert pressure on a third party);
12 he hides another important objection (i.e. he cannot or does not want to buy).

Obviously, the salesman who wants to be successful in such price discussions must at first analyse which of these motives (or which combination of motives) lies underneath the customer's bargaining tactics.

How about using this as a topic for your next sales meeting, sales training or simply in discussion with your fellow-salesmen?

Objection 11 Excuse. Ignore subterfuges. The more the conversation revolves around price objections, the stronger this excuse becomes, and you lose your chance of a sale. In such cases try first to find out what other point of sales resistance lies behind the excuse. Otherwise the sales talk degenerates into an irritating price discussion that can even turn into unpleasantly genuine resistance, for if you take his excuse seriously the customer will have to defend himself and so harden it into a real objection.

Objection 12 A general reluctance to buy is the result of a failure of the salesman (or the goods) to awaken the customer's desire. In this case any price will seem too high.

Objection 13 The customer who uses price objections to conceal his real reason for not wanting to buy (objection 11 is a special instance of this) forces the salesman to become a detective while being a salesman. In this situation, all you can do is try to guide the conversation so that it will reveal the real reason for the customer's resistance. Until you have found the real reason and dealt with it in your sales talk, you haven't the faintest chance of getting the order. But remember, nothing is easier for a customer to say than: 'Your price is too high!' It may conceal anything and everything.

Objection 14 When a customer needs your article and suspects you of holding him up because he needs it, he may buy despite his price objection, but it will be more difficult to get the next order unless you can quiet his suspicion. Here, as is the case with many objections, the cure needs to be made before the complaint. The cure is to establish a reputation, for yourself and your firm, of dealing fairly with customers and not taking advantage of their necessities. If it is not already established—that is, if the customer is evidently suspicious—you need to offer evidence and proof that you are dealing fairly with him, and you must offer them in the most friendly and frank manner you can. Further hints will be found in the following paragraphs.

Justifying the price

5 A logical method for playing down the importance of a price objection is to justify the price—high price or low price. High prices need to be justified because people would like to avoid spending too much money; low prices need to be justified because people don't want to get inferior goods. Most customers tend to suspect any surprisingly low price as evidence that the seller is trying to work off a poor-quality article or one that doesn't exactly fit the needs of the market. The canned-foods distributor who cut prices 25 per cent awakened this kind of suspicion; he might not have awakened it had he cut the prices only 10 per cent *and* explained how he was able to do so *and* offered a money-back guarantee of satisfaction.

There have been practical examples in which an item only started to sell well after a considerable price *increase* (e.g. in connection with a change in packaging).

The pricing unit

6 Wherever possible, use the following tactical resources:
In arithmetic, £14.40 per ton and 1p per pound are equivalent, but

they are not necessarily so in customer psychology. If your product is used in small units it is good tactics to quote prices in small units. It may be good tactics to make the pricing unit even smaller than the usual use unit. A book publisher seldom uses less than 4000 pounds of paper in printing an edition of a book, but paper manufacturers compile their price lists in 100-pound units. Although chemicals are sold in car loads of 20 tons, almost all American and European manufacturers quote price in pence per pound. The first impression made by such a price list is undoubtedly more favourable than if it were compiled in pounds per ton (or even per car load). Scandinavian Airlines advertise 'your flight in Sweden costs only 32 öre per kilometre' and a shower manufacturer uses '1p per shower!' It may be better to offer men's shirts at £1 each in dozen lots than £12 per dozen. A shaving cream has been advertised as costing 'less than ½p per shave.'

If you walk into a shop and enquire for the price of the best coffee, it sounds 'cheaper' if the sales clerk tells you '25p for half a pound' rather than £24 per bushel. These are points of no tremendous significance, but they can help keep the price aspect in its place. Can you present a sales appeal along similar lines? Have you done so? If you haven't, why not?

Price comparisons

7 A high-priced article seems less expensive when it can be compared with an article that is much higher in price. Some manufacturers offer a very high-priced line precisely in order to set up this kind of comparison. The article need not necessarily be compared with something directly substitutable; the psychology works if there is any significant relation between the articles. The salesman who has a high-priced article for sale should always, therefore, prepare for his sales interviews by gathering material for comparison.

Demonstrations

8 Sometimes the comparison can be introduced into the customer's mind by demonstration. A hydraulic jack, for instance, costs more than a cheap lever-and-ratchet jack, but if an auto-supply salesman

can get a customer to try the two in a demonstration the customer will invariably want the hydraulic jack and will buy it if he can afford it.

Compensation for the high price

9 The salesman who knows his prices are in the high range can also deal with the customer's price objections by presenting all the compensating factors. If he has reviewed and rehearsed these, he need never stand tongue-tied when the customer challenges his price and threatens to direct the sales interview up a blind alley. You must study the article you are selling to find every aspect of it that compensates for its high price, and try to get these compensating factors into the customer's attention before he raises the price objection. (For more along this line, see Chapter 18.)

Miniaturising price differences

10 When a price difference is not of any real importance it may still be necessary for the salesman to bring the fact home to the customer. A difference of £2 in the price for printing 10,000 mailing pieces is a fiftieth of a penny per piece. You can well get this thought into the sales conversation, and then follow it up with a remark about something in your offer that more than compensates for the trivial price difference: reliability, prompt delivery, superior quality, convenience. But use this manoeuvre carefully, a penny-pinching prospect can easily suspect you of thinking he is a penny pincher.

Stretching the price thin

11 Articles that have a long life cost surprisingly little when you break the price down into an amount per day or per month, or even per year. If a £30 appliance, say a vacuum cleaner, will last 10 years, its total cost per year is £3, per month less than 25p, less than 1p per day. If your appliance costs £33 and the customer wishes it cost only £27, the difference amounts to less than 5p a week over the ten-year life. If the appliance has a money-saving use feature as compared with something it is to replace or as compared with a rival article, the stretched-thin price may be less or very little more than the money to be saved. 'This gadget doesn't

cost you anything—it pays itself in saved wages' argues one salesman. If you have this kind of a selling point, use it in heading off the
price squawk.

Equivalent spending—and the high cost of not buying

If a customer can be led to think of the price of an article as 'a
petty-cash item' or 'no more than car fare,' or 'cigarette money,' he
cannot think of the price as high. But a pack-a-day smoker in 1973
spends nearly £100 a year on his cigarettes. A London man spends
£55 a year on subway fares to work and home. Some fairly high-
priced articles therefore involve spending equivalent to no more
than such petty-cash routines. A clever radio salesman says he can
often lead uncertain customers to the buying decision by proving
that the set does not cost more than his cigarettes over a certain
period of time. A Swedish daily advertised '1½ cigarettes—or Dagens
Nyheter in your mail box—costs the same.' And an Austrian salesman of electrical appliances says, '½p a day for electricity—less than
a box of matches.'

The equivalent-spending appeal can be applied to large purchases when they cost the equivalent of something relatively minor
that adds up through repetition. An air-conditioning salesman made
the point that a business firm could have clean, cool air at a capital-
outlay cost equivalent to its annual spending for janitor service to
clean floors.

In modern times, when technical improvements follow so fast one
after another, facts often arm a salesman with a powerful selling
point. A building owner once thanked a salesman for calling on
him, but explained that his heating plant had at least ten years' life.
However, he bought a new plant and scrapped the old one when the
salesman showed him that a new plant would save him ten per cent
of his fuel costs and the wages of a furnace man. When it will cost
your customer money *not* to buy your article, you need not fear his
price objection.

A pertinent and psychologically clever price discussion presupposes a very thorough knowledge of the offer. There can be no
insecurity in your mind, or you will find that it is not the price—
but the way you handle it—which causes the problem.

This chapter about price has been a very long one because we
have examined a great many ways and approaches to prevent price
objections from spoiling sales. We could take up still more, but most
of them would resemble those we have already considered, or else

be applications of the same principles. If the article you sell really has a place in the market, and if you have mastered the principles and methods just examined, you need never be speechless when a customer objects to the price you ask for the article.

Mention the price of the article at the right time. Relate the price to the return value which the customer receives. And beware of price defeatism! Be a creative salesman. Use your imagination.

The price area is the seventh area of creative selling, where sales are made and sales are lost.

EIGHT

The inner conviction area : Must the salesman be an R E P believer?

Can you answer these four questions?

1 How can a sales manager help a salesman to get over a slump?
2 What may prevent a top salesman in one line from being successful in another, aside from technical knowledge of the new line?
3 How does the reputation of the selling profession affect sales activities?
4 What is meant by 'selling the salesman to himself'?

Can you solve the following five problems?

1 Carl Peterson sells paint and varnish. He has been visiting wholesalers and the biggest retailers for about ten years. He is the top salesman of his firm and has repeatedly proved that he is experienced and accomplished in the technique of selling. He knows his territory thoroughly. But the sales manager discovers, with surprise, that Peterson's sales results have suddenly fallen off, as compared with the last season's, his figures show a big drop. Peterson cannot think of any reason why. He doesn't feel up to par, but he has done better when he was feeling worse. Come to think of it, competition seems to have become considerably more active...What reasons could be behind this drop? What action would you take if you were the Sales Manager?

2 Sales are dropping and the sales manager is determined to bring them back up. 'There's only one way to do it—make more calls. Our salesmen are making six calls a day—they'll have to make eight or nine and we'll get more orders. No excuses—see eight customers a day. If you don't, you're out. Selling is a hard job and it calls for hard work. If you don't like hard work, look for some easier job ... You've got to be tough with salesmen—their hides are too thick for anything else.' What do you think of this attitude?

3 A new salesman—only 21 and on his first selling job—is making the best volume record in a sporting-goods firm. He seems quite young in many respects—for instance, he spends his leisure in Boy Scout activities and in coaching a Little League ball team. Aside from these, he is completely wrapped up in his job and sells an amazing quantity of hunting and fishing and camping equipment although he doesn't seem to know any of the tricks of selling. How can you explain his success?

4 A firm that needs a new sales manager takes on a man with a doctor's degree in economics and marketing. He is smart, quick to understand basic business situations, and soon knows more about the field than did his predecessors. But sales fall off. The salesmen do not click with their new chief; they can't quite name what it is he lacks, but they say he lacks 'something.' Can you name it?

5 Today has been strictly foul for Frank Rowland, who sells life insurance. He was set to close the sale of three policies, and had hopes for progress on two other calls. But at ten in the morning his first prospect told him, 'I've got to take this policy from my wife's brother or else—you know how it is.' So Rowland was a little early for his appointment with Mr Cooper, an accountant who needed and wanted a really big business-protection policy. 'I'm sorry, Frank,' he said. 'My wife's father died suddenly last night and I've got to pay for the funeral and bring her mother to live with us. The policy will have to wait till the estate gets settled.' That left Mr Harrison, newly married, whose relatively small policy now began to look like the day's business. But Mr Harrison had received a letter from the Internal Revenue office disallowing an income-tax reduction and calling for prompt payment of the amount in question; so he can't take his policy 'just now.' Rowland has called on some new people who were on his list for next day, and they haven't been cordial. He wonders whether it's worth while to make his planned afternoon calls, and decides against it. 'This isn't my day—I'd louse up those calls too, the way I feel.' What would you have done?

The star salesman—then and now

Once upon a time, as they say in children's stories, people thought the star salesman was a man who reaped success after success with the aid of some magic formula. Nobody in those days believed it was necessary for the salesman to have his heart in his job and to believe in it, if he wanted to succeed. The call was for hard-boiled, cunning salesmen who did not throw up the sponge when they encountered uninterested customers, but instead opened fire and carried on with the battle. Sales managers worked to recruit experienced men of this type.

Today, experienced sales managers no longer put high hopes in experienced salesmen who have come in from other fields and other companies. They do not uniformly succeed—the tendency is the contrary, and lack of factual knowledge about the field does not explain the tendency, for some men who know the field well do not succeed with new employers.

People who cling to storybook ideas may ask how it is possible for an experienced salesman to turn in a poor sales record. There is no need to find the fact surprising. Experience in itself is often not enough for success—in many fields. Neither is skill enough in itself —many skilled strokemakers do not win golf tournaments.

The R E P conviction

As a salesman, you must be able to *convince your customer.* For you to succeed in doing so, it is essential that *you yourself be convinced* of the value of the article you offer, of the high character of the firm you represent, and of your own ability. Three things: the *Representative,* the *Enterprise,* and the *Product.* All successful sales activity is based on this R E P requirement.

Belief in these three creates enthusiasm; enthusiasm makes selling success possible. Lack of belief in the enterprise is dangerous; lack of belief in the goods is disastrous; lack of belief in the man, in *yourself,* is deadly poison.

Nothing could seem more obviously true than this statement about belief and lack of belief. But nothing is so neglected in directing the everyday work of salesmen as this necessity for establishing wholehearted belief in these three essentials. Sales managers and the marketing brass assume, *mistakenly,* that every normal salesman is all wrapped up in his job and just naturally believes in everything that has to do with it. So they hire new salesmen, give them first-class factual instruction about their goods and about the market,

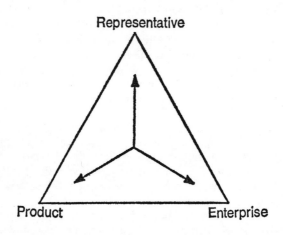

perhaps also some coaching in the selling techniques, and of course teach them the paper-work routines. And that's about all, except for a possible check-up to make sure the salesman has learned what he has been taught. Only rarely is any effort made to bring the salesman to a belief in his goods, his enterprise, and in the man he is. Even more rarely is this effort made when he is experienced and has transferred from another firm or another line. And almost never is any effort made to renew and strengthen R E P beliefs in the older salesmen who have been with the company a long time.

Carl Peterson, a proved star salesman of paint and varnish, found his volume falling off and only dimly suspected that the cause was a competitor who had begun to operate skilfully in his territory; he was not the kind of man who looks for excuses, and supposed that of course the fault was somewhere in himself. The sales manager told him, 'Don't worry. Just keep plugging, and plug a little harder.' Such perfunctory 'encouragement' doesn't help a salesman, and his sales slump is likely to continue. As it continues, the man loses belief in his goods, in his firm, and in himself. And the firm loses a valuable salesman who could be saved by just one think: support from his chief, selling the salesman to himself.

The more a salesman is dependent on himself in his work, the more he is isolated from his house, the more likely he is to lose his R E P beliefs. The man who represents a London firm in Yorkshire is alone at the far end of a long limb. But so is the man in the home-office city whose firm accepts the orders he brings in and never takes any other notice of him until his sales fall off. It is rare for a salesman to be self-stimulating as is the young man in the sporting-goods firm, in Problem Three at the beginning of the chapter. He is an active sportsman with a natural enthusiasm for sporting goods in general and a loyalty to 'his' goods.

Selling the product to the salesman

The R E P backbone of sales activity presupposes that facts will support the beliefs. A salesman can't be asked to believe in products of doubtful quality, or in·an enterprise that markets them by high-pressure methods, or in himself if he associates himself with sub-standard goods and an off-standard firm. The salesman in such a position cannot have the incentive that leads him to success.

Convincing the salesman of the merits of his product is primarily a question of supplying him with information about them. He will have a more vivid and useful conception of this if their advantages and disadvantages compared with competitors' goods have been clearly explained to him, and he is kept up-to-date with this information. This knowledge can be reinforced by keeping him informed of all essential details about the company's shares as well as the market in general (success stories are useful for sales talks). If possible the salesman should use the goods himself, as a consumer, and learn to assess them in this way. A chance to see the actual manufacture of the goods he sells, knowing about technical developments, meeting technical experts etc will provide a further basis for his conviction about the value of his goods.

Selling the salesman to himself

Always remembering that the goods and the enterprise must be worthy of the salesman's belief in them, the sales management's primary job is to *sell the salesman to himself* in order to provide a basis for his success in selling the goods entrusted to him. It must convince him that *he* is the right *man;* that, knowing the reputation of his organisation and its products, knowing the products and knowing how to sell them, he *can* sell them. It is vitally necessary to keep this conviction constantly alive.

Selling the enterprise

At one time, as far as considerations of these sales problems went, it was generally held that the salesman's job finished when he got the signature or agreement of the customer. The responsibility for the goods after that was left to another department who had to see that they were delivered. It was often the case—although not necessarily, for there have always been far-sighted and exceptionally capable business-men (in this sense, true 'marketing men')—that the development, successes and achievements of a business establishment were only made known to the so-called inner circle. As a rule little was done to ensure the proper guidance and information of the sales staff.

If an enterprise has a high reputation, the salesman benefits from it during every day he works. His self-confidence is bolstered up and so he has a greater sense of assurance in his work. But a good reputation has to be won and maintained daily and this is achieved, among other things, by the careful guidance of their representatives and frankness towards them. The prestige of the supplier is important in a buying decision; other things being equal, or even not quite equal, the salesman for a well-known firm is likely to get the order instead of the salesman for the firm the customer never heard of.

Selling is not robot work where ruthlessness and compulsion can produce the desired effects. Inner strength and tenacity are valuable qualities in a fair fight over sales and turnover. These qualities can not be produced by dogmatic harshness, compulsion or intimidation on the part of the sales manager, as was the case in problem 2. Methods like those produce insecurity and complexes but not a salesman who can go out and meet his customers on an equal footing.

Self-confidence

How can a sales manager create self-confidence in a salesman—the belief in himself and in his ability? Self-confidence is born of a man's knowing that he is master of his job, and this knowledge stems from successes. A salesman needs success even more than an entertainer needs applause, for success convinces him that he can convince others, that is, that he can sell to them. The more a salesman can be convinced of his ability to sell, the greater will be his sound self-confidence—an asset which strengthens him against inevitable set-backs. The kinds of depression that overtook Frank Rowland, the insurance agent in Problem Five, can never be wholly escaped in the course of intense sales activity. It is the task of a sales management to plan the selling programme of a salesman so that it does not confront him with problems that break down his emotional strength. A salesman's territory or list should include some easy customers with whom the salesman can experience frequent and confidence-building success. Then he can and will approach more difficult interviews with better chances.

If a salesman's orders fall off, the manager is wrong if he assumes that the only logical remedy is 'plugging a little harder' or correcting a selling technique. He should explore other possible causes. Could not his inner conviction have weakened? A salesman who does not really believe any more that his work will be of service to the customer can no longer convince him—at least not without high-pressure sales methods. Who is not convinced—cannot convince—and cannot create the desire for his goods. And so he is left with the reprehensible 'please buy for my sake!'

There can be a real difference between two sales managers with the same capabilities and qualifications. One may be able to inspire his colleagues with enthusiasm for his work and have the ability not only to be their 'boss' but also to lead them on the basis of confidence. The other may have got his job because of his knowledge of the field and of business in general, but his lack of human insight is a fatal shortcoming. A sales manager must be a natural leader of men.

Enthusiasm

'I can tell in a few minutes whether or not a man is capable of being a good salesman,' says one successful sales executive for a large industrial firm. 'I just want to listen to him talk a few minutes about his goods, his firm, and his work. If his talk doesn't show that he is enthusiastic about his activities I know that he cannot possibly be a good salesman.'

An enthusiastic man expects to succeed. He goes into every sales interview expecting to make a sale. But the man who enters the sales interview wondering whether he has a chance has in fact failed before he has even started. The salesman who is indifferent towards his own proposition will lead the customer into the same indifference. Indeed, the customer is normally indifferent and the salesman must expect this indifference. He, the salesman, must believe in his own success—the customer in the beginning is not interested in the salesman or in his goods. The salesman has to make his customer interested, and his enthusiasm and ability to create interest make him a creative salesman instead of an order taker. He can never expect to just find customer interest—he must create it.

Practically all sales literature stresses that the salesman should try to 'be enthusiastic.' Unfortunately, no one can tell him how to try. There is no patent medicine and no one-two-three routine for generating enthusiasm at will or at command, although the management can help instil enthusiasm into salesmen. But the salesman can help himself in this matter. He can protect himself against blunders by planning his sales talk. He should, before facing a customer, collect his thoughts and review all the selling appeals that should inspire the customer to desire his goods. By this systematic procedure he prevents his attention from drifting to earlier defeats. He is reminded, instead, of successes, where these selling points brought about sales, perhaps in spite of unfavourable circumstances.

The sales manager's role

The sales manager needs to be aware of the private life as well as the business life of his salesmen—for the private life may influence the professional life for good or for bad. The man who won't get enough sleep, either because he carouses or because he can't put away his butterfly collection, will have neither strength nor enthusiasm for his selling job. A disturbed family life affects a man's morale and robs him of emotional security and balance; in such circumstances he can scarcely be a convincing salesman. Though he knows, as in these examples, why a man is slumping or failing, the sales manager need not condone defeatism or inertia. He can drive out pessimism and indifference—not by empty phrases like 'keep plugging' or by mechanical pats on the shoulder, but instead by working at the real trouble, discovering the causes of it and helping to remedy them or at any rate not aggravating them. Creative sales management fosters the salesman's ambition, his inner conviction, and his competitive impulses.

Men who are drawn to the selling profession have inherent competitive instincts, and the sales manager should encourage these in every possible way. In particular, he should reward accomplishment —negotiating an important and difficult sale should bring praise and a bonus. Sales contests, designed to take into account relative success, will include rewards for achievement by new members of staff and improvement by generally low producers.

The sales manager can and should expect his salesmen to stay on the job and cover their territory systematically. Without expecting clock punching, he can and must discourage taking days off whenever the whim strikes. Customers should be able to count on finding a salesman when they want him, and so should the sales manager. Frequent and regular visits to customers are needed to bring sales results. But the salesman who is 'driven' to make these visits will not achieve good results; he should be convinced rather than forced. One way to convince the salesmen is to show them—to do their work when necessary, and prove that the sales manager can sell as well as supervise.

The sales management which can lead its salesmen according to these principles, and thus can form a real working team, will not only achieve high sales results but will also give its salesmen something that many salesmen lack—pride in their profession.

The salesman's status

In Europe the salesman has not got the social recognition that he enjoys as a matter of course in the USA. There the profession of salesman is greatly respected and people do not adopt the uppish attitude that a salesman's job really isn't quite nice. A man is judged by his achievements whatever his position, with top marks for the successful salesman. Here the salesman is often looked down upon either out of a lack of understanding or because we are behind the times. College classmates often shy away from the man who becomes a salesman and in many circles the attitude is 'Well, perhaps he is a decent fellow even though he is a salesman'. Many parents would prefer to see their son in a 'respectable' profession even if he is quite satisfied to be working as a salesman, and successful at it. People say things like 'He couldn't get on in any other profession so he became a rep' which shows a strange idea of the selling profession.

Often more respect is given to technicians than to salesmen in the works. The non-selling departments of an enterprise often downgrade the salesman instead of giving him support and yet it is the salesman who ensures the others' jobs and wages. After all, wages and salaries are paid by customers—whom the salesmen have made into buyers.

This public state of mind is to be deplored. The salesman and trader have built empires and spread civilisation. They have built the public buying desire that supports mass-production industry and the comfort of modern life. You cannot get away from the contribution the trader has made to the world. As far back as one can see, up to our own time the trader has always been the pacemaker of progress and development and always will be.

The exchange of experience

One of the ways to strengthen the salesman's conviction and to improve knowledge, ability and attitude is the organisation of well-planned and relevant, regular sales meetings, conferences and training courses.

Some progressive Companies have them weekly or monthly with good success, but others are afraid of the cost, argue that their salesmen should 'sell, not meet' and never call them together for any such reason.

Encourage your salesmen to participate more in the life of the Company, have them exchange their experiences, make them meet other members of the Staff, and you will immediately feel the resulting improved spirit.

If in addition you can procure genuine knowledge or improve abilities, the salesmen will grow confident of their capabilities and their power to convince.

How does the salesman himself react to being a member of an honourable profession? Unfortunately he often buries his head in the sand. He could do far more to gain for his work the respect it deserves. He should show more professional pride.

The salesman's task

Selling is not just taking orders. If a salesman is content merely to bring back orders that the customer has decided to place, the salesman is superfluous because a messenger would do as well. He is not on the job if he visits or telephones his customers merely to ask whether they 'need anything today.' That kind of salesman doesn't always end the day empty-handed, but he is no more than an order clerk and is far removed from creative selling.

If you are going to be a salesman you must accept the certainty that FOUR FIFTHS OF THE PEOPLE YOU VISIT WILL TELL YOU THAT THEY AREN'T INTERESTED *in whatever you have to offer.*

You have to live with this fact, keep it in mind all the time, use it as the start of every selling talk you plan and deliver. Then the customer deals you no blow when he tells you what you already know—that he isn't interested. You are going to *get* him interested. Salesmen had to get customers interested in the first automobiles, the first vacuum cleaners, insurance policies, cash registers, fire extinguishers, refrigerators, adding machines—and just about everything else this side of food in a famine. Four-fifths of their customers 'weren't interested.' But if these pace-setting salesmen had been put off by such customer resistance, these everyday realities would still be daydreams or novelties.

Creative selling means interesting uninterested customers. Selling to them demands all-out mental and emotional effort, more than the salesman can put forth unless he is an REP believer.

The inner conviction area is the eighth area of creative selling, where sales are made and sales are lost.

D

NINE

The reasoning area: The man who 'wins' arguments

Can you answer these four questions?

1 Can an entire sales presentation consist of an application of the question technique?
2 Why does success in an argument so rarely become a success in selling?
3 Must the salesman win agreement on every point to be able to sell?
4 What are some of the methods of changing the views of customers?

Can you solve the following five problems?

1 Dillon Evans was an old and experienced salesman of agricultural machinery. He knew every piece in his line of equipment in complete detail, and almost every piece in his competitors' lines, and was familiar with every advantage and disadvantage of every piece he knew. He knew, and knew why, the machines his firm made were the best. In fact, he knew the subject better than anyone else, and he made no attempt to conceal the fact. Whenever he ran into a farmer who thought himself pretty well up on farm machinery, Evans really unwound. Before long they would be in a contest as to who knew the most, and Evans would always win. Demonstrating his superiority in this way was a mighty satisfaction to Evans, and his

expert knowledge grew with years and experience. But not his sales figures! Even men who accepted his judgement in technical matters were never quite ready to order from him. How would you combat a tendency to be like Evans if you were in his place? When and how would you impress your customer with your expert technical knowledge?

2 Wharton Rowbotham is a salesman of office equipment and an expert on filing systems, the major items in his line. Secure in the expert knowledge of his field, Rowbotham considered his selling technique and decided that the mood and approach of his sales talks were too soft. He would make much stronger bids for attention, shake the customers out of their lethargy. He began making such direct—and truthful!—statements as, 'The filing system in your office is out of date. You can save six hours of clerk time every day if you switch to our equipment.' Rowbottom was invariably right when he made such contentions, but customers rarely took him up on them. Most of them would evade discussion or commitment; a few would challenge him with 'I don't believe it.' Rowbotham would start to prove it but rarely finished the proof because the customers so often exhibited impatience and irritation. They would question his statements, refuse to agree on obvious matters of casual fact, or look out the window and wish Rowbotham would just go away. Rowbotham reviewed his call notes one week-end and found nearly every customer ticketed, 'Simply won't listen to reason,' or 'Won't admit a fact when he knows it.' From the logical point of view, Rowbotham's way to proceed was not wrong, was it? Would you nevertheless criticise it? Can you prove a deficiency to a customer without criticising him? How ?

3 The sales manager of a big wholesale firm is discussing an expansion of the sales force. His chief favours taking on men already familiar with the trade, who have gained experience working for competitors. 'I don't care for the idea,' says the sales manager. 'Anyone we get that way will have a right to think he's pretty good, and he'll be hard to control. He'll want to use his own selling methods, and why not?—he's been making a living at them. He'll figure he knows the business, and why not?—that's why we'd be hiring him. Let's take some young fellows out of our own office force, maybe out of the warehouse or off the trucks, and train them. They'll be willing to learn and they'll work the way we teach them.' The chief can't see anything wrong with hiring men who already have developed their own effective methods and know the business. 'They'd be all right,' says the sales manager, 'if we could keep their heads down to

their hat size. But they'll get into arguments with customers. They'll be on the spot and think they have to sell right away, and they won't be able to relax.' The chief says, 'Well, I suppose you know salesmen. But I still think we could train experienced men our way sooner than we could train beginners.' 'The experience is just what I'm afraid of,' the sales manager persists. What is your thinking regarding this problem? Are both gentlemen right in some aspect?

4 There is a type of customer that enjoys baiting salesmen. These people like to needle salesmen and see how they act, new and inexperienced salesmen in particular. One such man always greeted a new salesman with, 'Well, what kind of white elephant are *you* trying to unload?' In one day he fired that one at seven salesmen. Two of them blew up completely—they didn't have any white elephants, they protested; they told him coldly or hotly that they represented reputable firms, and they asked him just what he meant by his question. One other salesman ducked the question and asked whether it would be more convenient for the buyer to see him some other time. Two others covered up quickly—they were just looking in, wanted to get acquainted, new in the territory, nothing urgent ...Two of the salesmen, however, mastered the situation and got orders. What do you think was their attitude?

5 'He was wrong all down the line,' the salesman reported to his boss. 'Wrong on every point, the jerk, and I proved it. He plain wore me out. Wouldn't admit anything. Rather win an argument than make money. I finally gave up and got out—I'd stayed with him for three hours, but it was hopeless.'—'It was hopeless after ten minutes,' the boss told him angrily. 'You laid an egg and boiled it for sure.' The salesman didn't get the point; he asked, 'What do you mean? Do you want me to give up after ten minutes?' What's your opinion?

Arguing and/or selling

All too often sales do not develop because the customer and the salesman have slipped from conversation into controversy and from controversy into quarrelling. We all know the man who wins every argument and loses nearly every sale. We know that we don't win customers by winning victories in disputes, and we know that a customer talked to a standstill has little desire to buy and much desire to get the salesman out of his office. Customers who are half sold in the beginning come completely unsold after a long argument. Everyone dislikes people who are 'always right'—and customers especially dislike salesmen who are 'always right.' We all have an antipathy to unsolicited advice from those who 'know better'; sometimes we feel the same antipathy towards solicited advice when it isn't quite what we want to be told. Yet in the face of all this knowledge some salesmen rush into hot discussions in order to prove that they are right—rush joyfully into them! But who on earth has not been told, who on earth does not know, that *it is impossible to convince a person against his will?* And yet, it happens time and time again, not only between salesman and customer, but also between sales manager and salesman.

Changing opinions

A salesman who wishes to change a customer's opinion must first succeed in making him ready and willing to change. The customer must be led and stimulated in such a way that the initiative comes from him—that he takes up the salesman's idea and makes it his own. For this reason, the 'argumentative method' is the worst possible way of attempting to convince a customer. In an argument, contact is quickly lost and the conversation becomes disagreeable to the customer, especially if he is losing the argument. You should watch your language and control your thinking as soon as you discover that your opinion differs from that of the customer. In the beginning of the conversation above all, avoid touching on matters about which you do not agree with the customer. Instead, create a basis for mutual outlook by stressing points on which you do agree. Let the customer realise fully the extent to which you agree with him, how well you understand his views, the number of matters in which you think he is right. As far as possible, avoid anything negative. Treat casually any differences of opinion that develop, unless they bear directly on the buying decision. Before you try to correct or refute any statement of the customer's, ask yourself, 'Do I have to take him up on that point in order to make my sale?' More often than not, you don't have to. If you think you do, first think at least once more.

The relation climate

The more you agree with a customer the better will be his opinion of you, and the more favourable will be the atmosphere—an element that is highly important for the successful outcome of a sales interview. If you genuinely consider the customer's viewpoint and skilfully match your own ideas to his, you will influence him favourably towards your proposal because such compromises tend to set up give-and-take obligations and to establish something in the nature of a bond. Avoid involving personal prestige—his, and yours. The salesman who worries about his prestige will soon have cause to worry about his economic existence.

You can keep the relation climate happy by not giving an unnecessary demonstration of your knowledge; such showing off may provoke the customer to contradict you. You do not need to 'teach' the customer; you can be well content if you sell him your goods. If you get the order, he can keep his prejudices, his idiosyncrasies, his opinions, his tastes—even though they are all wrong. It is poor tactics to try to alter or 'improve' the customer, even if it seems desirable; if he needs change or 'improvement,' probably others, closer to him, have tried to accomplish it and have already made him stubborn.

The question technique

A frequent source of arguments is the natural difference of opinion arising out of claims made by the salesman for the article he is selling. But it is easy to avoid such arguments—the salesman needs only to avoid asserting the claims. Instead of making an assertion, you can ask the customer his opinion on the matter. Assertions can always be challenged; some people automatically challenge them. In any case, assertions tend to be provoking; questions are rarely so.

Wharton Rowbotham need not have written so many gloomy call notes if he had asked questions instead of asserting claims. Suppose he had asked: 'Would you like to save the salary of one file clerk? ... Would you like to see a filing system that will do it for you?' These simple questions would have got the conversation off to a constructive start. If you use questions in this way you flatter your customer instead of challenging him. Doesn't everyone like to express an opinion? Through such questions, also, you arouse the curiosity of the customer—soon *he* is asking *you* questions.

Even if a question is not successful, it doesn't block the conversation. If a customer parries it or ignores it, you can still ask another question; you can keep asking questions even if one of them turns up an answer you don't want. But if you make an exaggerated claim, a mistaken assertion, or even a true statement that the customer doesn't believe, you arm him for a counter-attack and you lose all control of the sales conversation. (See Chapter 19).

It is not at all easy to relinquish the assertive approach, which is the innate tendency of most salesmen, and to put forth all your sales points by the question method. But it is worth while trying. It pays off!

Neutralising a conversation—an example

The question method is effective for dealing with the salesman-baiting prospect. One salesman, in Problem Four, answered the heckling buyer with 'Do you want a white elephant— I can get you one, but we don't have them in stock?' The other one asked, 'Will you talk to me next month if I sell you a white elephant today?' Asked with a little obvious display of good nature, a grin or a smile, such questions can get a conversation started towards the serious business of selling.

The sales conversation often reaches a deadlock when factual opinions are in significant opposition. A feeling of irritation is likely to arise in either the salesman or the customer, or in both. In this situation the creative salesman knows that he needs to neutralise the conversation, or switch it to another subject, or even suspend it for a short interval.

Do *you* know how to steer a conversation out of irritation, tension, argument?

You might study the following conversation as illustration of dangerous discussion and of various traps in the selling process. It is much simplified and condensed; in a real conversation the traps might not be so easily seen or escaped, the prospect not so responsive or amenable. An auto salesman, John Murphy, has finished greeting Mr Knight, who walked into the showroom to inquire about a sports car.

Murphy: This car is very comfortable, Mr Knight.

Mr Knight: (grunts).

M.: (*seeing his mistake*) How about trying the driver seat? Tell me if it's comfortable.

K.: I'll tell you if it isn't. (*But he gets in.*)

M.: How do you find the seat adjustment? Are you comfortable at the wheel?

K.: Seat's okay. Wheel's comfortable enough. But, Good Lord! There's not much room in here!

M.: Not much room! Why, it's four inches—

K.: (*cuts him off*) I don't care. To me it feels crowded.

M.: (*sees his mistake and stops contradicting*) Well, you're a big man. How about the floor? Have you got enough leg room?

K.: I haven't got too much...But I guess it's enough.

M.: And as you said, you're comfortable at the wheel. Did you notice that's real leather you're sitting on? There's nothing better than leather! (*An opinion asserted as fact.*)

K.: I don't know about leather. It's hot in summer and cold in winter. I've never liked it. (*Murphy should have asked, not told. Now he's been contradicted. He is all set to counterpunch when he remembers that it doesn't matter.*)

M.: Well, you ought to know what you like. We have other upholstery, anyhow—anything you like, hard or soft finish. (*He changes the subject.*) How do you plan to use the car? City or country driving?

K.: Mostly home and office. Sometimes to the golf course. About a thousand miles a month.

M.: (*getting set for the economy appeal*) Then you want a car that goes easy on the fuel, don't you? (*Although this has the form of a question, it is really an assertion with a 'don't you' tied onto it. Dangerous!*)

K.: Of course I don't want a gas hog! But skip the miles per gallon. Whatever you're going to tell me, the car won't do it.

M.: Well, it depends on how you drive.

K.: What do you mean—how I drive?

M.: A lot of things—how you start, how often you park, traffic lights—

K.: That's peanuts! What burns me is these ads about twenty, thirty miles to the gallon; then you buy a car and you're lucky if you get fifteen. Fellow in my office got a...(*long story follows*).

M.: (*restraining himself from telling the customer that he's all wrong—which he is*) Look, why don't we check the gas this car burns? With you driving it? And you can tell me how it acts.

K.: All right. (*They drive off.*)

M.: Does your wife drive much?

K.: Some. Hauls the kids and so on. We have a Bigblank station wagon. But we aren't trading it.

M.: (*working around towards the easy-handling selling point*) Does this car handle easier than the Bigblank? Would your wife like to try driving it?

K.: Oh, not today. Of course it handles easier—that Bigblank's work to drive. Except for that I'd get another Bigblank— they give you your money's worth. (*Now the real sales resistance is emerging!*) Why in the devil do they price these little scooters so godawful high? (*Thanks to this remark, Murphy now knows that price is important to the customer—the car is all right as to size and suitability, but Mr Knight feels insulted by the high price. But if Murphy were to contradict Mr Knight and try to prove that the price is not excessive there would soon be a real row going on. So Murphy chooses a roundabout way to come to the point of fair value at the price.*)

M.: You've driven all kinds of cars, haven't you?

K.: Yes—all kinds, all prices, all ages.

M.: Then you know about what to expect. (*By recognising the customer's experience and acknowledging it, he has created a more congenial atmosphere, and he can proceed more safely than before.*) Tell me, what is it you're looking for, this time?

K.: Well, of course it's got to take me places. Almost any heap would do that. But I want something a little different this time—and good looking ... sporty ... high grade construction.

M.: (*at last he knows what interests Mr Knight most*) Something different, eh? Anybody you know got anything like this car?

K.: Not yet, they haven't.

M.: And how do you like its looks?

K.: It looks good—good enough, anyhow.

M.: Would you like to get under it and see how it's put together? On the lift rack back at the shop? (*Knight will see his money's worth in the mechanical quality, and the importance of price will shrink.*)

At last Murphy is on the right track and knows which selling points he should push and which he should duck. He stresses the merits of the car, particularly as to novelty and appearance and construction and—of course!—prestige appeal. Mr Knight wants 'to look around and think it over,' but Murphy knows he's got the car sold. In the next interview he writes the order.

Winning an argument is no great art. Avoiding one demands far greater skill. The creative salesman is clever enough to sidestep arguments and thus keeps the channel open and unobstructed for a successful sale. Questions lead there quicker than assertions.

The reasoning area is the ninth area of creative selling, where sales are made and sales are lost.

TEN

The objection area: How to overcome sales obstacles

Can you answer these four questions?

1 How should a creative salesman react to pretexts for not buying?
2 Why should a salesman consider the customer's objections of more help than harm?
3 How many reasons are there for heading off objections—that is, for disposing of them before the customer brings them up?
4 Do you know how to deal with objections by the boomerang method?

Can you solve the following five problems?

1 Two salesmen are discussing their last experiences. 'I was talking to a real tough buyer today,' says the first. 'Brown calls me on everything I say, and he's continually raising objections to the line.'—'Well, how do you handle him?'—'Not too well. He brought up a lot of things I couldn't answer right away. *Now* I know the answers—but you can't ask a buyer to wait while you dig up the answers.'—'Why can't you?'——'Why *can't* I? *How* can I?'—'Easy! Here's the way to do it ...' Do you know the way? How? Does not the customer get the impression that you are insufficiently informed?
2 Orlando Myers, who sells structural steels, visits a Mexican customer who is about ready to buy the steel for a big project. He goes over what his firm can offer—specifications, quality, price, terms,

delivery schedule, guarantees—everything, with well-considered thoroughness and everything supported by concrete evidence. The whole time the purchasing agent listens attentively but does not participate in the conversation in any way. After a full half-hour the gentleman thanks Mr Myers for the information and says that he is not interested just now. But Myers knows the time for decision is near, and makes two more visits at decent but short intervals—both without results. Then, in a fourth visit, Myers starts almost from scratch, covering the first interview ground in detail. For twenty minutes the customer listens in polite silence—then he raises an objection indicating a possible reason for not buying Myers' steel. Slightly disconcerted at first, Myers shakes off his fears and answers the objection. Again thanks; and again no decision. But the next time Myers calls he gets the order in ten minutes. Later, when he studies the course of this long negotiation, he discovers what error of judgement he committed. He might have got this order much earlier, whereas he almost failed to get it at all. What has been Myers' mistake? What importance can such errors have in the sales conversation?

3 At a sales conference, the sales manager of an office-equipment manufacturer asks his salesmen to report the objections their customers raise frequently. One young and very energetic salesman turns in a long list of them, remarking that many customers throw the whole package at him. The sales manager suspects there must be some fault in the young man's approach if he regularly encounters such a massive list of objections. He asks the salesman to act out one of his sales conversations and his suspicions are confirmed. The salesman alters his tactics and the sales results improve. Surely you have discovered why this salesman was subjected to so many objections?

4 A real-estate broker is discussing with his client the possible purchase of a house. They look at the building together, and the broker senses that the customer is by no means uninterested. The broker volunteers, 'It's a good house but I can see three places where it might be better. The heating plant needs an overhaul, the garage needs a paint job, and the rear lawn will take a couple of years to clear out the weeds and fix up the turf.' The customer says he appreciates the tip-off and the discussion proceeds. Was the broker's method right? Was it a good thing for him to point out the three defects?

5 'That's a problem nobody ever reported before,' is the spontaneous answer of Kenneth Newbold, a machinery salesman. 'I don't know the answer, but there's a man in our plant that does. I'll ask him. Can I phone you tomorrow and let you know what he says?' And

then he goes ahead with his selling talk. Next day, the plant expert answers Newbold's question but adds, 'You didn't have to ask me—you know that as well as I do. You probably gave your customer a lousy impression of you and the firm.'—'Of course I knew the answer,' Newbold agrees. 'But I didn't want to shoot it right at him.' —'I don't see your point,' says the expert. Do you see Newbold's point?

The customer who offers no objections

It is a rare sale that goes through without any objections from the customer. Objections are obstacles in the selling process, and selling has much in common with obstacle racing. If you take part in the race you must undertake to clear the obstacles. The customer who says only 'yes' and 'very good' and buys is a rarity. *A customer who has no objections is usually a customer who has no buying interest.* Myers, in Problem Two, thought he was well on the way to getting an order because the customer raised no objections. But Myers had not given the customer any chance to participate in the selling-buying process; he did not organise the conversation so it would lead the customer to declare his position and utter his objections.

There are nearly always some details about a proposition, if the customer is at all interested in it, that he would like to change or improve; these are what appear as objections. Even in the case of an advantageous offer, the customer has to forgo something else in order to acquire the article. In addition, there are specific objections concerned with the offer itself; every product is made up of compromises and has advantages and disadvantages.

The salesman concerned with the offer must, whether he feels inclined to do so or not, search out and satisfy the customer's objections if he wants him to buy. There is no sense in suppressing objections or in pretending that they don't exist. Only through getting them out into the open can the salesman hope to meet them. There is one and *only* one type of objection that is dangerous—the objection to which no satisfactory answer is given (whether because the salesman is at fault or because the article is at fault).

Objections are just the verbal signs of sales resistance—not dangers but warnings of danger. The sales resistance constitutes the danger; the verbal expression of it does not. Objections are, therefore, in a real sense a *help* to every good salesman. No customer objects to a proposal which leaves him *completely* untouched. The first objection of the customer, if it is not an unconditional rejection, is in reality the first sign that he is beginning to become interested. Objections are signposts indicating the position of the customer. They line up the target and enable the salesman to aim at the bulls-eye.

The following points are important:
1 Some salesmen lose their nerve and think they have lost the sale as soon as the customer raises any serious objections.
2 Some salesmen are not well enough prepared to counter objections properly.

There is one condition that must be satisfied before you are qualified to answer objections—a thorough knowledge of your own offer, of your customer, his problems and of any competition and the market in general.

Training yourself to deal with objections

There is an excellent method of training yourself to deal with objections. It is so simple that only a few salesmen actually use it. You take a sheet of paper and draw a line down the middle of it, then list on the left side all the objections you are likely to hear from customers—the ones you have heard and the ones you can imagine.

If a large number of objections occurs to you, you can keep the list to reasonable length, or at least keep it in order, by grouping similar objections. The number of different possible objections in connection with any one article seldom exceeds five or six. Any more are likely to be variants of different wordings of a few basic objections.

When you have listed all the objections you can, then on the other side of the line write your *best* answer to each objection. If the same answer isn't best for all situations, write down the other answers; you will need them all. Then ask your fellow salesmen, your sales manager, your other colleagues, for their best answers, and write these down. Now you have more answers than objections! Out of the long list of answers you will select some, using your judgement and experience, that are especially effective. But you will be wise to study the list, repeatedly, until you have mastered all the objections and all the answers. You will discover new objections, add them to the list, devise replies for them, improve the replies you have devised, eliminate replies that prove ineffective, adjusting the list in the light of day-to-day experience. You and your colleagues can help each other by acting out sales talks, playing the salesman and customer roles, and exchanging objections and answers until you can give them both in your sleep. If you do these things you will almost never be caught without an answer to a real buying objection. Knowing the moves as you do, you will enjoy an encouraging feeling of confidence and security when you call on a customer.

The basic kinds of objections

To deal with objections properly you must know (1) what kind of answer to give, (2) when to give the answer, and (3) how to give the answer.

In order to know what answer to give, you must understand the kinds of objections you will encounter. Here are ten types:

1 *Unspoken objections,* which are always present but which you have to bring into the open before they can be answered.

2 *Excuses* (pretexts), which are best sidestepped, as they do not represent real objections.

3 *Prejudices, preconceived opinions*—illogical and strongly emotional objections which cannot easily be countered by reason.

4 *Malicious objections*—customers' efforts to disconcert the salesman, arising from bad temper, or an attempt to confuse or mislead him. Sometimes the customer even expresses ideas that he has heard somewhere, and which do not really reflect his own opinion.

5 *Wishes for information*—objections raised with the purpose of obtaining additional information from the salesman.

6 *Objections on grounds of prestige*—factually groundless objections raised mainly to show off the customer's idea of his own importance or knowledge.

7 *Subjective objections*—such as: 'The article is good but doesn't suit *me*,' or 'Our problems are different.' These need not necessarily imply criticism of the proposition itself.

8 *Objective objections*—remarks aimed directly at the article or the offer. It is important to distinguish these from the subjective type.

9 *General sales resistance*—a quite general and indefinite attitude which meets the salesman at the beginning of the selling talk.

10 *The 'last effort'*—the final objection raised shortly before the buying decision. Often an objection which the customer has used

before. Tone of voice and measure of intensity indicate that the customer is ready to buy.

Basic methods of dealing with the basic kinds of objections

Here are just a few suggestions, schematically arranged for the sake of brevity, as to how the salesman can deal with these cases.

1 *Unspoken objections.* The salesman can minimise the number of unspoken objections by cutting down his own talk and letting the customer do his share (questions and answers). The more the customer talks the more he reveals his viewpoint for and against the proposition. Sometimes it is necessary almost to force the customer to express his opinions. The method of questioning (in some cases even provocative questioning) can be an excellent help in such cases.

The conversation is to be concentrated on the customer's present situation and problems—not on the offer as such. This method offers no difficulties : it demands only self-discipline and self-control to avoid talking too much. If you feel that the customer has some objection on the tip of his tongue it is best to choose the direct route to the obstacle: ask him what he does not understand, whether he has some objection in mind, or if you have said something he does not agree with. The customer will usually answer freely and be glad to be able to speak his mind, particularly if he has been tactfully restraining himself from saying anything disparaging. Make it easy for the customer to voice his objections. Only when an objection has been mentioned can it be tackled.

2 *Excuses.* Don't waste too much time on excuses. They do not represent real objections. Even if you could answer them the purpose of selling would not be materially advanced, the customer might be irritated for no good purpose, and time would be lost unnecessarily. And why force a customer to defend his excuse and thus harden it into a real objection? As a rule excuses are distinguished by the fact that they reveal no direct connection with the customer's general line of argument. There are various methods of dealing with an excuse. You can pretend not to have heard it. You can offer to return to the point a little later—hoping that he will not insist once the conversation has developed. Some excuses can be disposed of in a few words. And, finally, you can leave them unanswered or yield the point and continue to sell.

3 *Prejudices.* Prejudices and preconceived opinions are difficult. Even if the customer is completely wrong, proving the fact does

not help. If the customer holds the opinion that the introduction of automatic time recorders in his office would destroy the joy in work, that a car has to be big to be any good, that green typewriters are ugly, that all French perfumes are better than American, and that trade through jobbers is bad business, then it is very difficult to overcome the idea. The view of the customer in such cases is based on emotion, and any purely logical arguments just bounce off. If you can avoid dealing with prejudices without endangering the sale, do so. Let the customer remain convinced that green is not a good colour for typewriters, if the appearance is of secondary importance. Admit that big cars are generally excellent, and turn the discussion to the advantages of your small car for his *special* kind of use. Under the influence of skilfully chosen facts the customer will forget his prejudice. Treat the perfume problem in a similar way by leading the discussion away from the question of origin. Pretend not to have heard the remark about jobbers; concentrate the conversation, instead, on the offer and the advantage to the customer of his being able to buy goods from a varied stock in a nearby warehouse.

The prejudice against automatic time recording is not so easy to deal with. You have no answer to such a statement as 'I don't like time clocks' or 'My girls would hate it.' So you agree that the objection has weight; but you go on selling. You mention firms that use the equipment, tell him what their experience has been in the matter of employee response. You may be able to ask him whether other efficiency-promoting measures, which he has put into the office, have damaged employee relations (be sure you know that they have not). You may offer professional service in preparing the employees to accept or welcome the change.

4 *Malicious objections.* First and foremost, don't be too hasty; and resist the inclination to be offended. If you can pretend not to have heard the objection, do so. The customer's display of bad temper need not necessarily have been evoked by you personally. Among the possible objections in the group are rumours which the customer may have picked up—concerning falling prices, import restrictions, and so on. It is not difficult to discover their true meaning. Generally speaking, malicious objections are distinctly related to excuses, and can sometimes be treated in the same way.

5 *Desire for information.* Objections which indicate the need for more detailed information must be welcomed positively. Besides being evidence of interest, they point out to the salesman certain flaws in his sales talk, and give him the opportunity of repairing them. Learn to recognise objections of this kind quickly. They are

more in the nature of a question than a statement—if not in form then in tone (for example: 'How can this material be of such good quality as the more expensive one?' or 'This sounds all very good, but we can't turn our whole system of soap-production upside down just on the *chance* of improving the quality, can we?') The customer needs a convincing explanation of proof. Accustom yourself to regarding most objections as invitations to give more and better information. Then your answer will be reasonable, balanced, affirmative, and convincing.

6 *Objections on grounds of prestige.* Many objections can be traced to the customer's desire to show that he has an opinion of his own. He wants to show that he can't be influenced, or that his position renders him independent. It is surprising how often objections based on obstinacy or the wish to maintain prestige are in inverse ratio to the advantageousness of the offer—the more favourable the proposition the stronger the effort of the customer to establish a contrary opinion. If you have just a little knowledge of human nature you can readily understand such an attitude. Often the customer feels driven to adopt it by the all-too-sure language and cocksure behaviour of the salesman. Therefore, be careful not to present your selling points as emphatic assertions; avoid a cocky attitude; and don't tell the customer—ask him. Don't give the customer the impression that you think all your ideas are the best ones. Direct the conversation in such a way that the customer finds confirmation of his own opinions in yours. Let him take part in the shaping of the proposal, and ask him for information and advice. Make him, in fact, your partner. Sometimes it is necessary to allow for his objections in your proposal and to attempt to achieve a compromise solution. This naturally places the customer to some extent under an obligation. Such compromises, which involve you in a certain degree of giving in, are very conducive to reaching an agreement.

7 *Subjective objections.* Every salesman must learn to distinguish between subjective and objective objections. Proving the excellence of an article is not enough to overcome the sales resistance of a customer if the article does not please him. (Study the connection between the quality and the utility of an article, dealt with in Chapter 6.) There are always people who believe that their problems are of a very special kind. Their problems and their work cannot be compared with those of others; and the experiences of others are not applicable to themselves. They may want to do everything in their own different way just because it is theirs, want to be different to assert their ego. Every time you encounter many such subjective

objections you can be almost sure that your selling talk is concerned too much with the offer and not enough with the customer and his problems.

If you use references and letters of recommendation you must be very careful over their choice. You should select expressions from enterprises and customers whose type, size, and problems correspond significantly with those of your present customer. Then you are less likely to get the objection: 'That may be suitable for those people, but not for us.' You must collect as much detailed knowledge as you can about the customer and his problems; in many cases you can do so only by investigation on the spot. Offers of trial installations, guarantees, the right to return, and similar inducements can also help to overcome doubts. Experience proves that a customer will drop his subjective objections and really participate, once he has convinced himself that the salesman is an expert who has made himself familiar with the customer's own special problems, or is prepared to do so. The more you can put your selling on the personal plane the better are your prospects of avoiding subjective objections.

A word by the way. Subjective objections are hard to overcome. There are no patent remedies—as there are none, in fact, for any objections—but only pointers such as those indicated. In some cases the customer is quite simply right. In others there is nothing at all that can convince him. No salesman can convince all the prospective customers.

8 *Objective objections.* Here the salesman is on his own ground. And he knows it—sometimes, perhaps, even too well. Before correcting a false impression entertained by the customer, let him know that you understand his view and could have shared it if you had been in his position. For instance: 'These performance figures really seem almost unbelievable when you see them for the first time, don't they? The fact is, we wouldn't believe them ourselves the first time we saw them. So we ran a check test, and here's what showed up...' (Further tactical hints are given later in this chapter.)

9 *General sales resistance.* Here the salesman is encountering an attitude rather than any identifiable objections. This situation exists at the beginning of the sales interview, when the customer may want to object but can scarcely formulate an objection. Thus his objections are not firmly formed, and cannot be. It would be premature for the salesman to meet directly this resistance that reveals itself in vague general objections—if he were to do so the situation might easily become bogged in controversies. At no time are the dangers of controversies so great as at the beginning of a conversation. To get around this kind of sales resistance, the salesman can

.make use of the hints about the Attention Stage in the discussion of The Selling-Process Area (Chapter 12).

If general sales resistance is unduly strong at the beginning of all his interviews, something is wrong either with the salesman's selling technique or with the offer as such—and then it is necessary to find out what is wrong.

10 *The 'last effort.'* This objection, the 'last kick' shortly before the 'yes' is said, is rarely meant seriously. Every decision to buy is accompanied by an uncomfortable sensation—the thought of the expense; apprehensions concerning the consequences of the purchase and the difficulties which may be connected with its use; the fear of having acted rashly, or having made a disadvantageous purchase. All such normal thoughts and feelings express themselves as last-moment objections. Frequently they are only repetitions of objections made earlier by the customer—which simplifies the treatment of them. But the repetition of an objection can also be evidence that the salesman did not answer the objection satisfactorily the first time. A careful analysis of the emotional background of the objection will orient the salesman as to whether he should go to the root of the objection or rather endeavour to increase the customer's trust in him. Often, however, this objection is a kind of shadow-boxing preceding the decision to purchase. Instead of answering such an objection directly the salesman can often put forward an indirect request to buy and thereby quickly close the deal. (*Customer:* 'This washing machine seems like a big proposition for our small family.' *Salesman:* 'Look—let's get it into your house and see how it fits.')

The time to deal with objections

Choosing the right time to answer an objection is much more important than many salesmen realise, and is often as important as the answer itself.

You can answer an objection (*a*) before the customer comes out with it; (*b*) immediately when he comes out with it; (*c*) at some later moment; or (*d*) never.

(*a*) *Answering the objection before it is made.* If you know or sense that a customer is about to make a certain objection you may want to head him off by taking up the question yourself, and answering it. This manoeuvre gets you out of the need to correct or contradict something your customer says, and reduces the risk of getting into an argument. You get the additional advantage that comes from deciding how to word the objection. You put it into the conversation at a time you choose. By putting certain pros and cons of your proposition voluntarily before your customer, you show him that you are not trying to hide anything. You make the customer feel that you understand his reactions. You may even get an objection into the open that the customer might hesitate to voice, or be unable to formulate—but which would stand as an obstacle against a buying decision. All these matters contribute to creating a basis for your customer's confidence in you. The objection tends to seem less important when the salesman brings it up than when the customer brings it up. And you may save a great deal of time that would have been needed to draw the objection out of the customer.

A salesman of any experience or skill soon learns what objections are likely to be raised against his proposition, and what kind of customer is likely to raise each kind of objection. There is your answer to the question about the real-estate broker's selling method. The more objections you can forestall by putting them into your own sales talk, the better.

(b) *Answering the objection immediately.* This is the most natural time to answer objections and the time at which you will answer them unless you have a reason for preferring another time.

(c) *Answering the objection later.* To postpone the answer is the right method in seven situations:

1 Delay your answer if you cannot give a *satisfactory* answer immediately. (Newbold, the machinery salesman, made his answer more satisfactory to the customer by attributing it to the plant expert. He showed that he did not treat the objection lightly and that he could be trusted to get an expert answer rather than deliver a snap answer off the cuff.)

2 If an immediate answer would break up the development of your selling points, or turn attention away from the point under consideration, try to delay your answer. You want to keep control over the timing of details in the sales conversation; if you let the customer assume the initiative you may find yourself being cross-examined.

3 Delay your answer if it would be or seem to be a flat contradiction of something your customer has said. A quick answer in this situation is likely to irritate a customer. It may give the impression that you are reeling off a memorised talk, that you have been too well coached and rehearsed. And even the customer may prefer to get the answer later, at a better moment.

4 Delay your answer when the objection is likely to dwindle in weight as the conversation advances.

5 Delay your answer if there is a chance that you will not need to make answer. Some objections almost answer themselves as the conversation develops. Excuses for reasons of prestige or a bad mood may, after some time, appear unfounded or unimportant even to the customer, in which case he will not expect to be answered if the salesman knows how to delay his reply for a while. The decisive point is whether the ensuing sales conversation gives the customer new reason for his objection.

6 Delay your answer unless you know it is a correct and true one. Salesmen are constantly making fools of themselves by trying to answer objections about matters they do not understand. Get the true answer, even if it takes time. If you don't know *the* answer and try to make up a quick one, your effort will be unsatisfactory and your customer will know that you are ignorant, or bluffing, or lying, or all three. He will know it very well, in due time, even if you happen on a plausible but incorrect answer. Admitting your lack of knowledge may sometimes (not always) delay the transaction, but it always increases your customer's respect for your reliability. A delayed answer may, admittedly, cause a lost sale; but it is less likely to do so than a wrong, bluffing, dishonest answer.

7 Try to delay your answer if your customer's objection is irrelevant to the discussion, or if it will be dealt with in the later course of an explanation that you have planned for a later moment in the interview. Some customers just generally bring up irrelevant ideas. Some objections simply can't be discussed usefully before the sales conversation has been developed to a proper point.

(*d*) *Not answering the objection.* As was said earlier, many objections need not be answered, or cannot be answered, or should not be answered. Prestige objections, excuses, malicious objections, prejudices, or the vague objections arising from general sales resistance at the outset—attempting to answer these can create dangerous arguments and make the sale hopeless. Justified objections cannot be answered but must be acknowledged; you should not throw away your fund of customer good will by attempting to deny faults or objections that are real.

Twelve approaches for dealing with objections

1 *Try to penetrate the screens.* You must deal with what your customer is really thinking, and this is often something other than what he says. No matter how earnestly a buyer states his objection, his statement may be misleading and may be intended to hide the real source of the sales resistance, the source the customer does not want to reveal and may not even know.

Few customers like to admit that they cannot make a buying decision without consulting someone else—a business superior, perhaps, or a wife. Such customers give other reasons for postponing the buying decision, or else find fault with the article.

People who can't afford to buy something hate to confess the fact. An embarrassed individual looks for defects with an emotional magnifying glass in order to have some other explanation than poverty. A business man who obviously needs and could use what you offer will invent almost any kind of subterfuge to avoid admitting that his firm is not making enough money to afford the purchase.

A somewhat similar kind of feeling prompts business people not to reveal that their volume is small. One man, for example, refused to install a postage meter 'because it makes letters look like junk'; he would not reveal that his firm's correspondence volume did not justify even the smallest postage meter.

Since so many stated objections are not the real objections, the salesman must analyse all objections before answering them—anything the customer says may be a cover-up. A few sales experts believe, with some justification, that almost every stated objection is a camouflage for another one. The way to locate the real objection is to keep the customer talking so you can pick up hints about his general background ideas and reactions. You can ask him to elaborate his objection; you can even put the simple question, 'Why?' For instance, 'Why do you think so?' (But be careful—you are in real fact trying to corner him, cross-examine him, catch him with a phony; and he will resent your questioning, unless you are careful to save his face.) The less well-founded his stated objection, the more the customer will have to talk, and the more he will reveal to you intentionally or otherwise. The more you learn, the better you can direct your reply to the real objection. Whatever the objection, your counter-questions will give you information and time for formulating your answer.

2 *Keep your composure.* You know better than to irritate the customer; you must not let him irritate you. Always answer the objection in a calm and friendly manner. An answer that betrays annoyance tells your customer that the objection has bothered you and makes him likely to press it more aggressively and to doubt your answers. Preserve an unperturbed manner, a relaxed attitude, a

smile, and a clear and convincing tone of voice. All these, in themselves, have a considerable favourable effect, particularly in the atmosphere of serious objections.

3 *Be civil.* Never contradict the customer directly, even if he is very much in the wrong. Your contradiction will never convince him or impress him favourably. You must try to overcome his objection by approaching it from another aspect.

4 *Be respectful.* Maintain and show respect for your customer's views—even if you think they are wrong and even if you don't share them.

5 *Be agreeable.* Many objections are due to the customer's need to strengthen his prestige and to show off. Therefore, agree with him more often.

6 *Be modest.* Restrain the tendency to cast yourself in the role of authority or expert. Offering your personal opinions as sales points is something of this sort: 'If I were in your place...' and 'I use it myself.' Such expressions may be out of place unless the customer invites them or accepts your views as expert.

7 *Be concise.* Give your replies without rambling. Don't talk your point away. Your customers are likely to grow restive and balky if you make them listen to long-drawn-out and roundabout replies. The longer your answer the more likely it is to have weaknesses. And while you keep on talking your customer is devising new objections based on such weaknesses.

8 *Be responsive.* Answer your customer's objections when you answer them; don't brush them off with a half answer. Watch him to see whether he is satisfied with your answer; until he is, continue to present every fact you can truthfully offer. Don't beat around the bush. If you aren't dead sure that you have answered a man, ask him straightforwardly: 'Does that answer your question?' or 'Does that leave anything up in the air?' If you don't ask such questions, you will have no assurance that your reply has done its job.

9 *Be progressive.* Don't dwell on an objection any longer than required by point 7. Change the subject and proceed with the negotiation.

10 *Study your product.* Learn every fact you can, and keep seeking for more facts, about the article you sell and the ways it has been used, can be used, is used.

11 *Study your customer.* Learn his personal preferences, his needs, his abilities and resources, his idiosyncrasies and prejudices, the ways you can help him. Keep abreast of them—he will change from time to time, and you need to know him as he is, not as he was last year.

12 *Study your business.* Keep posted on the experience people have had in using your product, on the objections they have expressed, the problems they have found and solved.

Fifteen hints on techniques and methods for dealing with objections

1 *The preventive method of presentation.* This method means, quite simply, building up your talk in such a way that the customer never feels or reaches the point of objecting. The customer has objections—if he hasn't, he isn't giving you any attention—but you anticipate them, deal properly with them, leave him satisfied about them, and go on with your sales talk. That is the right way to prevent objections; the wrong way, often seen in particularly aggressive salesmen, is to rush from one point to the next without giving the customer a chance to think or state his objections. But you can't silence a customer, and a particularly aggressive or rushing presentation provokes contradition.

Many objections are put forth by customers who haven't been able to keep up with the factual and logical development of the sales talk. You can prevent these objections by dividing the stages of your sales talk into still smaller stages, one-point stages, and presenting each in the form of a question that the customer answers. If his answer then should be an objection, it is a form of co-operation with you and not an act of controversy or contradiction.

You want to make your selling points in sizes and ranges that the customer can take in. Remember that you ought to know your subject much better than your customer does—and very likely you do know it. So you cannot assume that your customer is keeping up with you at every step of the sales talk. What is a-b-c- to you may be meaningless to him. You may have to do some of your customer's thinking in these matters, leading him slowly and gently to your way of seeing things. It is important to get along with the sales talk, but it is important not to leave the customer behind you in a fog.

It was clear to the sales manager in Problem Three that his young salesman needed help in the preventive method of sales presentation. When he learned to apply it his sales interviews moved more smoothly, interrupted by fewer objections.

2 *The 'Yes, but—' method.* The salesman must at all times avoid provoking the customer and getting him into a mood where he can't listen to truth or reason. If you can agree with your customer up to a certain point, you can carry him with you when you state the differ-

ence between what he has said and what you must say. For example: 'You are entirely right there—the light weight does reduce the resistance to vibration. The question is—how much? Also, what is the influence of this reduction on stability? Here are the results of some very critical but practical tests, which have also been made by the Technical Institute of the…University.' Note that although the idea is 'yes, but,' the language isn't. For the 'yes, but' manoeuvre is not only one of the most effective selling tactics but also one of the oldest. Every customer is alert to it. A man in Yorkshire even had cards printed that read: 'Don't but me! If you're a talking billygoat you belong in a circus.' The buyer of any experience when he hears 'yes,' expects to hear 'but'; when he hears 'but,' he hears the rest of the remark almost as if it were the flat contradiction not preceded by any 'yes.' The 'yes, but…' method is still good selling—but watch your language, and use it with discretion.

3 *The boomerang method.* However the customer may intend them, some objections lead to positive reasons for buying, and can be used as starting points for sale-closing developments. It has worked like this in automobile insurance:

Customer—'I don't want collision insurance. If I get a fender dent that costs twenty pounds to fix, I have all the red tape to get three pounds. That seventeen-pounds deductible stuff is for the birds.'

Salesman—'I'm glad you brought that up. Can I show you how that clause really saves you money? … Investigating accident claims costs insurance companies money, and the only money they get is from premiums. Sending a man out and getting reports on a claim costs anywhere from £2 to £10. Suppose we had a claim to service every time somebody got a £1 fender scratch? The claim-service costs on nearly every policy would go up to £15 or to £20 a year—we all get a few nicks in parking lots and that sort of thing. Those costs would have to be piled on top of the premiums. The way we do it now, your premiums don't go up every time an old lady scrapes a parking-meter post, but you are protected against a bad crash that might not be anything you could avoid.'

4 *The deferring method.* Here the salesman defers his answer until a more suitable time. Even a few seconds, or a few minutes, can be valuable thinking time. You can repeat the customer's words to make sure that you have interpreted the objection correctly. You can also ask the customer to be a little more explicit, to produce examples, to elucidate his objection, to provide evidence. Furthermore, you can break up the objection into its various elements, and

so on. When the customer is led in such a way to analyse his objection he may realise that he has not thought the matter out completely and may withdraw the objection.

5 *Agreement plus compensation*. To deny the correctness of justified objections is a short-sighted policy and distinctly high-pressure selling. You gain more by admitting the correctness of the customer's views and then naming compensating advantages. You should be ready to do this—for you should know whatever sound objections exist against your proposition, and you should by all means know the advantages it presents. By being ready, you avoid the embarrassment of sitting speechless when the objection is raised.

6 *The repetition and damping method (rephrasing)*. It is difficult to deal with an unfactual or exaggerated objection. You may have to help the customer make sense of his objection before you can answer it! The technique is to restate the objection in a way that makes sense or damps the exaggeration, and then to answer it if it still needs to be answered.

Example: 'Is this another price boost! What right do you have to keep this up? Fertiliser can't be worth that much!' *Response:* 'I know how you feel—it's gone up 2 per cent all along the line. And I guess you can't see any reason for it.'—'I certainly can't see any reason.' Now the steam has been blown off and the objection has been worded so it can be answered—by presenting the reason.

If a man says, 'You're asking too profanely and obscenely much for that little tractor,' you can rephrase his objection and agree with him: 'You feel the price is excessive, don't you? You have to sell a lot of wheat to pay for a tractor.' It *may* then turn out that a tractor in 1974 costs fewer bushels of 1974 wheat than a tractor in 1964 cost in 1964 wheat—and you *may* be able to get the thought tactfully into the conversation.

7 *Partial agreement*. This procedure is similar in essence to the 'yes, but...' procedure. A good example is furnished by the insurance man who had been told, 'I think life insurance costs more than people get out of it. Something has to pay your commission and your president's big salary.' He agreed with part of what his customer said: 'That's simple arithmetic; if you could be sure of living till seventy-five you could have a bigger estate by putting your premium money into government bonds... But what does your family have if you don't make it to seventy-five?' This answer has a much better chance of keeping the conversation constructive than the perfectly true answer, 'The state insurance inspectors make sure you get your money's worth for every cent you pay in.' The agreeing answer is disarming in two ways: It is ingratiating to the

customer to the extent that it is agreement, and it puts attention on to the reason why people buy insurance—to exchange a small certain outlay for the risk of a greater uncertain loss. Sometimes you can even go further and agree with the customer completely or temporarily—particularly in a question of minor importance.

8. *The forestalling method.* The usefulness of this method has already been suggested. If you are certain to come up against an objection, it can be decisively weakened if you bring it up before the customer does. If you are selling a family its first pressure cooker, you can ask: 'Now, have you been wondering about too much pressure? That's what this safety valve is for...' Everyone has heard of pressure cookers blowing up; but how can a person stay fearful if the salesman acknowledges the fear and disposes of it? Of course, you don't want to start the customer worrying about something she never heard of; but even if you start the fear you have a chance to stop it, whereas if the lady goes home and her husband starts her fears you may never get a chance to stop them. Another example: 'Now, we realise that you have a lot of valuable experience with X material. We know it cost you money to accumulate this. So we think it's just plain good business to...' Another: 'I know as well as you do that Y alloy hasn't been specified for hot-liquid valves before now. What we've done is...'

9 *Combining several objections.* The effect of several objections is weakened if they are dealt with in one sweep. Disposing of several points with a single remark makes each point look very minor. The real-estate broker in Problem Four used the forestalling method and this combining method and thereby gained his client's confidence. But there is a contrary principle: Just as objections are weakened by grouping them, so also are positive selling points weakened by packing them together. These principles are important in selling psychology.

10 *Demonstration of absurdity.* If the consequences of an objection are spelled out, with all their implications, the customer can often be induced to recognise and acknowledge its absurdity. *Example:* 'You're just trying to be polite when you say my stuff is too high-grade for your customers. Please—you run a *good* store, in a *good* neighbourhood—and you tell me *your* customers would rather buy some off-brand junk than pay a few pennies more for our high-grade goods? People don't go to junk shops to buy good stuff—they go to good stores like your...' When you use this technique, though, be careful not to ridicule your customer.

11 *Accepting the objection.* Especially in the case of the subjective

objections, which are always difficult to counter, it may be good practice to forgo making any reply and to let the objection stand as an uncontested fact—providing it does not seriously detract from the advantageous character of your proposal. *Example:* 'You might be right—I won't say you're wrong. But this deal still makes you money, doesn't it?' One well-known sales instructor and advertising space salesman uses the following version: 'Let us assume this problem can be solved...'—with other words—he asks the customer to accept his assumption!

12 *The method of comparison.* An objection is often best countered by citing comparisons rather than meeting the point directly. You should know examples from other users in your customer's general class or neighbourhood, or you may know of parallel instances from your customer's own experience. In business: 'Of course air conditioning means a capital investment. But will it pay off? When you put in the PAX phone system it meant a capital investment? Did that pay off?' To a couple undecided about a television set: 'Sure it costs money. Can you afford it? Could you afford the first car you bought?' In private life or in business: 'Do you know how Jones made out with his new heating plant? He got rid of one nearly as good as yours, and he's glad of it. He told me that...'

13 *Delaying tactics.* If your customer bombards you with a shotgun load of objections, especially if he uses a militant or distrustful tone, it is normally wise for you not to answer directly—better to try to keep the conversation going. After he gets talked out and relaxed, he will very probably come back to one or more of the objections, less vehemently, and he may be more cordial in hearing your answer.

14 *The questioning method.* This procedure involves the least risk of getting a dispute started, since in its very nature it lets customers make assertions and salesmen ask questions. You ask the questions; your customer answers and can't object to his own answers. If you think out your sales conversation in terms of questions, you can lead your customer straight to water *and* make him drink. Suppose you have called on a customer to renew his annual contract for trucking. He sells refrigerators and your firm has been delivering them for him, also taking care of miscellaneous hauling. But he tells you: 'Joe, next year I'm going to buy a truck and hire a driver. I'm getting too big to depend on delivery service I don't control.' You see a big chunk of business vanishing, and you know his decision is going to cost him money. It would be quite normal for you to buckle right down and tell him he's better off using your service. And it would be quite normal for him to be loyal to his brainchild. But by

using the question method you lead him to talk himself out of the brainstorm (not just this way, because it wouldn't be quite so simple):

You: 'Well, congratulations, Bill! I guess you figure on a big jump in your business volume?'

Customer: 'Not too much—about 10 per cent.'

You: 'Do you figure to save money with your own truck and driver?'

Customer: 'Oh, I think maybe £300 a year. I'm not kicking about your charges, Joe. Mostly I'd just like to own my own equipment. And money saved is gravy.'

You: 'Did you say you might save £300?'

Customer: 'That's how it looks—give or take a hundred.'

You: 'How much will you pay for your truck? I'll help you buy one at our fleet price if you want to pay cash.'

Customer: 'Joe, that's mighty nice of you. Well, I thought I'd get a little two-ton pick-up for about £2,000.'

You: 'Does that include the body and paint job?'

Customer: 'Huh?'

You: 'Body and paint job—we can get you the chassis for about £1,800, fleet price. Body and painting cost us about £400.'

Customer: 'That's bad news—even with your help it's about £220 over what I figured.'

You: 'Did you check with the union on driver's pay?'

Customer: 'I heard it's about £20 a week.'

You: 'Bill, I have news for you. It's £25 a week, plus pension contributions and Social Security and Unemployment Insurance and Blue Cross and Workman's Compensation.'

Customer: 'That just about soaks up the gravy.'

You: 'Bill, would you like to drive down to our office and look at the cost sheets on your account? See just what you'd have to carry in fixed charges and insurance and that kind of thing?'

Customer: 'No. I want you to forget all about it. I sure as blazes don't know the trucking business.'

You: 'Do you want a month to think it over? We'll go on with you for thirty days at last year's rates if you want to figure it closer.'

Customer: 'Not unless you're raising your rates a lot—how much are you raising them?'

You: 'About 4 per cent—sorry we have to. And with the oil business in a panic, we have to put in a fuel-price adjustment clause. Want to go over the details?'

Customer: 'I just want to sign up before I get any more brain waves. Give me that contract.'

Throughout this imaginary talk you have asked your customer the questions. His answers have made his decision. Of course, to save time, you told him what his truck would cost and what his driver would cost—but these were simple bits of factual information, and you invited him to check them. Your customer told himself that he hadn't based his daydream on anything very close to reality, and in the end he made the buying decision when you were not pressing him. But this was imaginary—you worked on only one selling point: cost. You might have to work on more sales appeals, or others. There is more on selecting sales appeals in Chapter 17.

15 *The use of testimonials.* The person whose judgement your customer most respects is himself. The person next in his respect is a competent man, whom he knows, who is in his line of business and in a position like his own. He can scarcely respect your judgement in this way; your judgement is too much and too naturally affected by your job as a salesman. For these reasons the best selling method is to induce the customer to deal with his own objections, by the question method. The next best method is to offer your customer the testimony of the kind of person he respects for good judgement and competence. When your customer objects on some point and you can't guide him past it by questions, you can proceed:

'Do you know the men at the X Company?... Morris Miller, the chief engineer?... You do know him? Good. Last year they had the same problem you're having. Would their experience mean anything much to you?' When your customer says yes—and not until he does —you report Mr Miller's feeling, and you ask, 'Why don't you give him a ring? I'll step outside and wait, or I'll call again tomorrow.'

The art in this presentation is that you don't make any assertion for your customer to dispute—Mr Miller gives him the information, in answer to his own question. There could be almost no surer way to avoid getting into an argument. The key to this method is the selection of your references. Before you talk about what they have said or done, you will do well to learn (by a few casual questions) whether your customer will feel influenced by their judgement or recommendation. When you offer a testimonial you must exhibit absolute candour. Let your customers communicate freely and out of your hearing. Don't talk about them or their businesses to each other, any more than is necessary to identify them and bring them together; in this way you display respect for business secrets and confidential knowledge that you may have. If your people do not know each other personally try to arrange for them to meet. Only through such strictly correct conduct can you build in your customer the impression that you are absolutely reliable. When he has this impression, you have gained the initiative and you can get the sales negotiations really moving.

Collect references. People who will speak well of you and your propositions can help you sell. Why not use them? You need not abuse them.

When you have dealt with an objection, don't dwell on it. This could produce further objections. Besides, you want to reach your sales goal as fast as possible.

Don't cradle yourself in false security if your customer raises no objection. There are no sales without objections. You cannot evade them. You have to tackle them. Learn what the answers are and learn how and when to make them. The right technique for handling objections is an essential part of creative selling.

The objections area is the tenth area of creative selling, where sales are made and sales are lost.

ELEVEN

The access area: The first step is often the hardest—how to get an interview

Can you answer these four questions?

1 In what circumstances should you give prior notice of a sales call, and in what circumstances should you call without notice?
2 How can you use the technique of alternatives in asking for an interview?
3 How can you avoid a reception-room interview?
4 Which should you ask to see—the real buyer or the nominal buyer?

Can you solve the following five problems?

1 Arthur Lincoln, a man with long head-office experience in a chemical firm, has transferred into selling and is calling on wholesalers. From the beginning he has shown excellent understanding of selling methods; he has picked up an extensive technical knowledge; and he impresses people well. When he started selling the sales manager travelled with him and introduced him to the customers; Lincoln succeeded so well and improved so steadily that he was soon put on his own. Everyone was surprised when Lincoln's orders fell off sharply after a few weeks of independent activity. The boss took to the road with him for another trip, to study his difficulties, but Lincoln's sales climbed again and the cause of the trouble did not appear. Now that Lincoln is on his own again, however, his sales

B

have fallen almost to nothing. What may be the cause? Why this difference in results obtained?

2 Walter Coleman, selling Diesel engines, is reviewing at a sales conference his visits to six industrial firms in a mid-western city. At four of them, Coleman never had a chance to start his sales talk—the buyers opened the conversation by saying they were not interested. Coleman dropped them immediately and concentrated on the other two firms, both of whom let him explain his entire proposition and demonstrate his equipment. The sales manager is pleased about the two encouraging receptions, but expresses regret that Coleman gave up on the other four prospects so readily. Is he right? Would you have done the same?

3 Elmer Smallwood, an insurance agent, has been trying to get some business with the Zeta Corporation, a medium-sized textile manufacturing firm. But whenever Smallwood calls, the president and the controller are either out of the office or in conference. Though he has made six such fruitless calls, Smallwood is stubborn and is determined to keep making calls until he gets an interview. He avoids giving notice of his intended visits either by phone or by mail. What would you suggest?

4 George Gruber, who represents a first-class manufacturer of electronic components, mentions at his sales conference that he has been running into purchasing agents who pop into the reception room, ask him what he wants, but do not ask him into their offices—sometimes do not even invite him to sit down. They say they are very busy and ask him to phone before his next call. Gruber wonders whether he should refuse to disclose his business in such public brush-off circumstances, whether he should try to sell or whether he should leave and call at a later time. Do you have a method to avoid being received in a corridor?

5 Henry Arnold, who sells building materials to large contractors, has a problem in procedure. 'Sometimes a prospect cuts in on me almost at the start and says to send him my proposition in writing and he'll look it over.' Does not the customer's answer eliminate the salesman's selling activity to a great degree? Would you forestall this, or do you have another solution?

Contacting uninterested customers

If all customers welcomed salesmen, office doors open and fountain pens ready to sign orders, their jobs would be as easy and profitable as some onlookers think they are. But sales talks normally begin with the customer saying 'No.' The 'No' may come through the receptionist—'No, Mr Jones isn't interested. He says to thank you but he won't waste your time.' Most customers, at the start, are not interested in your proposal, and their interest has to be created—by you, a creative salesman. Your problem is to achieve access and then to sell. (Compare Chapter No. 8.)

Walter Coleman (Problem 2) will never sell many engines if he drops all customers who declare they aren't interested. Salesmen in some lines must expect this reaction on every first call, just as in some other lines salesmen can normally expect to find buyers ready to see them. When the customer shows no interest, or refuses to see the salesman, the salesman's job has just begun. If the customer were interested of his own accord he would be looking up suppliers, not waiting for salesmen to call on him. Since lack of interest at the beginning of a sales interview is a normal condition, it is never a reason for giving up the selling effort.

A colleague of Coleman's, commenting at the sales manager's request, pointed out quite rightly that Coleman might have paid no attention to the customers' statements of non-interest; or that he might have replied, 'I didn't really think you would be interested. Why should you be? But here are some performance and operation data that may make you sit up and take notice : it's an overload test report you can read in less than two minutes.' Some such answer as this would have dealt with a real though perhaps unspoken objection of the customer—his lack of time. Good customers are often very busy people—the better customers they are, indeed, the busier they are likely to be. And since salesmen have a reputation for being long-winded time wasters, these busy and good customers try to keep clear of salesmen unless they need their help at the moment. If you can lead your customer to think your visit will be brief, that he can quickly ascertain whether he is likely to be interested in your proposition, you are very likely to get into his office.

Increasing sales efficiency—more and better interviews

The ability to get interviews is the prime condition for a successful sales activity. Strictly speaking, there are only two possibilities for a good salesman with a sellable merchandise to increase his sales: *Visit more customers or visit customers more often!* To make this possible, it is necessary for the sales organisation to assume the administration chores for the salesman and—during selling time—to release him from forms to be filled out, call reports to be prepared and similar paperwork, so that he can use his time productively. The salesman himself should be careful to perform 'unproductive' tasks only during the hours he cannot visit customers. The first step to a successful sales activity is the proper use of selling time. Only about a quarter of the roughly 220 days or 1760 working hours which are at our disposal each year can be used for active selling, i.e. time for actual sales conversations. To increase this time (more active selling time) and to use it effectively (productive selling time) is a most important planning task. The second step is to develop a suitable technique to get more interviews.

If you are already spending all your time in making calls, the only way to get more interviews is to make your interviews briefer. You can make the interview briefer by cutting down on social talk and gossip—and when you do so, you make it a better interview. The time is past when talking around the point was an aid to salesmanship. The briefer and better interviews are far more satisfactory and useful to busy customers, hence the customers are ready to see you more promptly and hence you spend more time selling and less time waiting in reception rooms. In the end, you find yourself selling more goods without any increase in your total effort.

Five requisites for a good sales interview

Before a busy man agrees to see a salesman, he wants to be reasonably sure that: (1) the salesman has something important to communicate; (2) the salesman's business is with him, not with some other man in the organisation; (3) the salesman's visit will be short; (4) seeing the salesman puts him under no obligation; and (5) the salesman will not high-pressure him. Meeting the last four of these requisites is relatively simple; meeting the first one is a much more demanding task, and is the key to making an interview worth the buyer's trouble. Lincoln in problem Number One was not able, when on his own, to get these points across and to obtain the interview. Therefore, he could only sell when his boss 'opened the doors' for him.

Making an interview worthwhile

If your customer is to be reasonably sure you have something important to communicate, *you* must be sure to have something to communicate and it *must* be truly important—otherwise you will have disappointed your customer and another interview will be hard to get. Unless you know you can fulfil this requisite you are not ready to seek an interview.

Hence you do not seek an interview until you have prepared a proposition that will be of some importance to your customer. When you present that kind of proposition to him you render him a service by your visit. His receiving you is not a favour but an action for his own benefit.

To be sure that you are indeed offering help and service you must look at your proposition through your customer's eyes. Putting yourself in his position, ask yourself: 'What kind of proposition would interest me as a customer, and how would I like to have it presented?'

If you have a proposition that meets this test, if you are convinced that your visit is truly of potential benefit to your customer, you have every right to persist in the effort to see him. Persistence in this kind of case is not high pressure, even though the customer is utterly uninterested. You need not be humiliated or driven off by an unfriendly reception; you must remember that none of your customers could ever get their own work done if they were to see and listen to all the salesmen who call on them. Your friends can tell you, and perhaps you can tell them, of many valuable business connections that were established only because a salesman persisted long enough to get the first interview with his customer.

Should you try to get an appointment?

An ever-live question for a salesman is, 'Should I give notice that I am coming, or should I walk in cold?' There is no general rule or practice in this matter. It is obvious that you should pre-arrange your visit if you can do so without increasing the risk of a refusal or of determined sales resistance. You will know which to do if you can answer the question: 'Must I take the customer by surprise in order to obtain a favourable conversation?' If you must surprise him, then walk in cold.

Making appointments, when you can, saves your time. Too much salesmen's time is wasted sitting in reception rooms and travelling to seek interviews that they do not get. When you have an appointment, you meet the customer at a moment that he has chosen, or at least accepted. This fact creates a favourable basis for the personal contact, and whatever you may say can be far more effective than it would be if you were saying it to a man caught in a hurry between one activity and another. Nobody keeps statistics on the sales that never got made because they were attempted when the customer just was not ready to pay attention. But they are numerous.

If you know that a certain buyer sees salesmen only by appointment, then you had better make an appointment. It is rude to do otherwise. Sometimes a salesman is tempted to get to such a man by deception. He may bluff or mis-state his business. 'I must give him some important information privately.' He may lie: 'I have an appointment,' or 'I am a personal friend of Mr X.' A good salesman does not try such manoeuvres. They are highly unlikely to bring a sale on the first effort, and they won't succeed a second time. Mr X will alert the receptionist to 'tell that phony I'm in Greenland.'

Should you phone or write?

Should the projected visit be arranged by letter or by telephone? If your firm, or your product, is unknown to the customer, an introductory letter followed by a telephone call may be the best procedure. A letter is preferable if you cannot rely on a telephone call enabling you to explain your business satisfactorily and sufficiently so as to secure an interview. Naturally, it would be wrong to end a letter: 'I shall be glad if you will let me know when it will be convenient for me to call on you.' A sensible conclusion would be : 'I will telephone you to inquire when I may call' or '...whether it would be convenient for me to call on you next Wednesday morning.' If you suspect that the phone call might bring a refusal, the letter could be ended: 'I will take the liberty of calling on you for a few minutes on Friday afternoon at three-thirty p.m. Should the time not be suitable I shall be grateful if you will advise me, through your secretary, of some better time.' Although, in this case, you cannot absolutely rely on being admitted if the customer does not answer, the prospects are favourable providing your proposition seems sufficiently serious and interesting to the customer.

Personal introductions

Personal letters of introduction may bring valuable appointments with important people. Printed or mimeographed introductions, worded generally as they must be, usually are ineffective or worse. But if an important figure in your firm knows your customer, or is well known in his field, the introduction may smooth the way for an interview. Such introductions need to be worded with all possible care and tact. Consider an essentially good one: 'Dear Mr Summers, We may be able to help you solve an organisational problem that presents difficulties to most companies when they are growing as yours is. Have you some time next week to see our Mr Smith for about ten minutes? He will not need any more than that, and you will be able to see for yourself what use you can make of our experience and equipment. I shall be very pleased if we can serve you. Yours very sincerely, Willis Wadhams.' Good letter? But suppose Mr Summers reacts with, 'Who in hell is Smith? Why doesn't Wadhams come around himself?' And notice that no specific time is proposed—will Smith be ready if Mr Summers calls on short notice? This letter needs a quick follow-up phone call. It's worth your trouble to devote a bit of time and effort to the best wording and presentation of the letter introducing a salesman or announcing his visit.

What to say

When you telephone for an appointment, especially a first appointment, be brief and to the point. For example: 'My name is Sharpe. I would like to have about eight minutes in your office to show you an interesting proposition. Would it be convenient to you if I come in Tuesday at 10.45, or would you rather I came in the afternoon?' Some salesmen can get appointments after saying no more than that, but most customers will ask you who you are, whom you represent, what your proposition is, and many more details. Some of this information you must give, and cordially of course. Whether it is better to volunteer it or wait to be asked is a matter of discussion. You do want to avoid being pulled into presenting your proposition over the phone unless you are ready with a good phone selling talk and your prospect is interested in hearing it. Such a telephone sales talk is every bit as important as a face-to-face talk; selling the idea of the article (Chapter 1) is especially important. But you will seldom take an order by telephone; you had better sell the idea of the office interview. You will almost always queer the sale if you reply, 'I'm hoping to interest you in our typewriters,' or 'I'd like to learn whether you need a public-address system in your shop.' Saying things like those makes it much too easy for the customer to be 'Sorry. Not interested.'

One Italian office equipment salesman answers the customer who would like to handle it all on the telephone 'Certainly I'd like to do that—but I've got something I must show you!' Ingenious and simple, isn't it? All he had to do was think of it!

Most customers, even though they know they are talking to a salesman and know how salesmen make their living, respond better if you avoid giving the impression that you are just after another sale. It is better for you to suggest a discussion or investigation of one of the customer's problems. You can say in honest modesty that *perhaps* you have a solution, perhaps (don't omit the *perhaps*) you can help him to earn or save more money. You want to avoid giving any impression that you want to turn his enterprise upside down or change his way of life. You also want to avoid telling him so much about your proposition that he can make the buying (or non-buying) decision without seeing you. You do well to start by talking about what he, the customer, wants—not what you, the salesman, want. Not: 'I'd like to show you...' but 'Would you like to see...' Not: 'I can tell you in ten minutes...' but 'You can tell in ten minutes whether you can...' Even if you are on cordial terms— *especially* if you are on cordial terms, preserve the cordiality by approaching your customer from his viewpoint: 'Joe, your copy of our new catalogue is in my briefcase. Have you got a few minutes for me to talk about it with you?'

Great skill is needed if you intend to avoid giving specific information about your proposition in a phone call seeking an interview. One salesman said quite truthfully, 'Mr X, my business won't take more than six minutes of your time unless you want it to take longer. But it shouldn't be discussed on the phone.' Thus he suggested briefness—a most important point. And he went on: 'May I come in now, or would you prefer tomorrow?' Whatever the procedure, know the name of the man you want to see! That is basic.

Postponed interviews

Customers quite commonly ask you to postpone appointments. You generally hear, 'Mr Sharpe, I'm sorry I can't see you today. Will you phone me Monday and see how I stand?' Often you get the message from a secretary. When you get a cancellation, try to fix a time for the postponed appointment; it is not good to leave the thing vague. At the very least: 'Monday? Fair enough—I'll phone at ten o'clock.' Perhaps a little stronger : 'Monday? I'll keep Monday morning clear and check with you about ten o'clock.' Even stronger: 'Glad to phone Monday. But if you have 12.15 clear, I'll be in the neighbourhood and can come in without making your phone ring again.'

Keep the initiative

In selling, the initiative is up to the salesman. He starts the selling process. He should never expect any initiative to come from the customer, and he should never abandon the initiative to the customer. The golden rule in selling is that *the salesman should always retain the initiative.* If the customer says he will telephone the salesman, he will probably neglect to do so, may feel guilty, and may thereafter avoid the salesman. So the salesman should relieve him of the obligation: 'You might be too busy to remember. I'll try you Tuesday if I don't hear from you sooner.' If the customer says he will order when his inventory is reduced, the salesman should be sure to get around and check the stock in good time; the customer won't order otherwise.

Should the salesman suggest a date, or leave it to the customer? You do better to suggest a time; if the customer objects, he is very likely to propose another time. It is really unnecessary politeness to offer the customer a free choice—more often than not, he would prefer to have a suggestion. And experience shows the customer feels he has less time if asked in too general a way 'when is it convenient to call?'

Offer an alternative

One way to keep the initiative is to offer an alternative. Ask your customer, 'Will Friday be all right at 10 o'clock? Or would you like Monday afternoon better?' If you are offering an alternative it is a good idea to suggest partly a definite time and partly a period of time such as an afternoon. This allows the customer a little flexibility. In suggesting appointments there are many advantages to proposing odd times—ten forty-five, eleven-fifty and the like. It improves the possibility of finding a free time and the customer has the impression that the talk will be short. When a man's calendar is clean, he is very likely to set appointments on the hour—ten, eleven, twelve. But very few callers stay an hour, so ten-forty-five or eleven-fifty are likely to be free. If, as the hour approaches, your business is not finished, ask the customer if you may continue the talk. If he has another appointment, suggest a time when you can come back. If he asks you to stay on, you know you have stirred up some interest. If you leave him unembarrassed with his next caller, you can look for a welcome in the future.

When you make your call without notice, especially a first call, you are in an entirely different situation. If you get to see your man, you are a new face to him and he hasn't had time to work up any uneasiness about you as he might if he were looking forward to an appointment in which he felt no special interest. But before you see him you have to get by his guard—the receptionist, the switchboard operator, his secretary, one or all, and perhaps a semi-police personality if the place has a security-national-defence tie-up. Their business is to protect their boss's time, but not to keep people away who might be helpful to him. They size you up largely on your manner—what else have they to go on?—and unless you show confidence in yourself they will gain no confidence in you. You are asking for the brush-off if you approach them in a hesitant or doubting manner. An experienced girl will be unfavourably impressed by 'Is Mr J seeing salesmen today?' What can she answer if you ask, 'May I trouble Mr J for a minute?'—her job is to save him trouble! 'I'd like to know whether Mr J would mind seeing me for a moment' is a pathetic plea for kindness, and will *not* get sympathy. 'Mr J is busy, I suppose' is a supposition almost sure to be confirmed —Mr J is always busy. Even if the receptionist calls in to Mr J, her tone can intimate that you are not worth seeing—if that's the way you make her feel; and Mr J is likely to play her tip.

The right way to announce yourself

When you call without an appointment you should know exactly what man to ask for. There is an obvious difference in the impressions that you create by two such inquiries as, 'Please tell Mr J that John Sharpe would like to see him' and 'May I please speak to the purchasing agent?'

Even when you have an appointment you do well to be civil to the guardians at the gate. Friendliness towards them can make them valuable allies in your customer's camp. You must respect their function; a secretary or receptionist who feels that you have by-passed her or high-hatted her can easily convey her poor impression of you to her boss; the same girl, if you respect her, conveys her respect. When you call without an appointment seeking a first inter-view, this mutual respect is even more important.

Should a salesman use visiting cards? Some people think they give a better impression than a merely oral announcement of your name to a receptionist. She may very well appreciate a card that saves her the need to ask you how to spell your name—especially if it is an unusual name.

A card can, however, be a real attention getter! But only if its design is striking, or if the salesman uses it to write a catching remark to attract curiosity. Does your card look like everybody else's? Why should it? It is part of your sales presentation.

If the buyer doesn't see you—

If the receptionist tells you that your man is out, you have lost some face in the very best circumstances—a great deal if the word 'out' is a diplomatic evasion. It is not good tactics just to say that you will call again; it is almost fatal if you go through the same process more than once. With each new and fruitless call a salesman loses prestige with the guardians and confidence in himself. He gives the impres-sion that his time may be wasted casually. If you want others to understand that your time is valuable, you must show by your actions that you consider it valuable. The insurance agent, Elmer Smallwood in Problem Three, failed to do this; each new visit made it more difficult for him to make his presence felt.

When you are told that your customer is out, inquire carefully to learn when he will be available. It is his secretary's business to help you and him in this matter, and if you invite her to do so as a matter of course she will almost surely do so. If there is no secretary, you can normally expect this service from the receptionist. If you can make an appointment through the secretary, she will probably feel obligated to ring you if the appointment must be changed or cancelled. If she can't make an appointment, you can ask her when her boss is expected back; if she can't tell you that, you can ask her when you can phone her to learn.

When you are told that your customer is in but that he is too busy to see you, you should try to settle on an appointed time for another call—either with him or with his secretary.

If you are asked to wait, you naturally and normally agree to do so. If you have another appointment that limits your waiting time, mention it to the secretary or receptionist, but not in a manner to force your customer's action; your object is to set up an easy exit if you must leave. Wait a reasonable time (usually not more than twenty minutes), then remind those concerned that you are waiting; it is not unusual for salesmen to be completely forgotten. If you are asked to wait a little longer, give your customer some more time, but don't show any exaggerated patience. Go on to your next appointment if you have one, and arrange to call back later.

The reception and your personal appearance

If the customer pops out and starts to talk to you in the reception-room—especially if he keeps you standing—you should not just accept the situation. Unless he starts the conversation by giving you an order, you are not going to sell anything standing up in a public reception-room. He may remark, perhaps, truthfully, that he has a man in his office—'this is just to say hello.' Very well—be friendly, say 'hello,' and make another date. Unless some such situation exists, he may ask you what your proposition is or otherwise intimate that you should start talking. If he stands silent, you can also stand silent and he will very possibly realise that he is being discourteous and suggest you come to his office; you can even look around, as if searching for a door or a desk. If you have material to show him, you can mention that it would be nice to have a table for spreading things out. If then you do not get a proper response, you can well put a civil end to the interview. It is better to give up for the time being rather than stumble on to sure defeat. You can explain that your business isn't a casual thing to be discussed in a reception-room, that he must be busier than you realised and you would both feel better at some other time when he is less pressed. You can do this in a way to exhibit respect for him and to insist on respect for yourself and your business.

If a salesman—one of your colleagues or yourself—notices that he is having more than normal difficulty in getting to see people, it is time for a check up. First he makes sure he has the right proposition and is approaching the right people. Then he reviews his methods to make sure he hasn't slipped off the track and begun doing something in a wrong way. Then—or sooner—he checks up on his own personality, manners, and appearance (fingernails, haircut, shoes, clothing, and other matters of grooming). Wearing smelly clothes or otherwise emitting unpleasant odours is especially repulsive to buyers; items to check here are sweaty clothing, bath schedules, armpits, garlicky food, flatulence, wet cigars, sour pipes, liquor breath. Sloppy clothing—unpressed or shabby—and beat-up hats are unattractive. And so on.

Who starts talking?

When you do get in to see a buyer, begin your conversation promptly. Do not make the customer start—if you do, you stick him with the initiative that he doesn't want and you should not surrender. You are really disorganised if he asks, 'What can I do for you?' For the question underlying the interview situation is what can *you* do for *him*?

The rare instances in which the customer has sent for you may provide some seeming exceptions to the rule of keeping the initiative by pressing into your sales talk. You may have to seek a lead from the buyer—to ask him what his present problems or needs are. You have good reason to wonder what unusual circumstance has caused a buyer to send for a salesman. He may be getting the offers of various competitors, and if so he will want to outline the problem. When you have the information you want, you take control of the development of the sales talk. By listening or asking questions at the beginning, you have not really surrendered control, but there is a moment when you take a stronger grip on it.

Whether the customer has sent for you or you have come seeking him, it is good to start the interview with questions designed to tell you what his problems are. A buyer is normally more interested in talking about his work and his needs than in listening to a salesman. Henry Arnold, in Problem Five, could have been getting answers and orders instead of brush-offs if he had started his interviews by asking questions.

The proper opening

Many salesmen believe that a sales interview should not begin with talk pointed to the actual object of the visit—the sale!—but with general warming-up conversation calculated to create a proper climate.

Their opinion is at once correct and incorrect: correct in that the proper climate definitely increases the prospects of a sale, incorrect in that this climate need not necessarily arise out of general conversation.

The best way to start a sales interview is to speak about the problems, needs, and desires of your customer. In these business areas you may be able to help him—you are much less likely to help his golf game if it is off, you can't help his ball team if it's in the cellar, and you can't bring cool weather or dry up the humidity. By talking about matters wherein you can be useful you develop a helpful climate and you concentrate also on the essence of your selling function and the reason for your visit. You do three advantageous things : you save time, you build the proper climate, and you start working towards the objective of your call.

This principle of getting down to business does have some exceptions. Some customers don't want to get right down to business. They may be in the habit of exchanging a few almost formal remarks about health, weather, golf, or baseball, and they may take the omission of them as curt or abrupt. Some, like farmers, just don't feel at ease in a fast conversation. You dare not fail to recognise these exceptions.

Getting to the right man

You must have had, for most salesmen have, the unlucky experience of being put onto somebody who has no authority to make a buying decision. In this situation you waste a great deal of time unless you recognise it soon. But many men who can't give you an order hate to admit it—to confess that they have no buying authority would cost them prestige. When you sense that a man likes your proposition, and yet you cannot close the sale, you can wisely suspect that your man hasn't the authority to buy; he is either not the right man or not the only man.

Sometimes you can check your suspicions by inquiring in the trade. You can even ask in the man's own firm. One salesman simply telephoned anonymously and asked who would buy a Diesel engine. Engines, the courteous receptionist told him, were 'naturally' in the domain of the chief engineer. Yet the purchasing agent had been stringing him along for nearly six months! Also take into account that perhaps several buyers work together. If the purchase has to be a joint decision it is hardly worth concentrating on one buyer.

Aim for the top

It is usually quite easy to speak to people at the top of a firm. They do not need to make themselves important, and they can always refer you to the proper subordinate.

The salesman who can talk to a top-level executive has many advantages. The top man has the broad viewpoint and the overall outlook that comes from being at the top. He can think freely of new ideas, of advantages that may require interdepartmental co-ordination. Indeed, only a man who tops the departments can decide a matter that affects more than one of them. If your first contact with the top man leads to nothing more than his routing you to the proper man, either under him or at his own level, you come to the second man with an advantage (unless you are very much lacking in tact). If several people must get into the buying decision, a top man can tell you who they are without endangering his vanity as a smaller man might.

The nominal and the real buyer

Naturally, you will exercise care to avoid going over anyone's head. If it is the system for the purchasing agent to interview salesmen and the president to decide on the purchase, you make concessions to the purchasing agent's awkward position. Many salesmen have been frozen out for years because they offended someone by going over his head. You must reach the real buyer through the nominal buyer, or with his consent.

The loose organisation

Sometimes the man you are talking to is the right man, but only one of the right men. In a small firm, or in a firm that has grown big with the same top people who started it small, organisation is often loose and individuals have overlapping functions. Executives consult each other and share decision; informal committees constitute themselves and dissolve almost from day to day. Someone will almost always talk to a salesman in such a place; almost nobody will give him an order that means substituting a new supplier for an established one.

When you meet such a situation you must expect to work your way into contact with the whole management in order to ask for the order and get it.

The technical adviser

As business grows bigger and its problems grow more technical, buying becomes a speciality and then many specialities. In a small firm, the head shipper buys a truck once in a while. In a bigger firm, the purchasing agent keeps the truck fleet up to strength as needed. In a really big firm, the purchasing department has a specialist on trucks, often with a technical expert to advise and assist him. When you set out to sell in that atmosphere, you had better be a technical expert or else take one along to advise you. If the customer has technical specialists, you can use your technical adviser first as an entry key and later as a normal link in the contact. Your technical man and your customer's technical man can become a real team serving both of your firms, and may very well deal with technical problems in a more natural atmosphere of mutual professional confidence that a non-technical salesman and a non-technical purchasing agent can achieve. But your technical adviser does not perform your function : you remain the creative salesman, responsible for the selling initiative and for developing the selling conversation to the point where a buying decision is made and put into effect.

The first call after a turndown

Many salesmen shrink from calling on a customer who has turned them down after an earlier serious effort to sell something to him. If you feel this way, you should correct yourself. If your turndown call was ended on friendly terms, if you had stated your proposition without high-pressure assertions, if you lost the order only because the customer preferred another proposition at that time, there is no reason why you should not look for a change in your favour at another time or with another proposition. You should have improved your earlier proposition; in fact, you should be constantly improving your proposition. Having something better to offer, you have a better reason for approaching the customer, a better chance to succeed in selling him. And if you learned anything from the former disappointment, as you should have, you must know better how to approach your customer.

Granted, there are serious problems in getting a businessman or any man to do something that looks like a reversal of a considered decision. But no turndown is final or unchangeable. There is the story about the luggage salesman who was turned down by a departmental store buyer on twenty buying days during eighteen months. But on the twenty-first visit the buyer recognised the salesman's sample case as the same one he had been carrying for a year and a half—and he saw that it was in excellent condition. Now he was interested, and he placed an order for the entire line.

A good time to revisit a turndown is a day when you're riding high after a successful sale and have free time until your next appointment. Then go around to see an old contact who never quite got around to buying from you, or a customer who hasn't bought much lately. You will carry the atmosphere of success into any interview you get—and maybe out of it.

There is one rigid taboo when you call after a turndown. Never, *never* ask your man whether he has changed his mind. Who wants to admit being indecisive? You don't. Your customer doesn't. Hence don't set matters up so that he can give you a favourable answer only by humiliating himself. Start from some different angle: conditions have changed, your product has been improved, you can offer better terms...

Don't let your customer apologise. If, as rarely happens, he brings up your earlier abortive visit (you must never mention it), make it clear that you made some mistake. If he says, 'I should have taken your proposition; the one I did take was a real lemon,' your cue is to acknowledge your own shortcomings: 'Well, I sure didn't sell it very well if you didn't buy it. Maybe the proposition was better than the salesman that day.'

Planned selling

Improvised selling interviews do not bring the results that come from interviews carefully prepared and planned. When you expect to see a customer, you plan your visit, of course. You look over whatever kind of card file or folder you have on his firm and the business you have done with them—his office hours, sales to him, complaints he may have made. But many salesmen have never had the experience of a well-planned or thoroughly prepared interview. Many base their plans on memory and hunches. Written plans are better.

Your written call plan becomes the starting point for planning the next call if you add to it a record of how the call went, the customer's reactions, and the things to be done after you leave the customer:

HOW TO PLAN A SALES VISIT

BEFORE THE CALL – PREPARATION

(1) WHO IS HE?	(3) WHAT CAN I OFFER?
— name of customer — position, authority to decide — peculiarities, habits, hobbies — problems, needs, desires — further contacts	— product(s) — other services — order of presentation — sales points (what)
(2) WHAT DOES HE WANT? — attitude — resistance — objections — primary buying motives — secondary buying motives — buying policy	(4) HOW SHOULD I OFFER? — sales points (how) — AIDA — DIPADA — special points

(5) WHAT DO I HOPE TO OBTAIN?
— objectives of the visit (sell, get decisions, influence, inform)
—co-ordination with previous and/or subsequent visits
— observations

AFTER THE CALL – EVALUATION

(1) WHAT DID I OBTAIN?	(2) WHAT MUST I DO NEXT?
— results — significant reactions	—follow-up, when, how, by whom — next call, when and how

Such detailed planning can make your selling truly creative. Without it, you will not accomplish all you could have done.

Under point 1) add interviews with persons in your customer's enterprise whom you would not normally contact but who could influence your sales success. Under point 3) mention additional products. If and when you have more than one item, or possibly a complete line to sell, there will always be some 'problem children' which are being neglected. Make a serious effort in every sales talk to sell these goods additionally—even if neither you nor your customer care about them!

You established points 3) and 4) with the help of the Sales Talk Analysis described in Chapter 18. Chapter 14 completes your knowledge concerning points 1) and 2), and Chapters 13-16 help you answer point 4).

Under point 5) you mention your own weaknesses, mistakes you want to avoid and positive hints for your presentation tips regarding your language, rhetorics, contents of sales talk and your personal appearance. The first point under 5) is the most important, the basis of your whole presentation. If you don't set objectives for your visit, an evaluation is impossible.

After the call you are interested in the exact result (if you were successful with a note the customer's special wishes and your concessions). The customer's reactions are important for your next contact, so that you pick the thread up at the right place. And finally point 2) should remind you of the things you can do to help your contact along a bit (letter of confirmation and thanks, additional information by telephone, follow-up visits etc.)

Study these slow items for the possibility that they may have special advantages for some special customer; if they do, see that he knows about them, for they may be extremely good buys for him.

Using the call plan

After you have prepared your first systematic call plan, Mr Salesman, get ready for a new experience in salesmanship when you make the call. You have studied your offer, studied your customer, studied his needs. You know you are offering your customer something advantageous, and you know what the advantages are. You know that you are rendering him a service. You've got a whole hand of high cards. This customer may have been difficult, but he will be less difficult now. And you have made sales to tough people before, when you were less well prepared.

Now, before you step into the customer's reception-room, you have to prepare yourself. Collect all your mental powers. Mobilise all the enthusiasm that is in you. Do these things consciously, intentionally. Enthusiasm is infectious and gives the customer confidence to make his buying decision. A tired and nervous salesman weakens the confidence and is doomed to failure. Nobody buys from a spineless salesman whose whole expression reveals pessimism, resignation, indifference, and fear of failure.

But you have no concern with these negative problems. You *are* prepared. During the minute before you expect to greet your customer, you can review your plan mentally as much as you like—not in anxiety but in confidence. You have your sales points firmly in mind or on notes that you can consult without embarrassment. You are ready for the selling situation you are about to enter and for the probable attitude of your customer. You are prepared for his probable objections and you have prepared to deal with them. You have studied the customer's problems, needs, desires, peculiarities. You have a plan ready for beginning the interview, and a plan ready for closing.

The model salesman

An especially successful salesman was once asked to explain his success, to suggest the reasons for it. He could not. He thought of his selling methods as not much different from those of other salesmen. He was no genius. Many less succesful men presented a better appearance. But people who knew him and worked with him could point out the secret of his success: he really liked making calls. As soon as he scented the slightest possibility of a sale he was on the train or in his car to visit the customer. He was often on the spot and talking before his competitors had written inquiring letters or made preliminary phone calls. He was often the first salesman to get on to an opportunity—often, in fact, the only one. If his offer didn't produce a result in a reasonable time, he visited the customer again, not taking it easy with a letter or a phone call. He led himself, perhaps, an uncomfortable life; but selling is not a comfortable job. This man was always on the spot, he never gave up, and he kept cheerful.

This man made his many calls and made them good because he insisted on knowing his business. Whereas even his good colleagues and competitors were content to put forward good propositions, this man always tried to offer the best proposition. He was especially happy if he could suggest an improvement over a customer's original concept of what he wanted. He always made such suggestions only after appropriate discussion, through which he demonstrated his deep and understanding interests in the customer and his special problems and needs. This sort of relation built itself up. He grew to understand his customers and their problems better and better—and better than they. Knowing his business and having such a uniquely intimate contact with his customers, he could give competent and persuasive advice. Thus any proposition he offered was much more likely to be sound and to match the customer's requirements than the competitive proposition. His propositions were made truly to measure. No wonder his sales volume was huge. 'Better visits' means 'more thoroughly prepared visits.'

Do not expect your customers to call you. If you want to get more orders, then you must make better visits. Many salesmen refuse to submit to this necessity. Some who acknowledge it cannot produce the necessary energy and perseverance to take advantage of their knowledge. Even shipping companies, railway companies, airlines, estate agents, banks, are sending people out into the field to attract customers. The retail trade is gradually starting to go out and look for customers and business. Progressive business men do not wait for customers to come to them.

Desk salesmanship is getting rarer. The telephone and letters do indeed have their place but nothing can replace face-to-face contact. Lasting sales success is founded on the untiring personal contact work of the salesman. But—you cannot do everything. A sensible arrangement of your work must begin with an examination of the circumstances which in your experience are decisive for your sales success. As a result you should do no more work but more efficient work. Check list 6 (p 254) will help you in this.

Many sales talks fail before they have really begun. Proper preparation, proper calling technique, proper timing, the proper offer made to the proper person, get you in and create a selling climate.

The access area is the eleventh area of creative selling, where sales are made and sales are lost.

TWELVE

The selling process area: How to prepare your next negotiation

Can you answer these four questions?

1 Do you know what 'empathy' means?
2 Why are we often disappointed about points we thought we already successfully settled?
3 Are you aware of the 'yes-yes' construction and the 'snowball principle' as a means of getting business?
4 How does one neutralise a conversation that has come to a standstill?

Can you solve the following five problems?

1 Henry Otway sells printing machines costing £10,000 and tape-recorders at £200–£300. He is considered an excellent salesman, is lively and ambitious. He has good prospects of selling a printing machine to the proprietor of a medium-sized printing works. When the salesman tackles him during a conversation he expresses a negative opinion of the tape-recorder that was left there on trial. Mr Otway seizes on this point and argues about it intensively so that the whole conversation revolves around the value of the dictaphone. The atmosphere remained strained until the conversation is adjourned. What mistake on Mr Otway's part would you have avoided?
2 George Pollit sells groceries to the retail trade for a leading wholesaler. He is a 'nice chap', excellent company, chairman of the

Carnival committee, but nevertheless a very serious chap. He has a particularly good relationship with his customers, shown among other things by the way he is familiar enough to call them by their Christian names. So he is understandably extremely worried when he notices other salesmen who are his competitors and do not have nearly such a good relationship with customers notching up more and more successes. He is too honest with himself to ascribe this fact to objective advantages. What do you think?

3 'If you have received the answer "No" three times in succession from a customer you can reckon that you will not be able to change his attitude at any subsequent meetings.' This is the opinion of Edward Robinson, the experienced sales manager of an aircraft corporation who combines long practical experience with a good knowledge of sales methodology. He is contradicted by one of his salesmen. 'But every business talk starts off with a "No". Surely the whole point of our work is to change this attitude?' Who is right? Edward Robinson? The salesman or both?

4 The negotiations had come to an impasse. Four representatives of a dyeworks (two salesmen and two technical staff) have spent the whole day since eight o'clock in the morning in the conference room of a textile manufacturer. They were negotiating sometimes with three, sometimes five members of the firm. A series of individual discussions had taken place in the works and to a large extent agreement had been reached. The foreman had even convinced the technical expert that the deal should be accepted. When they all met together in conference a spanner was thrown into the works when the boss and chief accountant brought up weighty financial objections. As this particular point had hardly been mentioned up till then the contractors had not regarded it as being of any importance. They agreed to have further discussion in ten days' time. Both salesmen would prefer joint discussions. The technical advisers want individual talks as the conference proved itself quite unsuccessful, even dangerous. What do you think?

5 'In selling the main thing is to be flexible' says a salesman to his colleagues. 'Preparation robs you of this flexibility, and anyway things go differently from how you thought. And every sales talk is different. What you have got to be able to do is to change gear and improvise quickly.' This pronouncement is not left uncontradicted. Can you make rules? Do customers react so differently from each other? Can you reconcile flexibility with planning?

Are all our different customers really so different?

To come straight to the point: the results of several investigations show that customer-reaction exhibits much more conformity and is much more calculable than we generally believe. There are always the same reasons for resistance, the same objections, views, doubts, attitudes or motives : 'too expensive; your competitors are cheaper; perhaps later; it may be all right in principle but does not suit us; I cannot make the decision; we are satisfied with our present suppliers; it would cause too much upheaval just now; we will come back to you.'

Are you familiar with these excuses? Yes? Just ask your colleagues if their customers say the same thing. As salesmen from other lines of business. You will be surprised to learn that things are not so very different even if people like to believe 'Well, we find in our department that...'

So it is possible for you to be prepared, and indeed you must be prepared. The whole theory of sales methods rests on this fact and the better prepared you are the more flexible you can be for you cannot be taken by surprise in unexpected or new situations.

How is this achieved, exactly? The following suggestions will give you a framework to help you to construct your own plans. You must work them out yourself for only you have the knowledge necessary.

Ten suggestions for a strategy for your sales talks

1 Make a mental picture of your customer. Get to the bottom of his motives and objectives. Make sure you understand his basic attitudes.
2 The 'you-approach' : getting under the customer's skin (empathy).
3 Find common denominators for
  . the plan of your sales talk
  . order of sales presentation
  . suggestions (sales points)
  . your opening
  . your direction of the negotiation.
4 Create the right atmosphere; relaxed, sympathetic, confidence, contact.
5 Projection (communicating ability).
6 Observe closely and minutely (recognise reactions. Watch the atmosphere of the meeting. Work step by step.)

7 Express yourself in a positive manner (yes, yes). Make use of the snowball principle and question method.

8 Plan your lines of retreat, alternatives, compromises. Win at least part of your objective.

9 Neutralise conversation if necessary.

10 Make sure that you get or lead up to proper confirmation. Introduce the next step immediately.

You will find further tips for your sales conversations in the following chapters. The ten suggestions above are a beginning and moreover they sum it all up. Here are some concrete examples for each one.

1 *Have a clear picture of your customer*

Who are you talking to? Shut your eyes for a moment and make a mental photograph of each of your customers. Concentrate on him (her) for several minutes. What does he want? What is he trying to do for himself? Career? Private life? What actions or reactions would advance or hinder his professional and personal success? What role does he play in the firm? What is his relationship to you? What is his basic mentality? Forthcoming? Cautious? Bold? Precise? Suspicious? Daring? Basic attitudes like these cannot be influenced—or at least not much—by external pressures.

If the gentlemen from the dyeworks (4) had taken the trouble to consider points like these they would have found it easier to see the problem in a more realistic light.

2 *'Empathy'*

If you are to be able to carry out suggestion 1) successfully you need a good sympathetic understanding of people—what psychologists call 'Empathy' (to 'feel *like*' someone). If I were the foreman, the specialist, the boss or the chief accountant of the textile firm how would I normally react? Are you one of those people who really understands others especially when they react or behave in a 'funny', 'strange' or 'misleading' way? Can you imagine what goes on in their minds? One small hint—in your next sales conversation try to consistently replace the word 'I' with 'you'. That will give the 'you' approach.

3 *The common denominator*

The link between finding the correct point of view vis-a-vis your customer and making your first bid or suggestion is 'the common denominator'. What does he want? What do I want? How can I reconcile these attitudes? Your plan of action arises from the answers to these questions, and how you proceed step by step gives rise to the order of your sales talk. Its contents are your suggestions and arguments. You need a suitable 'peg' for the opening of your talks (see Chapter 13). If you have prepared and considered your talk you will be able to guide the negotiation (instead of the customer asking all the questions and directing it).

4 *The atmosphere*
I am sure that you know intuitively when your sales conversation is taking place in a 'good' atmosphere. You are relaxed and can talk openly to each other, informally. There is sympathy between you as well as mutual trust. You don't need to weigh up every word nor worry about antagonism, and the atomosphere is generally free of tension. If the atmosphere deteriorates think of suggestions 6, 7, 8 and 9.

One other point: if you are going to influence someone who is a stranger to you, you have to close the gap (as if you were friends). You have to do just the opposite with close friends. You know how difficult it can be to influence members of your own family. Suddenly a stranger can say something that is accepted straightaway —and you are somewhat put out. 'I have been saying that for ages and you wouldn't listen to me.' In this case you have to create a gap as if you were a stranger.

Perhaps you understand Mr Pollitt's position (in problem 2) better now, and also Mr Otway's mistake? By the way, salesmanship is a means rather than an end.

5 By 'projection' I mean active influence.
You may understand your customers but it still does not mean that you have any influence over them. What counts is your own conviction, and also your will to influence the customer, as well as eloquence, intensity, your will to succeed. Your whole personality, your strong feeling of being of service to your customer by your suggestions play a role too in putting forward a sense of positive suggestiveness as a result of your 'projection'.

6 All your preparation will indeed seem a double-edged weapon
if you obstinately stick to a preconceived plan without closely observing your customer and his reactions (see problem 5), but you can fit your arguments to his reactions and be careful to move step by step. If the friendly climate changes you can turn to suggestions 8 and 9.

7 *Be positive. Yes-yes formula and 'snowball principle'*
Saying 'the glass is half full' and 'the glass is half empty' means the same thing logically, but there is a considerable difference from the psychological point of view (see 'Empathy'). Negative arguments do not have the same pull as positive arguments. When you are unable to meet your customer's demands in every detail it is more advantageous to tell him what you *can* do than what you cannot. ('First thing tomorrow morning' instead of 'not today'.) Beginning with the yes-yes formula presupposes 1) asking a question instead of making an assertion and 2) shaping your questions in such a way that your customer automatically answers with 'yes'. Repeat this several times. 'After three "Noes" you almost automatically get a fourth; after three "Yes's" you get another one.' The 'snowball-principle' follows the same idea. A series of small successes will automatically develop into bigger ones. Here you will find that asking questions help you especially if they are rhetorical. 'You want to guarantee your business future, don't you?' 'You want to avoid being left behind by your competitors, don't you?' 'You want to do everything to develop the sales potential of your products, don't you?' 'You have been considering using cheaper material, haven't you?'

These formulations correspond to suggestion 7. By the way, which of the five problems would be most easily solved by this process?

8 *Prepare your lines of retreat*
This suggestion is a precautionary measure which is hardly ever given enough attention when preparing negotiations. If you rely on only one course of action which may not be acceptable in the circumstances, you are left with no way out and let yourself in for unsatisfactory compromises, if you achieve anything at all.

Consider these points. If I cannot do exactly what I set out to do what other solutions are possible? What alternatives can I think of? What (modest) part of my objectives can I achieve so that the conversation does not end with no chance of any sort of result or success? Possibly, for instance, ending the conversation in a new way, or letting the customer keep the goods to try them out or agreeing a further meeting, may be possible retreat goals.

9 Mr Otway would have been well advised to follow this suggestion, wouldn't he? He would have found another of the preceding suggestions useful. I am sure that you know which.

10 *Confirm, in any case*
Even if you find you have a decisive success do not be content with an uncontested confirmation on your part by the customer or even verbal confirmation. Much too frequently it turns out later that each interprets the agreement in a different way, or that new considerations crop up to put the whole thing into question, or that you have not understood each other properly. You will save yourself much disappointment with a written agreement, binding to both sides, or by immediately introducing the practical realities of the purchase.

These ten suggestions should make your sales negotiations easier in the future.

Prepare yourself thoroughly for your sales negotiations—much more thoroughly than before. To be armed for all contingencies gives you a sense of security and that is what you need in order to convince others.

The selling process area is the twelfth area of creative selling, where sales are made and sales are lost.

THIRTEEN

AIDA and selling : How to arouse attention

Can you answer these four questions?

1 What are the salesman's best methods for holding his customer's attention?
2 Should you mention the goods you sell in the attention-getting stage?
3 How can you best recapture the attention of a distracted customer?
4 At which point of the sales interview does the customer decide inwardly whether he is going to listen to you?

Can you solve the following five problems?

1 'I would like to show you some advantages of our excellent new carbon paper.' Ward Wilson begins his sales talk in this way and prepares to demonstrate just how good his paper is; but often by this time the customer has cut in to say that he is not interested. Or else he listens, or pretends to listen, a few minutes longer as a mere politeness, and does not become interested. After a few months of strenuous and virtually fruitless effort, Wilson gives up selling carbon paper and takes a job in a retail radio shop. There he becomes one of the most effective salesmen. How can you explain this?
2 In a sales meeting : Salesman A maintains that before each sales call he decides upon the exact sentence or thought with which he is going to start his sales conversation. Salesman B does not think this possible. He reckons this should grow out of the momentary situa-

tion, as otherwise he would give the impression that the conversation was memorised. The other participants of the meeting have differing views. What is your opinion?

3 Salesman Hofman normally tries to establish contact quickly with his customer with some general conversation. It frees the customer from the feeling of a 'special event', which might make him too cautious. Usually, he starts with the words: 'I happened to be in the neighbourhood, so I thought I'd drop in!' Do you agree? What do you think should be part of a good beginning of a sales talk?

4 Beginning of a conversation at a repeat visit, following the customer's 'no' during the last call 'Mr Client, I would like to refer to our last conversation. Maybe, in the meantime, you have come to a different conclusion?' Good or bad? How would you do it?

5 'Mr Newberg, you are throwing £30 out of your window each day' salesman G starts his conversation for the introduction of a new lubrication oil. Some customers listen to him amused, others get angry. In some cases, G is successful. 'Well, if I don't get any attention with that, how should I?' he says. What is your comment?

An analysis of the selling process

To separate and identify the parts of a sales process is almost as complicated as a psychoanalysis. But there is no doubt that a sales process passes through certain general phases of development. An old-time analysis of the development, and one that is still sound, is represented by the initials AIDA, for Attention, Interest, Desire, Action. It may call for variations, and there are other plans for sales-process development. But the salesman must always get the customer's attention, get him interested, stimulate his desire for the offered proposition, and bring him to take action—to buy it! In all our five problems, the salesmen concerned failed to meet one of the A I D A, requirements.

You can safely use the A I D A pattern as a rule for constructing your sales conversation or as a check pattern for analysing it and locating deficiencies and defects.

Of course, you do not go through all four stages of the A I D A technique if the customer takes the initiative for the sales conversation. In the case of retail store selling, the customer comes to the salesman with his attention already developed. (Many shoppers complain that it's hard to get the *salesman's* attention!) He will have some degree of interest and desire, but the creative retail salesman may still build sales on the A I D A formula—bringing an undecided shopper to action, inviting his attention to other items and following the process through to buying action. It is useful, nevertheless, to study the differences between retail-store selling and the kind of creative selling that is the principal subject of this book. Chapter 14 especially illuminates this difference.

We must recognise as two significantly different processes :

1 The serving or attending process, where the initiative comes from the customer. He approaches the salesman, tells him his interests and wishes, and buys the article he knew he wanted when the conversation began. 2 The creative selling process, where the initiative comes from the salesman, who must secure his customer's attention, awaken his interest, stimulate his desire and cause him to feel it as a need, then bring him to decision and action.

The difference between the two processes, one of decisive psychological importance, is far too seldom stressed in sales literature. Many people like Ward Wilson, the carbon-paper salesman in Problem One, cannot succeed in getting orders in the field but are highly successful in selling over the counter.

The four-stage A I D A sales process is not confined to a definite time limit or to an exact sequence. It can occupy three months or three minutes. The attention stage may merge within thirty seconds into the interest stage; or the desire stage may persist for hours before it can be promoted to action. Sometimes, even, the sequence of the first three stages may be shuffled or one of the stages skipped.

Four key questions

Every salesman should examine the structure of his sales process in the light of the four-stage plan, asking himself these four questions:

1 Does the sales talk arouse the *attention* of the customer at once?
2 Does it awaken the personal *interest* of the customer?
3 Does it create the *desire* to have what is offered?
4 Does it lead in logical development to buying *action*?

Eighteen ideas

Here are eighteen case stories about devices for getting attention. Some can be used as they stand, others require adaptation.

Case 1–The doorbell rings. The man who confronts the housewife is well-dressed and carries a briefcase. 'Do you happen to have,' he asked, 'a good clothes brush?' Slightly startled but curious, she tells him, 'We have one that we use—it's not too good.' She is on the point of stepping to get it for him when he says, 'Here's a *good* one,' and draws it from his case. Let's not follow through—maybe the lady won't like the trick. Her attention has been aroused, however, and she can no longer turn the salesman down almost absent-mindedly as she would almost surely have done in response to the dull opening, 'I wonder whether you need a new clothes brush.'

Case 2 Throughout his career, a vacuum-cleaner salesman has successfully aroused attention by asking 'May I show you how you can simplify your housework?'

Case 3 Another house-to-house salesman inquires, 'Do you know Mrs Blank?' The housewife usually does know Mrs Blank, for she is a neighbour to whom the salesman has sold some item from his line. If she does not know Mrs Blank, the salesman carries on, 'She's your neighbour. She has a toaster...'

Case 4 A man coming home from work has just put his old car in the driveway when a stranger in working clothes asks him, 'Do you have a tow rope?' Since most people do not have tow ropes, the usual answer is no. 'I'm not stuck,' the stranger hastens to say, anticipating the offer of a push. 'But you may need this tow rope— genuine nylon cord, five-ton test.'

Case 5 A tape-recorder salesman arrives at the office of a prospective customer who is just talking on the telephone. The salesman is asked to have a seat and wait. But in the meantime, he sets up his equipment, and when the customer has finished his conversation, it is played back to him. Of course, he is immediately interested.

Case 6 Salesman asks a retailer, 'How would you like to sell out a truckload in a hurry?' Note the words 'sell out'—not buy. Then the salesman proceeds to develop his Company's merchandising plan, including advertisements, posters and demonstrations designed to help the retailer in his sales job. Can he ignore the question or give a negative answer?

Case 7 Many brokers handle the renewals of household fire insurance policies as routine. But one man asks, 'Did you know you can add burglary protection to that policy for just a few pounds?' He writes much more business than when he used to ask, 'Would you be interested in burglary insurance?'

Case 8 'Would you like to cut down on the time you spend pushing stuff around your shop?' asks a salesman of materials-handling equipment. What factory manager doesn't? But would he give his attention to a salesman who asked, 'Can I interest you in materials-handling equipment?'

Case 9 'Good morning, Mr Johnson,' a metals salesman greets a small manufacturer. 'Fellow from Germany read us a good paper on machining aluminium at the metallurgy convention last week. Might be in your line. Here's a copy if you'd like it.'

Case 10 'We've got something coming up that might cut your production costs,' a steel salesman begins. 'Could you tell me a couple of things?' What manufacturer would not pay attention to 'something coming up' that would save money?

Case 11 'I've been admiring your show window, Mr Rowland,' says a salesman of fancy imported canned food. 'You must do the best quality-market business in the city. I'll bet the supermarkets don't compete much with you—do they?' The opinion is flattering and the question is one every independent grocer would like to answer 'yes.' The salesman has his attention before he even mentions canned tropical fruits.

Case 12 Robinson gets his chance to talk to the purchasing agent of a firm that sells mechanic's tools to truck-fleet and taxi garages. 'Would you like your salesmen to take on a line that could get them £30 extra orders on every call they make next month?' he opens. Obviously the agent would like to know more, and consequently the opening was successful.

Case 13 'Just handle this stuff—see if you can tear it,' suggests a salesman as he offers an auto dealer a sample of transparent plastic. The dealer has fifty new cars stored in an open lot, and the salesman means to suggest that he put them under individual protective coverings. Tear-resistance may be only one useful quality of a car-cover material, but inviting a man to tear something gets his attention.

Case 14 'Can I show you something your typewriter will do?' asks a successful colleague of Ward Wilson, the unsuccessful carbon-paper salesman of Problem One. He slips an original-plus-eight-copies pack into the machine, and types: 'Can the carbon paper you are using give you this many good copies?' He hands the pack to the customer with the invitation, 'Look 'em over and count 'em.'

Case 15 A textile salesman turns a flashlight beam on a piece of rayon print. 'Bright and shiny,' he comments. 'Can you see the pattern reflected on the wall there?...' He works up these quick shows to avoid growing stale on customers he sees regularly.

Case 16 Late in August, Simpson makes quick calls on all his customers. 'This is Paul Revere's ride,' he tells them. 'Prices go up on October 1. You can save X pounds if you give me your order now for the same quantity you bought last October.' He knows each.

customer intimately and uses this knowledge to sell, not to oversell.

Case 17 'I want to get an order from your boss,' the salesman candidly tells the busy man's secretary. 'And,' he adds, 'please tell him I've run on to something outside my line that will save him more than he spends on my order.' He has a report on a recent tax-deductible-expense ruling that his customer can use to save several hundred dollars.

Case 18 'You don't fire people when their jobs get beyond them, do you?' the office equipment salesman asks. 'We sure don't,' says the office manager. 'We've got money invested in these people. We shift them to some kind of job they can do.' 'Then how about shifting this old filing system of yours to a branch-office job where it would be an improvement—and putting a modern system in here at the head office where you need more capacity?' The salesman gets serious attention through the dramatic parallel that also shows his keen understanding of the customer's needs and problems.

How can *you* gain your customer's attention right away?

Maybe these ideas will help you—they are meant to be understood, not copied. Each shows a method to arouse attention. Adapt them to your situation. Between you and me: it works for you, too!

Get into your proposition promptly

A conversation opener that will arouse immediate attention is as important in selling as a good catch line is in advertising. Two reasons : (1) During the first sentence the customer is more disposed to give his attention than at any later time. (2) What he hears at the beginning often determines the customer's attitude towards the proposition and towards the salesman as well. During the first few words, many people decide either consciously or unconsciously whether to get rid of the salesman or hear his proposition. If the customer's attention is not aroused, seized, and held, the rest of the sales talk often has no effect.

In some selling fields—insurance, door-to-door selling, and selling by telephone, for examples—the first two sentences may decide whether the salesman gets any chance to sell at all. Whatever and however you sell, examine and consider the opening of your sales talk. You can often improve it by omitting meaningless introductory expressions that might not be true if you were to have them taken literally: 'I just came in to tell you...' or 'The reason why I'm here is...' or 'I have called to...' or (this is especially bad) 'I'm sorry to bother you, but...' Always remember that your first words must ride in over any random thoughts running through the customer's mind and lay a foundation for interest in your proposition. Indeed, if you can get interest as well as attention with your first sentence, why not? Put yourself in your customer's place and ask, 'What would any widget salesman say that would make me care a hoot about widgets?'

The first sentence

The eighteen ideas for getting attention suggest how the first sentences of the sales conversation can intimate some ideas which are of direct interest to the customer. They need not necessarily convey information directly concerned with the article you are selling. The function of the attention getter pivots less on the article itself than on the idea of the article (remember Chapter 1, The Idea Area—What Do You Sell?). To mention the article itself in the first sentence is usually psychologically wrong. Even when it may be mentioned, the *idea* of the article should predominate. The customer is inherently interested in his own problems, and since the salesman must help him to solve them it should not be difficult to word an introductory sentence so that it points towards them.

Be different

One guiding principle for introductory attention getting is to be different: different from what the customer expects, different from your competitors, different from your habitual or customary behaviour. Try to make yourself as distinct as possible from your competitors. Although a gimmick may be a useful thing in itself, it loses all value as a result of repetition and imitation. In being different you become creative, not imitative. You search for new ways of looking at problems, ways that no one else uses; you search also for good ways, old ways, that are good but have fallen out of use and are ready to be tried again.

Say it with questions

An introductory sentence that embodies a question may be especially good. A question starts a man thinking of the answer, thinking about the subject you want him to think about. It catches his attention and holds it while he thinks. It demands an answer. It launches an exchange of ideas.

Your introductory question, if properly worded, invites an answer that will help build your sale. Such questions must suggest positive answers. You can see instantly what is wrong with, 'I suppose you wouldn't care to talk about ways to simplify your billing?' You can imagine a dead-stop answer to 'Are you well supplied with tweed suits?' You are not telling but asking the customer to predict your future when you word a question, 'Can I interest you in better lighting equipment?'

If you see a man regularly, then above all avoid slipping into habitual, unexciting conversation openings. 'There comes Joe. He'll pull that corny gag as sure as fate!' When the customer is in this frame of mind, or sooner, is the time for you to open on a new theme, to put the customer's imagination to work, make him say to himself, 'I never thought of that—it's a new angle.'

New angles, news, reports of technical innovations—these are always good for getting the customer's attention. Keep alert to discover them so you can report them to your customers.

The beginning of the conversation should be desirable for the customer. To frighten him is dangerous (although it may work on occasion). If you feel that your customer is going to say he does not need your proposition right now and would therefore like to see you 'some other time', you can start like this : 'I would just like to give you some information so that you can form your own opinion on how much this equipment will save you when you need it.'—Or 'for your own information, so you have it in your files when you need it.' Now be careful to avoid contradiction!

Distractions

External conditions can sometimes prevent the customer from giving a salesman his undivided attention. Telephones ring, messengers, secretaries, and others are present in the room or walk in and out. Many people always feel free to cut in on a salesman. The situation may reach the point where you need to say—in good nature and sincerity!—'I see I've hit your busy time.' Then your customer is likely to do something about the matter, if he can. At worst—or it may be better—he may clean up the interruptions and then give you his more earnest attention.

The other people in a customer's office are not always intruders —your customer may have invited them to sit by as observers, consultants, or as mere moral support. You should include such people in your conversation and respect their situation; it may be they who determine the customer's decision. The third man in the office has built up—and brought down—many a salesman.

After an interruption has occurred, do not merely resume the conversation but instead ask a check question to make sure your customer has not lost the thread. You can ask, 'Had I mentioned that...'; or you can say, 'I forgot whether I said that...'

If you notice that the customer's attention has wandered as you are talking, you should control the natural impulse to raise your voice. A short, abrupt pause, preferably in the middle of a sentence, is much more effective. The more sudden the pause, the more effective the contrast.

An important aid in holding the customer's attention is to look him directly in the eye. Thereby you compel him to look at you. You are not staring him down—you are giving him your close visual attention, as he has the right to expect. Without eye-to-eye contact you cannot hold the attention of the customer, however well you may talk.

You have to stimulate attention from the outset. Your first sentence must grip the customer. Check yourself on how you begin your sales conversations. In any hundred salesmen, ninety-nine can improve the way they open their sales talks. You have one or two sentences in which to sell the customer on wanting to hear you.

The attention sub-area is the first sub-area of the selling process area of creative selling, where sales are made and sales are lost.

FOURTEEN

AIDA and selling: Arousing the customer's interest

Can you answer these four questions?

1 When is the appropriate time for a demonstration?
2 What do you know about the various demonstration techniques?
3 What aids does a salesman always need for a demonstration, even if he cannot show the actual item?
4 What importance has the suggestive technique in a demonstration?

Can you solve the following five problems?

1 Salesman Clark has some exceptionally good sales material at his disposal. Tests, statistical information, letters of recommendation, illustrations, price lists, all put nicely in order, were handed him by his Company. He decides to leave his bulky files in the car, so that he does not give the receptionist the impression to be a salesman. He thinks that later he can still get his material, if he needs it. Is this correct?

2 Mr White sells tape-recorders and visits various Companies. He prepares the introduction of his sales talk carefully. He is successful in arousing the customer's interest and in explaining the advantages of his equipment. But after fifteen minutes he finds it difficult to hold the interest much longer, and his calls seldom exceed thirty minutes. Therefore, White then prepares a second visit, as he does not believe it possible to lead the customer through all the stages to

the buying decision during one conversation. But his method is not too successful and he is dissatisfied with himself, until he finally has a simple and obvious idea, which immediately produces better results.

3 Salesman Long was not particularly bright, his appearance inelegant, his speech caustic, his mannerism irritating. On the other hand, salesman Small was smart, well-educated and well-mannered. Long always took out his catalogue at the beginning of his call and showed the picture of his products. Even if the customer said he knew it all (which happened at almost every visit) he was not confused and just went on showing. As a result, he brought back a series of orders. On the other hand, Small thought this method too obtrusive.

4 One salesman, during a sales meeting: 'You say that the customer should participate in the demonstration. But our machines are so complicated that he could very well make a mistake and therefore get a wrong impression. I'd rather not risk it and let him watch me.' Some of his colleagues agree. Do you?

5 'Many of the demonstration methods salesmen in other lines of business use seem like dirty tricks to me,' an elderly salesman of chemicals states. 'Our customer wouldn't go for that, and a Company like ours couldn't use them.' Some of his older colleagues agree, but most of the younger ones don't.

Repetition is no proof

Interesting a customer in a proposition means *making him realise clearly* what he gains by accepting it. The advantages which have been indicated (most likely as an appeal to his attention in the introduction to the conversation) have to be proved.

Claims and assertions are not proof; repeating them is not proof, either. The best way of proving advantages is to *demonstrate* them. A skilful demonstration transforms the attention of the customer into a direct interest in the offer. The interest step is the step of demonstration. You must almost invariably demonstrate, whether or not you have the article itself with you. If you don't have it, you have to use aids, imagination, pictures, or the like. The less you talk and the more you show, the better. Let the customer examine its qualities himself, as soon as possible. Nothing is so convincing as what he sees and handles with his own eyes and hands.

Demonstrate

How do you demonstrate an insurance policy? Give your client a pencil and scratch pad—guide *him* while *he* figures what his insurance policy must do. The demonstration of a life or casualty insurance policy takes place in the customer's mind—that's where you operate to sell him.

If you talk about the strength and capacity of a jack, your customer says, 'Uh huh, of course...of course.' If you let him lift a truck with the jack, he has the interest of personal experiment in ascertaining its strength and capacity. If your paint is odour-free, let the customer smell it and then smell its strong scented competitors (unnamed). If you want to stress the foolproof qualities of your gadget, let your customer abuse it and then see it function. If your car climbs hills easily, convince your customer by letting him drive it up a steep hill. If his offices need your air conditioning, try to interview him in your own comfortable air-conditioned office on a hot day; if he still takes convincing, help him figure the value of employee time lost last summer when hot weather caused heat prostrations or forced early closings or just made everybody mope around the water cooler.

Ten demonstration hints

1 *Always demonstrate whatever you sell.* The sooner you demonstrate, the better. The demonstration promotes the sale even though the customer knows your article already, and even though he exhibits no enthusiasm for the demonstration. Whatever your offer, refusing to use demonstrations is like hopping on one leg instead of walking on both.

If you cannot have your article with you, use models, samples, photos, drawings to make your offer tangible. Never forget pencil and paper. Remembering figures is difficult, writing them down has in itself some of the quality of demonstration. The act of quickly sketching a diagram is a demonstration. Favourable differences in size, in weight, in durability, in anything measurable, can be demonstrated by drawing lines or bars on paper. You need never worry about being an unskilled artist; your clumsy motions in drawing a circle can be more interesting to the customer than the unexciting precision of a perfect draughtsman. With some imagination almost every sales point you make can be represented in a drawing—even if only a check mark. The more abstract the proposition, the more important it is to accomplish some kind of visual demonstration to render it concrete.

2 *Demonstrate your article in use.* Perfunctorily showing a customer your article is not a satisfactory demonstration. You may have to think in order to devise a demonstration of your article in use, of its potentiality for the customer. Unless you do find good demonstrations, however, you are throwing away sales out of sheer indolence.

3 *Give your demonstrations a dramatic touch.* Sometimes interesting demonstrations can be built up to dramatic effect.

A man selling glass-wool insulation convinced many homeowners by wrapping an ice cube in his product, then heating the package in a red-hot frying pan and showing the unmelted ice cube after the pan was cooled.

A salesman of fire-foam extinguishers found his customers reluctant to let him smear the foam on their desks for a test demonstration; he took to coating his hand with the foam and then turning a blowtorch on it!

A stain-remover salesman would use his handkerchief to wipe grease off his automobile engine, or swab up a spot on the pavement, then clean it snow white with an application of his product.

When a two hundred pound toy salesman jumps on a child's chair he really proves it is soundly built.

The strength of a glue is dramatically demonstrated when a heavy telephone book is lifted and supported by a single glued page.

A waterproof ink is dramatically proved when a freshly written name on a business card does not run in a glass of water.

In the early days of safety glass it was impressive to see a test pane laid on a plate of metal and hit with a hammer.

A tractor salesman didn't use the driveway to the farm but drove right across the uncultivated land.

A watch manufacturer displayed a watch which had been attached to the wheel of a locomotive and after having travelled five hundred miles was still working.

A salesman of canvas covers used to hand his customers a pair of scissors, asking them to try and cut through the sample of material,

A manufacturer of cranes asked a schoolboy to work his crane, and proved its easy handling.

Salesmen of tubeless tyres used to ask customers to use a hammer and drive nails into the tyres.

The easy touch of a book-keeping machine was proved by typing with a cigarette.

As proof of a fine quality toilet water the sprayed liquid was suddenly set on fire.

These examples are a few among thousands. All of them show how an unexpected and dramatic demonstration can grip the interest of a customer and be more effective than any mere talk. All good salesmanship is to a certain extent good showmanship.

4 *Draw the customer into the demonstration.* Lead him, when possible, to do whatever is the demonstration. It goes further to bring the sale home than anything the salesman insists on doing.

Auto salesmen know that no man's old car will ever be satisfactory to him after he has driven a new car in a demonstration.

Sometimes a demonstration can have the character of instruction, as the customer learns to operate an appliance. The more you interest your customer in learning how to handle your article, the more readily he sees himself in the position of owner. Many hi-fi music systems, toys, appliances, and the like are almost wholly sold by the method of customer demonstration. Instructing a customer as to how a gadget works, and letting him learn by handling it, is much more convincing than letting him watch you or your technical operator display a confusing and practical proficiency. If all salesmen were taught how to get the customer into the demonstration, all sales would boom.

Figures and calculations which the salesman uses during his demonstration should as often as feasible be noted and calculated by the customer.

5 *Be careful with printed matter.* Printed matter can boomerang as demonstration. The customer whose attention is not yet engaged can too easily take the offer of a brochure as an end stage of the interview: 'A booklet! Good! I'll look it over and give you a ring.' Printed matter is to be shown when it underlines the oral presentation, e.g. if certain details, which the salesman has mentioned, are very evident from the brochure. It should not be handed over, but explained in drawing the customer's attention to important facts. A brochure must also be demonstrated!

6 *Concentrate your demonstration.* Never string a demonstration out until the customer grows bored or fears he is wasting time. Show one thing, or a few things, that your customer can interpret easily and understand perfectly. If you get him bewildered or exhausted, he is likely to think your proposition is bewildering or exhausting rather than your demonstration.

The factory visit is often a horrible example of an overlong demonstration. Taking a man through a big modern plant, past machinery making millions of little parts automatically and too fast to be seen, walking him footsore, overdosing him with process information, add up to a demonstration that leaves him dazed and unable to talk business. Let him recover before you continue the selling process. Better still, don't wear him down.

7 *Bear in mind the influence of suggestion.* A customer gets strong suggestive impressions from your manner, your attitude, and your voice as you demonstrate your article. You avoid suggesting fragility in an automobile door by avoiding any delicate touches in opening or closing it. You avoid suggesting workaday ruggedness in sheer nylon stockings by avoiding any rough or casual handling. You don't drive a tractor in front of a farmer or operate an air conditioner for a housewife until you are ready to give them the impression of utter ease and simplicity. And you must not give the impression that you are an expert who makes a ticklish job look easy—be just an ordinary guy doing an ordinary simple thing.

Mannerism, voice and attitude all have to convey the impression of security, and to a certain extent should reflect the character of your proposition.

8 *Help your customer draw the right conclusion from your demonstration.* You cannot be sure that your demonstration means the same thing to you and to your customer. A salesman once demonstrated a light plastic garden hose to a department store buyer. To prove how tough the frail-looking stuff was he tied it in a knot and pulled it so tight the water ceased flowing. The buyer said coldly, 'Most people aren't as strong as you are.' The salesman might have introduced the demonstration by intimating what he would try to prove; and he might have said, as his knot choked tight on the flow, 'Can you beat that for strength?' or 'Did you ever see anything that tough?' or 'No one ever pulls a hose that hard.'

Customers may miss the point entirely, or they may see the point but not concede it. Until they do see it and do concede it, until they confirm the conclusion the demonstration is intended to establish, your demonstration has not succeeded no matter how skilfully you have conducted it. This point is overlooked by many salesmen.

You cannot assume that the customer is convinced because he says nothing. He may be only polite, or embarrassed. So you ask him, for instance, 'Did you ever see anything that tough?' He may reply in three typical ways:

(a) 'That doesn't prove anything.' If you draw this feeling out of him, you can sometimes save a sale that would have been lost had you let him keep silent. If nothing better, you can suggest, 'What test would you like to see?'

(b) 'It looks pretty good, but...' Though you have not wholly failed with your demonstration, you had better dig out whatever comes after the 'but.' Sometimes the doubting customer's thought is 'Will it work that way for me?' If you can hand the article to him and say, 'Now you try it,' you can often clear up the suspicion that the demonstration depends on the salesman's skill. Sometimes the customer thinks you are showing him a better-made article than the one you will sell him. Then it may help to ask, 'Would you like this one, or a new one?' Or if you are shooting at a quantity order, you can suggest, 'Keep this one for a sample and use it to check the lot we ship you.' A car manufacturer has come to the conclusion that in future he would only use cars for demonstration that had been driven for at least 10,000 miles. The point here is as before: you have drawn a comment from the customer that can enable you to perfect your demonstration.

(c) 'I never saw anything like it. It really is tough.' You have proved your point and your customer is interested. Now go ahead and sell—stir up the desire to buy if you have not already done so, and ask for the order.

9 *Don't try to force the customer to make up his mind right at the beginning,* particularly if you show him a choice. The customer should never feel that he is being pushed or given unfounded advice before he has had the time to thoroughly examine your offer and obtain all pertinent information.

10 *Don't expect too much of your customer.* Don't show him too much. Don't tire him out. Only show what you want to prove. The customer should not already feel surfeited in the second phase of the selling process. A demonstration must be carefully planned, prepared and executed. It should not follow momentary inspiration or chance. Your sales technique cannot be any better than your demonstration technique is. Reflect on how to improve it, and give yourself some regular training!

The most effective method of selling is the demonstration. Use it! Try always to have the customer watch your article in use, to use it himself. The best spoken sales presentation does not grip a customer half as well as a good practical demonstration.

The interest sub-area is the second sub-area of the selling process area of creative selling, where sales are made and sales are lost.

FIFTEEN

AIDA and selling: How to stimulate and strengthen the customer's desire

Can you answer these four questions?

1 What does it mean to lead the conversation in terms of the future?
2 How do you recognise the growing readiness to buy?
3 What is the difference between arousing a desire and creating a conviction in the customer?
4 What is necessary except proof of a need and the possibility of a good solution for it in order to create a readiness to buy?

Can you solve the following five problems?

1 Salesman Wilson reports: 'I had proved all advantages of the buy. He recognised them all. He also agreed that our offer was particularly favourable. He had the money and could have spent it. And yet, he showed no readiness to buy, I cannot understand it.' Can you?
2 Insurance salesman Jones argues: 'They always tell us we must create a desire in order to interest the customer in the buy. Then you tell me how to arouse desire for a life insurance!' Not quite easy, is it? Can it be done?
3 'Very interesting,' concedes the buyer of the X factory in seizing the bar in Duraluminium. 'I realise that this new light metal alloy is a great success. You have probably already seen the people over at Y factory. They ought to be interested in this.' Now the selling

engineer, Mr Brewer, gets nervous. He was sent by his Company as a specialist to this particular customer, and for the last one and a half hours he had been explaining all the advantages and applications of this new alloy. Now that he should reach the conclusion, the buyer tells him to go and see Company Y! Brewer recognises the mistake he has made, but it is too late to change anything in the buyer's attitude. He, therefore, asks if he could see the Technical Manager of the firm, and the buyer has no objection. This time, Brewer does not make the same mistake, and finally it is the Technical Manager who 'makes the sale' with the buyer. What was the difficulty? Have similiar situations occurred to you?

4 'It would certainly be nice to have a new vacuum-cleaner,' agrees Mrs Knight with a glance to her husband, while the salesman changes one of the parts. 'Work would be much easier, and I wouldn't get such dirty hands. But there are so many things one would like and cannot have!' Mr Knight agrees—a vacuum-cleaner would be convenient—but it's true—there are so many things one would like. There is no doubt that both Mr and Mrs Knight would like a new vacuum-cleaner. And yet, somehow, the salesman cannot make the sale. He continues to demonstrate his equipment and even increases the Knights' desire, but by the time he realises what is wrong, they want to go out and there is no more time for the conclusion. However, he believes that he has discovered the reason for his failure. What is the root of the problem? What can be done?

5 'You cannot be the only one to use that old colour scheme!' salesman Bald tells the foreman of a textile company after having convinced both the buyer and the Technical director of the necessity to change. 'May I prove to you again the advantages of the new scheme?' But even after this proof the foreman remains negative. What would you have done?

Need and desire

A customer who has no desire for your article, even though you may have interested him in a qualified kind of way, cannot as a rule be led to buy it by your assertation or even by your proof that the article is excellent. It's the best? But he doesn't want it? So what?

The main reason for a man's buying an article is a combination— that it satisfies a *need* and that he has *the desire* to buy it. No demonstration will sell your accounting machine, though you prove ten times over that it is the best in the world, unless you succeed in arousing his desire for more efficiency, more convenience, more accuracy, more speed, or more something than he is getting with his present machine or procedure. No desire, no order.

In Problem Three, Mr Brewer made his mistake by building up the purchasing agent's interest, but neglecting to build his desire. He remedied this ommission when he talked to the metallurgist. If your customer, like Mr Brewer's purchasing agent, does not decide to buy after you have made a convincing demonstration and led him to acknowledge that it proves your point, the reason is that you have not aroused his desire for your article. If you analyse the sales you didn't quite make, you may find in a surprisingly large number of cases that the fumble grew out of this fact: interest is not the same as desire.

To arouse the desire of a customer, it is essential above all other things that you should have some knowledge of his predominant wants, interests, and needs. Only when you have this knowledge can you hope to make him conscious of his need for your article and arouse his desire to have it. If you can get this information, you arm yourself with it before you visit your customer; if you can't do it in advance, you try to discover these decisive facts during the course of your sales conversation—you ask your questions, watch your customer's responses and reactions, and you shape your appeals to your customer's buying desire in accordance with what you learn.

Desires are specific

The desire that must be stimulated in order to arrive at a sale is the *individual's* desire. Salesmen who know this fact nevertheless attempt, too often, to work on *general* desire, to have one sales talk for all customers. But there is no sales talk that will work for all customers, for customers have differing patterns of wants and needs and interests. *Most* of your customers have wanted speed in the car they might buy; *this* customer may want safety and may object to speed. For most uses, *people* want cloth to be durable; but *your present customer* may need it for only a one-time use. *Most* varnish buyers want high gloss; the *one* buyer now before you may want a low gloss, for any of many good reasons. *Most people* want the savings feature that is part of an ordinary life insurance policy; *your present customer* may not want these savings features and may, therefore, demand term insurance.

You stimulate desire when you aim at the wants and needs of *the person before you*. He is not an *average* man; he is *one* man, different from every other man.

Stimulating desire

When you wish to stimulate your customer's buying desire, you must skilfully portray to *him* the satisfaction, the advantages, the enjoyment your proposition will bring to *him*.

'You can get out more with your children,' the salesman tells the young apartment housewife, 'if you have this time-saving automatic washing machine.'

'You can feel easy when you have this policy,' the life insurance salesman promises truthfully. 'It means money for your retirement, or money to take care of your wife or pay for your son's education if you don't retire.'

'Isn't it an appealing thought and a consolation to know that you do not have to worry about your own and your family's economic future, even if something should happen to you?' is another argument used by an insurance salesman.

'You can dictate your report on the spot,' says the salesman offering the portable dictating machine. 'Any place, any time, day or night, and never mind whether you can get to a stenographer.'

'Did you ever want to get out a quick announcement without waiting on a printer?' the salesman asks the store owner. 'That's when your own duplicating machine shines : when speed will sell more than four-colour printing.'

'Mr Harrison, what if you get a flat up there a hundred miles from a garage? You want some good tough tyres for those mountain roads—better let me X-ray the ones you've got. And you need a good jack and a good pump and wrenches and a puncture kit. If you never unwrap 'em you'll be glad you have 'em anyhow.'

'Since your daughter is playing the piano so much, Mrs Thompson, you'll enjoy hearing her more if it's kept tuned. She can be sure it will sound right whenever she plays—for practice, for parties, for your guests. And regular tuning keeps up the value of the instrument, too.'

'These bright lighting fixtures will draw a lot more customers to your windows, Mr Smith. Wilson, in the next block, says he's had people cross the street for a look. Your store front will be the most modern-looking in the block. And imagine all the bright light on your Christmas decorations!'

'Air conditioning helps in cold weather too, Mr Manager. You get fresh air without opening windows and wasting heat. Your people won't get drowsy or have headaches from stale air. No draughts to complain about.'

Emotion and reason in buying desire

Neither you nor any other salesman creates buying desire by marshalling logical reasons. Your customer must *like* what you offer and *want* to have it. The desire to buy is emotion—not reason, however reasonable and logical it may be. Stimulating the customer's buying desire is not the same as proving that he has a need. A lawyer or doctor, who has a clear and pressing *need* for life and retirement insurance, is quite likely to *desire* a vacation cottage instead. What many executives *need* is a dictating machine; what they *want* may be a personable secretary. When the stenographers know that they *need* new typewriters, the office manager may *want* new filing cases. In many homes the housewife *needs* a new vacuum cleaner, but the whole family *wants* a new television set. Many people *need* new tyres but *want* new gadgets. Many stores *need* new wiring but their owners *want* new fixtures.

If your customer gets stuck in the conflict between a desire and a need, he may avoid deciding between them by buying something else—from some other salesman, not from you. You will not help him to satisfaction unless you can make the desire felt as need or the need felt as desire. He needs to be freed from conflict, to be convinced that his preference is right.

Appeal to reason too

Problem Four—that of the hesitant vacuum-cleaner customers—represents a situation that many salesmen have experienced. The customer's desire has been stimulated, he has come almost to the point of buying; then he hesitates, starts to think it over, becomes doubtful—all very disconcerting to the salesman, who has been counting the sale 'in the bag.' Such situations do not occur when a purchase is a more or less spontaneous matter, not involving any considerable outlay; then buying action normally follows buying desire and the order follows directly upon the salesman's invitation. But when a purchase is of major significance to the customer—when it demands a financial sacrifice or a change in his habits—the salesman must do more than stimulate mere buying desire. He must also convince the customer rationally that the purchase is justified and sound. It is especially important to achieve this conviction if the buyer is not acting on his own behalf but as agent and must be prepared to explain the reasons for his decision.

Sales instruction often overemphasises the emotional factor in selling. However true it is that the selling appeal must be directed to the emotions of the customer, it needs to be emphasised that these appeals to emotion are not sufficient for obtaining an order of any consequence and should not crowd out selling appeals directed at reason and intelligence. Your offer surely contains merit based on fact and reason, which can be presented as appeals beyond the appeal of buying desire. Use them to give your customer a supporting assurance that his emotional desire to buy is justified by reason. Although Mr and Mrs Knight, in Problem Four, would have liked to get the new vacuum cleaner, they were deterred from doing so because they feared to spend a comparatively large sum on something they needed less than other things. Or *thought* they needed less. A few questions by the salesman about repairs needed on the old cleaner—recently or soon—might have turned their thrift and caution into the direction of buying the new trouble-free cleaner. Likewise, some facts regarding the real value of the best care for rugs and furniture, the possibility for Mrs Knight to use the time she saves productively in assisting her husband in his business, the low cost compared to an expected life of ten years, might have made the sale.

Five examples of reasoning to support desire

Here are a few typical examples of the use of logical arguments to overcome customers' misgivings about the soundness of their buying desires. The two last offer especially enlightening illustrations of the point.

Case 1 A dictating-machine salesman has found the general manager of a large firm fed up with stenographers and office femininity in general. 'If it was my money, I'd buy your machine in a minute. But it's stockholders' money, so...'—'You might *save* money for your stockholders by putting in the machine... Could you say how many hours a week you have girls at your desk taking dictation?'—'Fifteen, maybe twenty.'—'And that's about half of a girl's time?'—At least.'—'At about how much a year?' Thus the initial cost of the dictating machine ceases to be a factor against the sale and the saving in office labour costs becomes a factor supporting it.

Case 2 Jim Henderson is proud of owning the best hardware store in the county seat. Naturally he carries guns, ammunition, and fishing tackle. Naturally the salesman would like to have him take on other sporting goods—tennis, golf, baseball, football, basketball, ski-ing gear. Henderson wants to go along, but '…most of my business is with farm and local people. They don't have much time for games and playthings. I'm kind of afraid.'—'But Mr Henderson, who sells this game stuff to the high-school teams?'—'I think they get it by mail order.'—'Or they drive over to the state capital.' 'You could get that business, couldn't you?'—'I sure could! Never thought of that!' Now business pride is supported by demonstrable business opportunity.

Case 3 The Gem Furniture Store proprietor has budgeted £2,000 for a new delivery truck. What that amount will buy is a rather light vehicle. The truck salesman points out a larger and more rugged truck for £2,500. 'I'd like to own it,' the Gem man confesses. 'Big, modern, husky looking…but I can use that extra £500 in lots of ways.'—'You might lose the £500 in other ways with the light truck,' the salesman explains. 'How often do you make two trips to deliver one sale?'—'Pretty often.'—'Ever run you into driver over-time?'—'Oh, yes. Six or seven hours a week, twenty or thirty times a year.'—'Suppose you had this big truck–would it save you much of that overtime?'—'Come to think of it, maybe it would. Let me look over my route sheets.' And the customer is joyfully out to justify his purchase of the big truck he really wants.

Case 4 'That shop of mine looks *so* dark and old-fashioned,' Mrs Griffith remarked at a Chamber of Commerce luncheon. The next day Mr Graham, the electrical contractor, stopped at her store and showed her some brochures on fluorescent lighting fixtures. 'Oh, I'd love them,' she told him, 'but business has been falling off…'—'You have to have them,' he told her bluntly, 'or your business will fall off still more. This old-fashioned lighting makes your best merchandise look like junk. Good light is a good investment, and the bank will help you finance it. Your business will pick up enough to pay it off inside of two years. Now…' And a good businessman-salesman prevented Mrs Griffith from destroying her business through mistaken economy.

Case 5 'Of course,' the factory owner agrees, 'I'd like to put our production on an assembly line. We've grown too fast to keep on with this small-scale method. But I'm still in debt for the tools…'— 'But you've had to turn down orders, haven't you?' the equipment salesman asks.—'Yes; and that hurts. And if I rip out machines to put in an assembly line we'll lose a month's production and have to turn down a lot more.'—'Why not build the assembly line in a new factory? No lost time then.'—'Please! I told you I'm still in debt.'—'Of course you're in debt. So is the Giant Steel Corporation, and they're building new plants. Let's figure tax benefits and increased earnings against the cost for a new plant and see how soon it pays out.' And the manufacturer is released from the entanglement of unexpected prosperity with unrealistic caution.

Which comes first?

When emotion and reason must support each other in building up towards a buying decision, it is easier for the salesman to stimulate the desire first and then present the logical points to justify it. This preference rules even though the salesman normally initiates the selling process because he knows the logical reasons why the customer needs the article. You must first influence your customer so that he wishes to buy. Wishing to buy, he is glad to be convinced that his needs justify him in buying as he wishes. If you start off by presenting logical points before the customer has recognised the wish and been moved by it, you are in effect giving unsolicited and perhaps unwelcome advice—which is an effective way to get into controversy and argument. When you have built up the desire, the confirming logical arguments give the customer support for doing what he wants to do—for buying your article.

It is important to stimulate buying desire. But it is not enough. You must both lead your customer to desire what he needs to buy and convince him that he needs what he desires to buy.

The desire sub-area is the third sub-area of the selling process area of creative selling, where sales are made and sales are lost.

SIXTEEN

AIDA and selling: How to conclude the sale

Can you answer these four questions?

1 Is there one decisive point in the closing stage of the sales conversation?
2 What does it mean 'to anticipate events'?
3 What is your reaction if the customer wants to postpone his decision for no good reason?
4 What do you know about partial decisions, alternative offers and concentration methods which are part of the techniques to reach the conclusion of the sales conversation?

Can you solve the following five problems?

1 A customer comes to a car showroom and enquires about a model. The salesman gives him complete information. After some time, the Sales Manager—afraid his salesman might miss something—joins the two. After thirty minutes, the customer leaves to 'think it over.' Next day, the salesman visits with him and mentions: 'you couldn't make up your mind yesterday!'—'Oh yes I could, but you would not let me!' is the customer's answer. What happened?
2 'When I take out my order book, I can immediately feel how the customer gets nervous. But this cannot be avoided, can it?' says one salesman in talking to his colleagues. What do you think?
3 District Manager Smart cautions a young but good salesman: 'When you have the order, don't stay with the customer any longer.

You lose your time and risk that you must start all over again.'— 'But I cannot simply disappear—this would look as if I had a bad conscience!' argues the salesman. Finally they reach an agreement with each other...

4 'You have to put the pen for the signature in some clients' hands,' says pharmaceutical salesman Jones in a sales meeting. 'Yes certainly, this can happen, but you don't like to do it,' agree some of his colleagues.

5 Salesmen of the food industry meet and discuss their experiences. One of the men explains: 'The worst is when I know that now I must ask the customer whether he wants to buy. I always hesitate. If he says no, the whole thing is a flop. That's why I wait as long as possible until the customer makes his own decision.'—'That cannot be a good method,' replies one of his colleagues. 'A decision must be made, therefore it is always better if you choose the time. But I agree that it is difficult to know when the customer is ready for a buying decision.' A third salesman adds. 'Besides, the sale takes an awful long time if you wait for the customer to make the decision. He very often may like to postpone it.' After some discussion they agree on how to close a sales conversation. And even if their method is not infallible, it certainly improves their sales results.

Asking for the order

When you have made your customer inclined to buy, and then have supported his inclination by logical arguments that enable him to see and feel his desire as a need, you have completed the preparatory steps towards a successful sale. You have a last difficulty to overcome—to produce buying action. To produce it, you need a sound closing technique.

An old piece of wisdom counsels you, 'Just keep right on talking and going over your sales points until the customer says "Yes".' That is wrong! Closing a sale is not so simple. You cannot talk a customer into a buying decision, least of all by talking him to the point of exhaustion. If you try to, you are likely to talk him entirely out of any buying intention he ever had. The glib salesman, chattering incessantly, is a bad salesman and has a very short career.

Sometimes the customer glides without help into a decision, and the salesman need not ask for the order directly. Such happy events can occur when the salesman has really aroused the customer's attention, interest, buying desire, and sense of need—through perfect understanding of the customer's problems and through a perfect sales talk. But normally, it is necessary to apply a closing technique.

In general experience, the decision to buy is one the customer resists making. It may be a decision so difficult and so important that the customer cannot, without help, summon up the strength to make it. It may require a financial sacrifice. It may be an either-or decision—either forgo some different thing, or forgo the thing offered. Therefore, almost every buying decision is connected with some negative aspects which have to be overcome· through an efficient closing technique.

The most skilful closing technique never brings a buying decision unless the salesman has aroused (or stumbled into) the customer's buying desire. It produces buying action only when the customer is already considering the proposition seriously.

The secret of closing

The art of closing is to introduce the suggestion to buy in such a way that even if the customer reacts negatively the sales conversation can be continued. You prepare your closing approach before you start your sales talk. And you prepare to go on with the sales talk after any possible response or objection—including a clear and outright refusal.

Don't let the moment slip

One cash-register salesman had a gift for finding the most suitable customers for his product—independent retailers—whose sales volume was too great for the one or two registers they had. He interested many customers in taking another or better machine, knew they wanted to buy it, and then encountered the familiar objection that they couldn't afford a new machine. Of course, they agreed, they would have to get it eventually. Meanwhile, they wanted to study out some way, if they could, to make do with present equipment. Almost invariably, however, they expressed themselves, they wanted to wait and not buy immediately. So as not to jeopardise his chances, the salesman thought it necessary to suggest taking a little more time for the decision. 'Fair enough. Think it over. I don't want to rush you. Let me come in again day after tomorrow.' Too often, on the day after tomorrow, the customer had backed even further away from making the buying decision.

It is normal for the customer to hesitate at the buying decision. If the salesman falls in with this hesitation he loses the initiative and weakens his chances. When he returns after the postponement, the only question he can ask suggests an ultimatum, a cross-examination, a calling-to-account: 'Now, Mr Miller, have you thought the matter over?' Mr Miller may have thought, but he rarely has decided. The salesman has no new points to offer in favour of buying, so he rehashes the stale ones of the day before yesterday. They are not so effective as they were when they were fresh. He is fighting a losing battle.

An old rule of selling is : 'The order within reach today is beyond the mountains tomorrow.'

Sensing readiness to buy

If a customer feels ready to buy, it isn't difficult for a salesman who pays attention to sense the fact. The customer's manner of speech and facial expression reveal his readiness clearly. You can be sure he is ready to buy—

If he asks about delivery time.

If he inquires about a trade-in allowance.

If he expresses concrete desires about quality or finish (even though he words them as objections).

If he asks you to 'figure the price a little closer.'

If he asks you whether you will put some of your selling points in writing.

If he asks how to care for the product.

If he asks whether you can hold the proposition open for a few days while he makes his decision.

If he asks whether he can have the article a few days on approval.

Sometimes your customer shows such evidence of buying readiness almost without effort on your part. Sometimes you have to draw it out of him, by asking questions or by otherwise inducing him to talk. (That is your job, as a salesman.)

Sometimes buying readiness shows itself in the 'last effort' objection: 'Is this really the model with the best trade-in?' 'Do you have to have the answer now?' 'Will this stuff really stand up?' 'If you could see it my way...' And so on. All these are buying signals.

Your insight and understanding of the real inner attitude of the customer, in this last stage of the buying process, determine your sales success. You can sharpen your insight and improve your understanding in various ways: by studying books on applied psychology; by systematically observing the remarks and gestures of your customers, their responses to your conversation. If you put the suggestion to buy in a skilful manner, you need not be afraid of the possible 'No,' because such a 'No' is more likely to refer to some part of the proposition than to be a sweeping rejection of the entire offer.

Five conditions for closing readiness

Before you can try confidently to close a sale, you need to be sure that five conditions have been fulfilled. We have stated them before this. They seem utterly obvious. But salesmen often overlook them —one or more of them—and lose sales. Here they are:

1 *The customer must understand the full scope and value of the offer.* After a lost sale, it often turns out that the customer had failed to understand the offer and had overlooked some point or points favourable to him.

2 *The customer must trust the salesman and the Company he represents.* A tempting offer can get attention, can stir up interest, can even arouse desire. But it rarely brings a buying decision unless the customer trusts the salesman. This is where the high-pressure salesman with his not quite trustworthy offer falls through.

3 *The customer must have a desire to enjoy the advantages of the offer.* Even when desire exists, a buying decision may come hard; if no desire exists, no buying decision will be made.

4 *There is no critical 'now or never point.'* There are moments of climax in every sale—not one, but several. If you miss one, you take advantage of the next. You watch for the buying signals, of course —but you need never be tense or anxious, for you are not going to miss an *only* chance. If you realise that a moment has gone, don't feel frustrated—there will be many more moments.

5 *The salesman must be ready for a 'No' answer.* If your customer says 'yes,' you write the order. But what will you do if he gives you a straight-out 'No'? If you are prepared, if you have planned your reaction to this possibility, you won't be stunned; you can go on with the conversation, get the sales process rolling again, and ask for the order again. Always know what you will do next.

Fifteen hints on closing techniques

These hints illustrate how you can induce buying action:

1 *Issue a direct or indirect invitation.* 'Don't pass up this break. Give me your order now, and tell me when you want delivery—we'll bill you then. How many do you need?' The quantity needed is the order quantity—an effective suggestion.

'Even if you've paid off your mortgage, you need fire insurance, Mr Williams. Better let me have your policy application now—then your protection starts at noon tomorrow. What's your valuation on the house and contents?' By answering the question, Mr Williams moves towards the buying decision.

'Pretty early Spring this year, isn't it? If you decide today, we can install your refrigerator before the 1st of May,' the salesman tells a food store owner with a glance to the Spring sun. 'What are your floor dimensions and load?'

The direct or indirect invitation is usually followed up with a question based on the assumption that the invitiation will be accepted. To refuse the invitation then requires greater energy from the customer than to accept.

2 *Offer alternatives.* When you offer a customer two different buying proposals, you help him to ignore the third alternative—not to buy. The lawn-mower salesman asks, 'Do you want the reel job or the rotary?' The question, he hopes, distracts the customer's mind from the decision, to buy or not buy, and directs it towards the decision 'which to buy.' Proposing two (or three) choices reduces the risk of a refusal.

The alternative may concern quantity: 'Do you need 100 gross, or will 75 gross do you for now?' ask the button salesman of the shirtmaker. (The expected order is only 40 gross, but proposing larger quantities may get a bigger order—say 50 gross if not 75 or 100.)

The alternative may concern delivery time: 'Would you like to have it sent right away, or later this week?'

'Which model do you prefer, Sir, the smaller or the bigger one? Which one would you like to drive?' a car salesman asks his customer.

Any other matter in which the customer has a choice or a selection may be the basis of alternatives: patterns, colours, sizes, styles, used or new, domestic or imported, one brand or another—the customer in the United States has almost infinite choice and the salesman guides him to exercise it.

The offer of alternatives is good tactics when you send a written offer in response to an inquiry. The inquiry in itself creates such a strong presumption of probable buying that it is almost absurd to draft a reply in terms of whether or not to buy; the question is already one of what or which or how many to buy. Also, offering alternatives gives you something more to talk about, lets you say more than a bald price quotation or other reply to your customer's inquiry.

You can almost always word a buying invitation in terms of alternatives, no matter what you are selling. Make a practice of planning alternative offers that would be realistic for the customer you are going to approach. The invitation should never be worded to suggest an ultimatum or a showdown: 'Will you decide on this?' 'Do you want it or not?' 'Can we bring it around today?' Closing invitations of this kind are aspects or poor selling technique. They have the quality of high pressure; they put the customer in an unpleasant position even if he is ready to decide—and they often catch him unready. They violate the rule of sales psychology which is our third hint.

3 *Avoid asking questions which can easily be answered with a 'No.'* Questions which present an ultimatum almost force a negative answer. ('Do you want it?'—'No.') Still worse are questions worded in the negative: 'You wouldn't care to stock a gross, would you?' 'You don't want to trade that machine in, do you?' 'You wouldn't consider aluminium siding, perhaps?'

4 *Use check questions.* During your sales talk, you get many opportunities to test your customer's readiness to buy through the use of check questions. Whenever you develop a selling point you can tactfully ask whether the customer agrees. Through this check-question technique many salesmen have improved their success in difficult selling situations, getting more orders and getting orders more quickly. And, most important, they always know exactly where their customer stands in relation to their offer.

The salesman takes the test dishes out of the dishwashing machine and asks, 'Three minutes, Mr Jones! Would that take a load off your wife?' Mr Jones agrees cordially—the machine would reduce drudgery. 'Would you like to know when we can deliver?' the salesman responds. This last question is the check question—Mr Jones's answer will tell the salesman whether to press for buying action or to develop more sales appeals and build up desire.

The customer says, 'I see your point. When you put it on a cost-per-day basis it really isn't expensive.' This provides an opportunity for the check question, 'Would you like to start using it this season?'

The customer says. 'I see what you mean. Of course an ad that pays off is worth whatever it costs.' This gives the salesman his lead for the check question, 'Do you think a half-page would pay off in the October issue?' If the customer turns down this suggestion his answer does not break up the sales talk; but it he accepts it, the sale is in.

The customer and salesman have checked some rough cost-in-use figures for a new duplicating machine. 'Looks as if you came up maybe £70 ahead in the first year,' the salesman observes, 'Are we right?' The customer agrees : 'I can't see where we could be wrong.' Then the check question : 'Well, do you want to begin saving that £70 right away?'

In these four examples, a 'yes' answer to the check question could bring a sale in immediately. Note, however that all of them avoid using the word 'buy.' Thus the customer does not refuse to buy even if he does answer 'no' to the check question.

The customer can give three kinds of responses to a check question: negative; neutral or noncommittal; or affirmative.

Unless the check question is badly phrased (and phrasing it well is the salesman's job), the negative answer is not a turn down of the entire offer but a refusal to concede that the selling point is conclusive. If the dishwasher customer answers 'No,' he may mean, 'Not till I ask some more questions,' or 'How do I know my wife can run it as easily as you do?' or 'I might find something she'd rather have.' So the salesman can inquire after the buying appeal that the customer will consider conclusive, dispose of the sales resistance accordingly, and build up desire to the buying point.

A neutral or noncommittal answer to the check question indicates that the customer is not yet quite convinced, or is hesitating for some undiscovered reasons, or just wants to put off the decision. The salesman is on the right track, but he still has some distance to cover.

An affirmative answer to a test question means that the buying decision is ripe to be made—or is made.

5 *Break up the decision process.* To make a decision easier for the customer put it to him in stages 'yesterday we agreed...today we must..., and next time we still have to...'

6 *Review the buying reasons.* Bring together and go over again all the essential benefits that the customer can be expected to derive from the purchase. Grouping all the reasons for a purchase is an effective closing technique. It is especially effective if you can get them into writing—your writing or (still better!) the customer's.

You can also establish a plus/minus list, which describes clearly all advantages and disadvantages of your offer.

Repetition has a strong suggestive effect. Your customer may not understand, may even not hear, a selling point until you repeat it for the third or fourth time. So you repeat, at the close, the selling points you have made. If now he first pays attention to something, you settle it.

But you don't bring up new selling points in the close. If you do, you are back near the beginning, with the job of establishing a selling point that the customer hasn't yet grasped or accepted. Meanwhile, your established points grow stale.

7 *Aim at part-by-part decisions.* Instead of forcing a customer to make a difficult over-all decision, you can aim at achieving the desired result in stages by putting questions that lead to decisions about parts of the deal—about particular wishes, conditions, and so on—*before* the customer comes to decide about the purchase as a whole.

Auto salesmen in particular have many opportunities for making use of this technique. Here is an example—a diagram rather than a faithful picture, perhaps—that illustrates the method:

'Which colour do you like best?'—'Oh, the blue.'

'Do you want power steering? It's wonderful for parking.'— 'We'd like it, but I suppose it costs another £30.'

'Well, it's an extra, but you may want it anyhow. Do you want your windshield with a sunshade-tint top?'—'No, I don't want to pay for it, and I don't want it anyhow. Interferes with seeing.' (*Negative reaction.*)

'Well, a lot of people feel that way. Especially tall men. Now how about the seat? Won't you sit in it and see if it's right? High enough for you?'—'M-mm-h. High enough. Can you get it up another inch?'

'Sure thing. Simple shop adjustment. Is there any other adjustment you want?'

And so on. Step by step, the customer is relieved of minor decisions that would enter into his formal and final buying decision.

When a customer says 'no' on an isolated point, as in the wind shield-extra matter of the example, the 'no' is not dangerous because it concerns only a single part of the proposition; and it becomes a 'yes' if the proposition can be changed to fit the customer's preference, as by furnishing a clear windshield or raising the seat. Even an outright disagreement is not likely to be serious if it concerns a minor point—as between, say, a flush tank and a flush valve for a toilet bowl.

Another example: 'How many outlets would you need in your offices?' asked Mr Palmer who sells telephone installation.—'Well, one here and two in the supervisors' office, one in the typists' room, one in the warehouse and one in accounting.'

'Is that sufficient?'

'Yes, that's all.'

'Wouldn't you need another one in the invoicing department?'

'No, that's not necessary.'

'Which of the two models do you prefer?'

'They both look good. But I guess I prefer that one at the left.'

'Would it be an advantage to connect the installation with the outside telephone so that calls from the city can be put through?'

'Well certainly—but that costs...'

'The difference is not that big. Let me show you the price list. Could we go through the offices and check on the installation possibilities? Would this be a good spot in your office?'

8 *Take advantage of your customer's special requests.* If your customer requests changes in your offer, or if you can suggest possible changes that would make it fit his desires better, you have an opportunity that may help you close the sale. Complying with requests or making changes has the effect of committing the customer to accept the modified proposal—not rigidly, but there is a tendency.

'I don't like this kitchen floor surface,' says a lady who is considering buying a ready-made house. 'Couldn't we get some darker colour?'—'Maybe we could arrange that,' the salesman replies. 'I'm sure we can if it's the only thing you want changed. In fact, I'll put that in writing and add it to our agreement.' The offer establishes a good climate or disposes of an objection that may be only an excuse.

'I want to use your paper,' says the printer, 'but I can't wait five weeks for delivery.'—'If I could get it in three weeks, would that help you?' the salesman asks.—'Yes, it would.'—'All right, I'll talk to the plant and let you know this afternoon if I make any headway.' How can the printer refuse the offer, if the three-week date will serve? Or fail to buy, if the salesman gets the three-week date?

Approaching the matter via questions, as in these two illustrations, is much more effective than the eager offer of unconditioned concessions. 'Of course we can change it to darker linoleum' would invite the customer to try for more favours. 'All right, I'll give you a three-week delivery' is almost insulting, for the natural thought is, 'Why didn't he offer me the best terms at the beginning?' But when the final assent to the request is conditioned on a favourable buying decision, even if the salesman must refer the concession to his office for acceptance, the effect is one of fair-dealing give and take:

A few further examples:

'If you want smaller collars on these coats, I think we might work it out for you,' the salesman offers. 'We're still in production, and it shouldn't be any trouble if I get your order while we're still cutting.'

'Would those chairs be okay with a firmer seat padding?' the salesman asks. 'We'll build you a gross that way if you specify.'

'This press won't do my work,' says the printer. 'What does it need that it hasn't got?' the salesman asks. 'Maybe we can put it on.'

The offer to redesign, or alter, or meet special specifications, almost puts the customer under obligation to buy. Therefore, if the salesman has the slightest chance to offer a change suitable to the customer (even if he has not expressed it openly), he should gratefully seize this opportunity to bind him.

9 *Push ahead of events.* This method, like those in hints 1, 2, 7 and 8, is intended to get away from debating the issue of 'to buy or not to buy.' Instead, the salesman discusses details of delivery, design, payment, and other buying conditions so that the customer's thoughts are directed towards the time when he has received and will use the article. The buying decision is not mentioned, but is regarded as an accomplished fact.

'Do you want this stock for now, or next month?' the stationery salesman asks his retail customer (using the alternative approach). The customer could reply 'Neither,' but is not likely to.

'What do you think about taking your cement in four deliveries while the job's in progress?' the salesman asks the contractor's purchasing agent.

'You can spread payments six months and we'll carry you without finance charges,' is a salesman's offer to small retailers who need modern display fixtures. 'Keep your cash and use it for stock to fill the fixtures.'

'Which machine are you trading in?' the tool salesman asks. 'We can just as well drill the baseplate on the new one to fit your floor bolts.'

'This copy of the order goes to the service department,' the salesman explains. 'The service crew will be around to help you check

up on the unit's operation as soon as the installation is finished—
and they'll stay with it till it's okay.'

'You can advertise these dresses,' the salesman suggests to the
retail buyer. 'Would you like to have photos on our model? Or have
us make them on your model?'

'Which patterns would you be interested in?'

'Which of these machines should be replaced first?'

'Could we start with the installation tomorrow?'

'If you make the first measurements after one week, you will
immediately be able to establish the savings.'

'Can our engineer check the installation quickly at the end of
this week?'—'You can introduce this new fashion when you open
your big Spring show. Would you like us to send you some man-
nequins?'

Questions and offers like these lead the customer's thought towards a definite buying decision by anticipating events that will
follow it. When the customer accepts the idea of these events, the
buying decision comes along.

But when you anticipate events, heed this warning: Take
extreme care to avoid tricks or high pressure. *Don't* hurry the
customer. *Don't* push your pen at him. *Don't* start writing an order
before he gives it to you. *Don't* pretend the order has been given
when it hasn't. *Don't* tell him his signature is just a formality, for
it is a thing of binding importance. And *don't* use this method, or
any other method, to con a customer into giving an order that will
hurt him.

10 *Show that you regard the purchase as an assured event.* When
you have come to the conviction that your article corresponds to a
need of the customer, then you should show the fact. If you wish to
convince the customer that he should buy your article, then you
must, yourself, radiate the conviction. You must show no doubts as
to whether the customer, when he has heard your selling points,
will buy. Word your sales talk, manage your voice, assume an attitude and general manner so that they all display quiet confidence
in the outcome. This confidence precludes such unwholesome
appeals as 'Do me a favour,' 'We're old friends,' 'We've put a lot
of time into this,' 'Since we gave you a break last time,' 'Because
we'd like to have your order,' or 'Because we throw a lot of business
your way.' Such language in a 'sales talk' is begging or wheedling;
it is not selling. Sooner or later the salesman is asked to pay, dearly,
for any orders he gets through such appeals. (*Customer*: 'Last
week I did you a favour. Now...') The temptation to employ such

high-pressure methods is especially strong in the final stages of a selling conversation. Don't yield to it.

The conviction that the customer is going to buy prohibits reference in your sales talk to what may happen *if* the customer buys. For this reason a steel salesman reworded a point from 'If you buy this stainless steel...' to 'When you work with this stainless steel...' The auto salesman would say, not 'If you buy this car,' but instead, 'When you've driven this car...' The air-conditioner man would say, 'You will enjoy a comfortable Fourth of July with this unit,' not 'If you have this before the Fourth.' The office-equipment salesman assures his customer, 'Those machines will have your billing up to date in a week'; he finds no need to suggest, 'If you put those machines in.' All the 'when' sales points are stronger than any 'if' points can be.

Show no trace of nervousness or uncertainty in this final stage. Either the customer will be unconsciously affected by your attitude, or he will notice how desperate your efforts to obtain the order are and will become suspicious. Control your voice and take care that it sounds clear, confident and calm. Be relaxed. How often has a strained and nervous attitude affected the customer, consciously or unconsciously against buying! ('I've only to see how a salesman sits on a chair to know whether he is nervous,' says a very experienced buyer.) When the points for and against a purchase are being weighed, little things can tip the balance. Excessive eagerness and apprehension on the part of the salesman act as a brake on the customer's will to a quick and positive decision. The more you need an order, the less anxious you should appear. Slow down the speed of your closing invitation, make pauses, allow the customer time to think, use 'no-pressure' selling. Don't create tension—there is too much in the air already. If you use an order pad, put it on the desk at the beginning of your conversation. *Never* ask the customer *whether* he wishes to buy but only *when, what, where, how* and *how much.*

11 *Let the customer try out the article.* Nothing helps a quick decision more than leaving an article with a customer for a trial period. Let him use the new vacuum cleaner for a week so that he cannot get on without it afterwards. If your customer has some business in another town, demonstrate your car by having him drive it there. Invite a bookstore browser to take home a book he is interested in and send it back within a week if he does not want it. It is likely that the book will stay. Book dealers who make a practice of sending books on approval when a price inquiry is received state that in three or four out of every five cases the books are bought. If

a small manufacturer is hesitating about the wisdom of changing from his old material to your new metal alloy, offer him a trial shipment and return privilege. If your customer is not entirely convinced of the advantages of your proposition, always offer the return privilege within a certain period of time. One office equipment manufacturer recommends to his salesmen to place as many trial machines as possible for a period of six-ten days. He expects to sell three out of five placed machines. 'It's purely a question of organisation' the Sales Manager states. 'During the trial period we service the customer's old machine—to make quite sure that while he has ours, he really uses it!'

This brings us to the most important way of proving the value of an article: the use of *guarantees and the right to return*. No sales argument is so effective as a positive guarantee or the option of returning the article (without reason and without cost). By this means you facilitate purchases and reduce the customer's fear of making a mistake. Your article should be able to carry a guarantee. There is often an incomprehensible reluctance to give guarantees, trial deliveries and time-limited options of return; nevertheless these measures considerably enhance the prospects of a sale. Of course, some articles, by their nature, do not lend themselves to these expedients.

12 *Strike while the iron is hot.* In most cases it is an advantage if the sale is concluded at the first interview. The customer, as well as the salesman, saves time. The capacity for decision is at its highest peak, the selling points are at their freshest, the receptiveness of the customer is at its strongest, and the risk of a tough battle over conditions is as low as it will ever be. Surveys have shown that a remarkable number of selling calls are unjustifiably long. The waste of time is most manifest at the conclusion which, often enough, is not a conclusion at all. The salesman is so afraid of a refusal that he doesn't dare to suggest a purchase, hoping that if he keeps talking the customer will eventually interrupt him with a buying decision! If this fails to transpire the frightened salesman assumes that the customer is not ripe and suggests, directly or indirectly, a postponement of the decision.

'Of course,' thinks the experienced salesman, 'I am bright enough not to tell a customer that he can think the matter over and I'll call again.' But wait a minute! Every time you do not specifically invite the customer to buy, every time you keep talking when you should be closing, every time you stall and wait for the customer to speak out, you are inviting him to keep the decision up in the air for the time being. An omitted invitation to buy becomes an indirect invitation to procrastinate. It is easier to talk yourself out of an order than to talk yourself into one. It is entirely possible to discover, by means of check questions, when the iron is hot and ready to be struck. When it is ready, don't hesitate to strike! If you have missed the right moment—be sure to be ready for the next one!

13 *Apply the key issue method.* This method is effective but rather difficult, and cannot always be used. In using it, you concentrate your whole sales effort into convincing the customer about one point that is decisive for his buying action. You cannot use the method unless there is some such point. You cannot guess at the point, pick it at random; you must find it and be sure you have found the right one. And you must convince your customer overwhelmingly and leave him happy about it. An example will illustrate the method:

Salesman: 'I hear you can't turn out enough work to keep up with your orders.'

Customer: 'That's right. If I could make more I could sell it all.'

'Then would you be interested in a machine that will increase your production by 25 per cent?'—'I'd buy it for any reasonable price.'

'Of course. But production capacity and reasonable price work out in arithmetic. Production's *the* thing?'—'That's it.'

'Fair enough. Then you'll take my machine if it turns out 25 per cent more than your present machine?'—'I sure will!'

'Now we're teed up and ready to drive. I would like to have you come over to Smith Brothers' plant with me. They have two of our machines running on stock a little heavier than yours, and each one turned out more than three thousand units last month.'—'I'll have to see them. If they really do that, I want them.'

The imaginary salesman has brought the whole buying action to hang on one deciding question. If he comes up with a satisfactory answer, he probably gets the order. He has saved the customer's time, his own time also, and has kept out of a lot of rambling conversation by limiting the issue to one crucial point, to be proved. How can you use this idea in your sales activity?

13 *Invite all remaining objections.* When an interested customer is still hesitating over a decision, he may have various reasons. Perhaps he feels he cannot properly survey all the facts; perhaps he can't make an independent decision (wife or boss must be consulted); perhaps he feels that the disadvantages of the proposition

stand off the advantages. The salesman's only way to learn the reason is to invite objections. Out of them the reasons will appear, plain or disguised.

'No, I'd like to think it over,' says a wavering customer. The dealer decides that this request need not break up the conversation. 'By all means,' he says accordingly. 'Maybe you're in doubt about something I could clear up in the meantime?' This last sentence is the key to keeping the talk going. Now the customer must reveal something. He can answer in several ways:

(a) 'Well, I hardly know what to say. I guess you just have to sit down and think this kind of thing over.' The lack of decision can now, probably, be attributed to the fact that the buying desire has not been sufficiently stimulated. Hence the salesman will have to present, with some new approach, his strongest sales points.

(b) 'It's a good proposition, all right, but I don't have to have the thing right away. There's no rush.' His buying desire has been aroused, despite his general interest. Now it is necessary for the salesman to employ appeals directed at arousing the buying urge; he must also present effective reasons against any postponement of the decision.

(c) 'Well, I still think the price is a little high.' Or: 'It's not quite what I had in mind.' Or: 'I don't really care too much for it.' Or: 'They look all right, but I'm afraid they won't stand up.' All these remarks express serious factual objections which the salesman has not quite dispelled up to this time. In some cases, he will have to go back almost to the beginning of his sales talk and go over all his points again; in others, it may be sufficient if he deals with the specific objections again, more effectively and with a new approach.

(d) 'I'd like to talk it over with my board of directors.' 'I have to clear this kind of deal with our export manager.' 'I can't decide on my own.' Either the salesman has not got hold of the man who makes decisions, or else the customer is not quite certain about the proposition and his own judgement of it. The salesman has to decide whether he should try to arouse still greater desire in the man before him, or to work directly or indirectly on the man behind the speaker.

(e) 'No, I can't think of anything in particular.' If the customer replies in this vein or in one similarly hesitating, the salesman knows he is likely to buy if only he is invited a little more strongly.

In addition, of course, the customer may answer the question evasively, or his unwillingness to decide may depend on several considerations. You can overcome this problem to a certain extent by asking a further check question following the customer's reply: 'Oh, I see. Is that the only thing that prevents you from making up your mind?' Then the customer's answer can only be one of the following types:

(*a*) 'Yes.'

(*b*) 'No, not only that. I think it is very expensive, too.'

(*c*) 'I don't know. I'm not quite clear about it.'

Case *a* is a direct admission; *b* is either a subterfuge or there is yet another reason for the indecision; in the case of *c* the reason is not known to the customer himself. It is useful to put these check questions to make sure that you are not wasting time by replying to a subterfuge. Always try to discover where the real resistance lies hidden. The stated reason may hide a real one. One experienced Sales Trainer recommends the question: 'And apart from that?' If it was the true reason, the customer will confirm it, if not he will be taken by surprise and come out with his real motive.

A very successful salesman of services to Top Management discovers many objections by saying 'You are so pensive.'

15 *If no decision can be reached, keep in contact and do not lose the initiative.* First of all you must distinguish between valid reasons why the customer cannot decide straight away, and pretences or general indecision. In the presence of valid reasons it is wrong to press for an immediate decision. In fact you yourself should advise postponement and thereby establish real trust. In the face of pretence, or general indecision you can counter with: 'Is there any special reason why you should wait?' 'Better decide now; then the matter will be settled.' 'If you accept the proposal now we can start installing the machinery tomorrow and you will be using it the day after.' Holding up in such a way the prospect of an early enjoyment of the advantages of the purchase is most helpful. 'If you put your signature here you will receive the first volume tomorrow'; or 'If we complete the arrangements today there will be no need for you to bother any more about the matter: I will look after everything else and you will not need to give up your time for further discussions.' In a few cases there is no need to take any notice of the customer's delaying tactics, if you are sure of your ground and know that the customer is merely reluctant to express his readiness to buy. Always try to be equipped with a talking point to indicate the advantage of buying immediately. And, as a last resort, point out the loss or damage he will suffer if he doesn't buy (now).

Any real need to discuss or examine the proposition with other responsible people in the customer's firm must naturally be respected. Nevertheless, there is nothing to prevent your suggesting that you might be present at the discussion, as you could perhaps supply some useful information, or suggesting that you might speak to the third person yourself (but don't do it behind the back of the person you are now dealing with). You can send supplementary material and arrange to collect it personally—which acts as a reminder. You can leave the article for testing. Or you can propose a trial installation. You can give a specific guarantee (a deciding factor if the sale is a hair's breadth from a successful conclusion) or show that you are ready to be accommodating.

The idea of saving up a selling point until the end is unrealistic. No sensible salesman will hold back an important selling point until the whole sale hangs on a thread.

A sudden relaxing of conditions at the end looks like high-pressure selling and arouses the customer's suspicions. Giving in to the customer on a few points after a long discussion is another matter.

Always worth employing is the practice of writing a letter of acknowledgement in which the proposition is repeated in concentrated form together with the most important reasons in favour of the purchase. This written reminder has a number of values:

(a) The proposition can often be presented better in writing after the oral interview. It is easier to find the right points, and avoid the wrong ones, when you can reflect on them in peace. You can improve on some of your spoken appeals. Furthermore you can take into account the newly-acquired knowledge of the customer, his attitude, and his special problems.

(b) It is easy for the customer to make use of the written material for further consideration. It simplifies his thinking; he will use it, and you thereby influence him though you are not with him.

(c) The written proposition has a general air of trustworthiness (this is often overlooked).

(d) On people with a strong visual sense, the written argument makes a more powerful impression than the spoken word.

(e) The letter is likely to be put before any company purchase conference where the decision is discussed. Thus it gives the salesman his chance to influence people he might never meet in person.

It is a fact that many salesmen are reluctant to write letters (good salesmen are often poor correspondents). For this reason many a sales manager has to force his representatives, by means of mild pressure, to write follow-ups. Experience soon proves the value of these letters.

Finally, the rule that has already been given elsewhere needs to be repeated: *The salesman should always keep the initiative.* It applies also to sales letters. They should not end with the words 'I hope to hear from you' but, for example, 'I will take the liberty of inquiring in a few days whether this information is adequate' (or 'what further information you require').

It is not the customer's job to re-contact the salesman. The salesman must claim this privilege. Do not, as a rule, be satisfied with a customer's promise, 'I'll take it up again next week.' Instead take care of the matter yourself: 'Will it suit you if I ring you at the beginning of next week or shall I wait until Friday?' (*technique of alternatives*). There are always some good reasons for making such a proposal, but often none at all need be given. Even when the customer says he will ring you on his own initiative it is usually possible to fix a date when you can ring the customer yourself if he has not phoned you.

16 *Even when the customer gives you a definite 'no', do not give up on him.* A 'no' is rarely irrevocable. There are innumerable possibilities that a new situation will arise which can induce the customer to re-examine his decision. Often you can ask directly what made the customer reject the offer. By asking this you can learn things bearing on your next call and things bearing on your past work. What the customer tells you may suggest better ways to help him and improve the chance of making the next offer a sale. It may also enable you to make a critical reassessment of your own sales work and to correct possible defects.

When you ask a customer why he rejected your offer, you do well to suggest by your question that something must have been wrong with the way you presented it—*not* with the offer.

A valuable word when you are seeking information is 'why'—a straightforward questioning word which calls for an equally straightforward answer, and often receives it. You can ask 'why' of your customer, or of yourself. You gain something from every visit if you examine why you got the order or why you didn't. It is no disgrace to lose an order, but it is almost a crime not to know why.

Unless you don't want to see a customer again, you must avoid reproaching him for his negative decision; you must not make it embarrassing for him to express his negative decision. You may feel strong temptation to do so if you have taken a great deal of trouble or if the disappointment is keen because you have been especially confident of making the sale. But embarrassing the customer may lead to his taking care not to have any further dealings with you. If you are tactful about losing an order you need not lose a customer; you can often arrange to return at some future time and take up the matter again. Do you always conscientiously establish the reason why you lose an order? This is very necessary if you want to improve your sales technique.

Ending the conversation

Should you or your customer make the move that ends the sales conversation? One sales manager advises his salesmen to break off a selling process that is leading nowhere. The salesman who does this saves some of his self-esteem; the customer respects him; and the salesman keeps the way open for future calls.

When you do call back after a turndown, you should avoid the common mistake of asking your customer if he has changed his mind. No one wants to think of his decisions as inconclusive and reversible. (This important psychological fact has been mentioned before.) Rather, you should take up the earlier main objection directly *if and only if* the situation has changed. If it has not changed, select a completely different starting point.

Do you give up too soon?

Many salesmen give up too quickly. They are easily intimidated when the selling effort has begun with a turndown. When they make a visit to a customer for the first time they are often afraid of him for no good reason. Above all, they are much too inclined to write off a customer for all time if a proposal has been finally refused after a complete selling process. Generally speaking, there is no final refusal in buying and selling.

When you have the order

When your customer has decided to buy, particularly after putting up strong resistance and weighing his decision for a long time, you should not leave hastily, as if to snatch up the order and rush out of the office before the signature dries. That behaviour looks like a confidence man's getaway. A salesman in a hurry after he has made a sale creates mistrust and misgiving, the more so if the buying decision has been made with some hesitancy. The customer continues to feel, 'Am I doing the wise thing? Am I being rash?' If the salesman leaves the customer fighting this inner battle with himself, the customer may regret his decision to buy. He may begin to wonder whether he has been high-pressured. He may phone the salesman's office to cancel the order—and it may be embarrassing or impossible to enforce the contract.

You should congratulate your customer in a tactful and cordial way on his advantageous purchase, repeat details about delivery conditions and the like, offer advice and help with regard to the proper care and use of the article. Thus you help to relax the tension that accompanies decisions, and you minimise the danger of the customer's regretting his decision. Your sale is not really final until the article has been put to use and the customer has ascertained that it comes up to all expectations—his own and those that the salesman's promises have built up.

Salesmen often violate the principle of paying attention to a customer after the sale. Such mistakes endanger the next sale.

'When you forget your customer, he forgets you' is a fact so important and so neglected that a European oil company once had it printed on posters and affixed to every letter it sent its retailers. Serving your customer after the sale is a premium you pay in order to keep him as your customer. Contact of this nature gives you a great advantage over all your competitors. Among its other advantages, it gives you further insight into the problems, needs, and circumstances of the customer. It gives you an invaluable opportunity to learn whether your product in use lives up to the expectations you and the customer had for it. After-the-sale service equips you with many more selling points, as experienced salesmen acknowledge. It produces many cues, leads, and recommendations for more sales. There is no easier way to work towards more orders. Do you use this resource? Using it will make you a more efficient salesman.

The chain reactions

Every contact you have with a satisfied customer provides new selling possibilities. You can sell:
(a) the same article to the same customer;
(b) another article to the same customer;
(c) the same article to another customer (the first customer's acquaintance, friend, colleague, or competitor);
(d) another article to another customer (also through recommendation).

These possibilities of chain reaction are not sufficiently exploited by salesmen in general. It is often cheaper and easier to sell more to the old customers than to chase after new ones. A satisfied customer is often in a position to drop a few hints about people in his circle who are likely to be in the market (unless exclusiveness is part of your deal with him, formally or informally).

Use every possibility for chain reactions. You make your work easier—and sell more! And your Company can sell more advantageously—thanks to more profitable orders.

It would be worth while for some sales managers to review their salesmen's work for possible extra sales to be developed through possibilities (a) to (d) above.

The salesman who ends a first-rate sales talk with a third-rate closing effort has built up an easy sale for some competitor. Plan your closing tactics. The customer has to be invited to buy. Make it easy for him to say 'yes.' Avoid all negative questions and ultimatums. Never give up on a customer.

The action sub-area is the fourth and last sub-area of the selling-process—the twelfth area of creative selling, where sales are made and sales are lost.

SEVENTEEN

The tactical sequence area: DIPADA—a new process for creative selling

Can you answer these four questions?

1 Do you know whether the DIPADA process can be used in your line of selling?

2 When a sales conversation is started by a customer's inquiry, is the DIPADA or the AIDA process called for?

3 Do you know whether identification, proof, and acceptance constitute one, two, or three elements of a selling process?

4 Is there any difference between the closing techniques of the AIDA method and the DIPADA method?

Can you solve the following five problems?

1 Barton Emsworth sells accounting equipment and supplies. A special feature of his system is economy in space. Also, through an ingenious coding system, two and often three sets of accounting records can be consolidated. The equipment has four other demonstrable advantages. Emsworth begins talking to each customer by pointing out the possibility of simplifying the work. This approach arouses attention. Then he goes on to explain the further advantages of his system. He gets a reasonable number of orders. One day he realises that he could sell even more by organising his sales talk according to a different plan. What may be his idea?

2 Jerry Strike, a former truck driver, sells commercial vehicles. He specialises in selling to metropolitan delivery contractors, whose

needs and mentality he understands well. He searches out the particular problems involved in their work, selects the vehicle that best fits them, and proceeds to arouse the customer's buying desire for the vehicle he has chosen. His customers are not very talkative; Strike's selling conversations are necessarily almost monologues. Strike knows that this method is not ideal and that when he does all the talking it is hard for a customer to follow the points he presents. He also realises that he frequently skips one stage of AIDA selling, a method he has studied. The real trouble is that he omits two stages in the DIPADA process. Which?

3 'We would like to look at some material for redecorating our premises. We thought...'—I understand. Just let me see... Now, we have a large selection of striking wallpaper designs. Here are some new imported ones. Outstanding! Just look at them! With these on your walls you are sure to increase your sales. You are the first people who have seen these designs. And...' The monologue sales talk is bad enough, but the stream of talk is not the only thing wrong here.

4 Wallace Earl is a good listener. Selling industrial equipment, he knows that he can seldom expect an order on the first contact with a customer. He also realises that he must make himself thoroughly familiar with his customer's problems. Accordingly, he sounds the customer thoroughly for information; and as a rule he gets it. Sometimes he devotes his first two or three visits to such inquiry. He is well aware of the psychological rule that he should speak primarily about the customer and secondarily about the articles he is selling. Conscientiously keeping to this principle, Earl succeeds in keeping the customer's interest alive during these early conversations. When he is satisfied that he knows enough about the customer and his problems he promises that on the next visit he will have a proposal ready for consideration—an improved assembly line, a better materials-handling system—with its advantages presented in great detail. Earl's sales manager is of the opinion that this method wastes too much time. He can't prove the opinion, however, because Earl is a comparative newcomer to the firm and his sales results do not cover enough time to permit objective appraisal of the advantages and disadvantages of his technique. What is your opinion? Could this question arise in your activity too?

5 'In some ways it is easier to sell to new customers than to old ones,' an industrial salesman remarks. 'Attention comes spontaneously when you're new to a buyer. After you've seen him a few times everything tends to get routine. You can't come in with something new every visit. Some people I know make out a lot better

with old customers, but I find it much easier to deal with new people.' These opinions touch off a wide-open bull session. The AIDA process and the DIPADA process get thorough going over; their use with new contacts and old customers is discussed; in the end, there is substantial agreement as to the advantages and disadvantages of both kinds of techniques. Which type of sales visit do you find easier? Do you conscientiously train the other?

The DIPADA selling formula has proved valuable in the construction of sales talks for wholesale and industrial customers, as well as for retail selling. It brings good results especially in the sales of all kinds of industrial products, complex plant and office equipment and intangible projects or abstract offers. The DIPADA method is markedly appropriate when the sales call grows wholly or partly out of some action taken by the customer—for instance, a request for information.

The DIPADA method may seem relatively complex, but it leads always to a sound and complete sales process which really engages the customer. In some periodic calls on old customers it is much better to use the DIPADA process than the AIDA. The DIPADA process has six steps : Definition, Identification, Proof, Acceptance, Desire, and Action.

The essence of the DIPADA method is best exhibited by presenting two approaches to the same sales problem—the customary, 'orthodox' approach first, then the DIPADA approach. The top management of a leading watch manufacturer has become concerned over the poor selling ability of the retail clerks in the stores, through which the watches are marketed. A survey of the stores, conducted by a research organisation, has prompted the management to inaugurate a salesmanship school for retail clerks.

One of the manufacturer's salesmen, Alton March, has this conversation with an old customer:

March: Mr Dealer, my management has some important news for you.
Dealer: Uh-huh?
March: Yes, they're offering to do something for you that no watch manufacturer has ever done.
Dealer: What is it? Are they going to give me discounts I can make a profit on?
March: Not discounts. This proposition is better than that.
Dealer: All right. All right. What is it?
March: Well, we're setting up a selling school.

Dealer: What's the idea? Don't your salesmen sell me enough watches?

March: Oh, no..Not for our salesmen—for yours.

Dealer: For my salesmen? You think they don't sell enough?

March: Well, some of them *could* sell better.

Dealer: Hmm... Isn't that something I ought to handle?

March: Of course—of course, Mr Dealer. We just want to help. It may be that we could—

Dealer: It might be. Okay, when I need your help I'll let you know. Now, what was that big deal you started to talk about?

March: The selling school. That was the deal I meant. It works this way—

Dealer: Interesting idea. Sorry I'm busy. Tell you what—give me a good fill-in on it next time. Right now, there might be some customers on the floor...

Sumner Trenton, presenting the same proposition, uses the DIPADA approach:

Trenton: Mr Dealer, could you tell me a couple of things about your sales?

Dealer: What about my sales?

Trenton: The methods, Mr Dealer. You're an expert salesman.

Dealer: Thank you.

Trenton: The whole trade knows it. But how about your clerks—do they sell as well as you do?

Dealer: I can't say they do. They don't sell as much. You can't expect too much of them.

Trenton: Do they sell as well as you could expect them to?

Dealer: Some do. I guess most of them don't. After all, they don't have much background. Some of them are really just kids.

Trenton: How do you go about training them?

Dealer: Training? Are you kidding? When would I find time to train anybody? If I see them do something wrong, I tell them.

Trenton: Mr Dealer. Suppose somebody else would train them for you? Make salesmen out of them? Would you like to have them learn real creative selling—how to make bigger sales to each customer, how to make customers feel your stores is theirs, make them want to come back? You know—the sort of selling you do yourself.

Dealer: Would I like that, you ask me! Of course! But who? How? Where? How much would it cost?

Trenton: Well, we'll do it for you. Mr Dealer. We're setting up a sales school for retail-store clerks. Teach them real selling. We've hired some of the best sales teachers in the country—

Dealer: Wait a minute. How do you teach them? Do you teach them to sell *all* my stock or just your watches?

Trenton: Your whole stock. If we just get our share, we'll be happy. And we'd appreciate your advice on some of the teaching methods.

Dealer: So?

Trenton: Here's the way we make better salesmen, Mr Dealer. Do you want to see how?

Dealer: Sure! Show it to me.

Trenton: (*explains the plan. Then*) There it is. Those two suggestions of yours just about polish it up. Have I told you everything you need to know, Mr Dealer?

Dealer: Yes-s-s...I guess you have.

Trenton: Don't you think it ought to work?

Dealer: Oh, yes. Yes—it ought to. But look here—this can't be a gift. It costs money. Who pays for it? Do I? How much?

Trenton: Mr Dealer, we pay all the costs of instruction, rent, light, books, materials, instructors. You furnish the students. We don't charge you any fees, nor do we charge the students. Getting the students to class and home is your problem and theirs; the cost will be different for every employer. But I can give you a rough idea.

Dealer: Let's have it, for a start.

Trenton: (*explains the estimate*)...so your actual outlay for each student would come to about £20. Does that figure?

Dealer: It figures.

Trenton: Now, suppose the course boosts your average clerk's sale by 5 per cent—will that pay out for you in six months?

Dealer: If they really go up 5 per cent, it will pay out.

Trenton: How about if they learn to sell half as well as you do?

Dealer: Then it pays out in a month.

Trenton: Mr Dealer, your best people are likely to benefit you most. Could you send us your three top people?

Dealer: I can only spare two.

Trenton: That's all right. We can work the others into the next session. Two, you said?

Dealer: Two is right.

Trenton: Thanks for the support. Here are the enrolment forms. I'll leave four—you might want to squeeze in more than two. I'll be around Monday to see you about your stock and I'll pick up the cards then.

March got stuck before he got moving but Trenton succeeded. In part, his success came from generally superior ability, in part from staying close to the DIPADA selling method. Now, before you look at the next paragraph (if you can avoid looking at it), check over Trenton's sales talk and see if you can recognise the various phrases in it.

Each new stage of the DIPADA process is tagged with the words, 'Mr Dealer.' Knowing this, you can check your analysis.

Now for a second pair of examples, in extremely condensed form. Philip Hughes is selling insurance. He will be talking to two prospects—both business men, both comfortably well to do, both fathers (their sons born within the past month). With John Seaman, whom he calls on first he starts off.

Hughes: Mr Seaman, have you ever heard of the savings plan for your child's education?
Seaman: I've heard of saving plans—probably not yours, though.
Hughes: Let me explain it to you. You put aside a certain amount of money every month, and—
Seaman: Put money aside! Hah! I haven't any to put aside. Doctor bills, baby stuff, new clothes for my wife. I can't put money aside.
Hughes: Oh, well, let me explain the plan anyhow. This Money—
Seaman: I'm sorry, Mr Hughes. Not now. Insurance is a fairly serious thing, and I haven't time to give it proper attention now. Suppose you call me later. Or let me have your card...

Hughes does have a chance for another interview with Seaman, say in six months. But he cannot be pleased with his result. The fault was in a bad presentation, as Hughes admits to himself. So at his second appointment, with Mr Bess, he uses another approach, the DIPADA method. It turns out to be better :

Hughes: So now you've got a son! Three to take care of instead of two!
Bess: That's how it counts up.
Hughes: Having your first son means a lot. Now, you have to arrange economic security for him as well as for your wife.
Bess: Yes, I'll have to make a living for him.
Hughes: You've probably thought of these things, but you may not have realised that you've got to plan about thirty years ahead —money for his education and getting a start in life. You want

that arranged in case you're not around. (*The thirty-year figure is chosen for two reasons—Hughes is going to offer a policy that matures in thirty years; and to mention a shorter time would suggest the thought that his customer could conceivably die inside the shorter time, a thought that would put him into an unhappy frame of mind for buying.*)

Hughes goes on to suggest to Bess the reasons why he needs to provide money, how much will be needed, and when.

Definition

We have seen Hughes working at the definition step in the DIPADA method. He has not discussed insurance; he has been speaking only of the customer's needs, which are to be covered by the insurance eventually to be mentioned. Such exploration of the customer's problems is, as has been said earlier, of interest to the customer, and this interest neutralises possible sales resistance. But to measure the customer's needs only is not sufficient. Hughes must also gain some insight into his wishes. He probes these: 'You do have college in mind for the boy, I suppose?'—'Of course, of course.'—'then you'll take him into your business?'—'I'm not too sure. I'd like to stake him to a professional education if he wants it.' —'That will cost money. You'd feel good if you could be sure he'd have it.'—'Of course I would. I want to be as sure as I can. As sure as anybody could make it.'

Thus the customer himself leads the selling process to step 2, identification. The definition of the customer's needs and wishes has been accomplished. (Emsworth, the office-equipment salesman in Problem One, was unconsciously skipping over the definition stage and endangering the success of the selling process.)

Identification

Now Hughes can mention the article he is selling—namely, insurance. Up to this point he has been working out with Mr Bess the defintion of Mr Bess's needs and desires—summed up as financial security for his family and for his son's education. Now he will be working towards the identification of these needs and desires with his article, insurance.

'Mr Bess, your present insurance would provide about a quarter of the amount we estimated your wife and son might need. The way—'

'Hold it! You ought to know I can't pay four times the premiums I'm paying now!'

'You're absolutely right—everybody has to be content with something less than 100 per cent protection. Now we have to look at the costs and set a figure.' And Hughes goes on to present his proposals.

Up to this point all is well. The definition has been accomplished, the identification established. Hughes must be careful not to neglect the stages of proof and acceptance, which Jerry Strike failed to complete in Problem Two.

Proof and acceptance

The necessity of proving to the customer his need to buy has been discussed earlier as an aspect of the desire stage in the AIDA process. Proof is recognised as the third stage of the DIPADA process, in which desire is fifth and next to final. Even so, the proving step is often neglected by salesmen, who think they have accomplished enough when they bring about identification. The identification is not really nailed down until it has been supported by concrete, point-to-point proof. So Mr Hughes now leads his customer through an item-by-item comparison, matching the desires and needs that have been defined against the insurance that has been offered. Thus he proves that the identification is valid—the article offered coincides with the wants defined. But he has not proved anything to Mr Bess until Mr Bess has accepted the proof. Therefore Hughes asks Mr Bess to acknowledge, as he proves each point, that the proof is conclusive.

Desire

Now, we come to the desire stage.

Hughes and Bess have worked up the *definition* of what Bess wanted and needed—money for his son's education and other purposes. Hughes developed the *identification* of insurance with money for these purposes. Hughes offered *proof* that the identification was exact and complete. Bess gave this proof his *acceptance*. Now Hughes undertakes to stimulate *desire* to buy.

In stimulating desire to buy, Hughes follows the idea and methods outlined in discussing the desire stage of the AIDA process. (See Chapter 15.)

Action

Action—that is, buying action—is the desired end stage of AIDA or DIPADA or any other selling process. The ways to bring about buying action—in other words, closing techniques—are presented in Chapter 16 and need not be repeated here.

The customer's initiative in DIPADA

Whenever the customer starts the selling process—in retail, wholesale, telephone, or other selling—the use of a simplified DIPADA method is recommended. From the very beginning the customer is aware of desires or needs, a fact which gives the salesman a running start into the stage of definition. Unfortunately, this head start is often wasted. Salesmen show articles to customers haphazardly. They make offers without paying attention to what the customer says (or would say if the salesman would permit him to). The customer becomes frustrated, then loses interest as he realises that the salesman is not listening to him and is making no effort to understand his needs and desires. (Do you recognise the situation of Problem Three?)

When the wishes and needs of the customer are clearly defined by the customer's inaugurating the sales process, the identification with the merchandise is relatively simple. The customer has named or described what he wants; the salesman shows or demonstrates an article or a choice of articles, one of which the customer identifies as what he wants. The stages of proof and acceptance take place almost simultaneously with the identification. The buying desire is already in existence, and the customer moves into buying action with no more than a gentle closing invitation from the salesman.

A simple variation of the DIPADA technique is the rule in retail selling (customer with intention to buy): the IDEPA method *Identification* of customer's desire, *Demonstration of* suitable solutions, *Elimination* of undesirable alternatives, *Proof* of the right choice, *Acceptance* of the buying proposition.

Starting at the right point

The DIPADA selling process compels the salesman to start from the right point—namely, the desires and needs of the customer—and to undertake a thorough examination of these desires and needs (definition stage) in relation to the article offered (identification stage). This identification must be supported by proof (proof stage) and verified by acceptance (acceptance stage). Strict adherence to these stages protects the salesman against the danger of slipping into high-pressure selling methods. The use of the question technique, especially in the definition stage, is especially natural in DIPADA selling, and offers manifold possibilities.

Selling demands a careful definition *of the needs and desires of the customer. After this follows the* identification *of these with the offer. Continuing from identification come* proof *and* acceptance, *before the salesman goes on to arouse a buying* desire *strong enough to enable him to close the sale with the customer's buying* action.

Tactical sequence is the thirteenth area of creative selling, where sales are made and sales are lost.

EIGHTEEN

The appeal area: What you say and how you say it, or 'petty details that make hungry salesmen'

Can you answer these four questions?

1 What is competitive-sales technique?
2 Do you know how to analyse each selling appeal, and how you can judge the efficiency of your selling appeals?
3 Do you know the relation between (*a*) possible, (*b*) usual or applied, and (*c*) strong selling appeals?
4 Do you know what a Sales-Talk Analysis looks like?

Can you solve the following five problems?

1 A long time ago, a trade association arranged for a survey of selling methods in retail drug stores. Shoppers were sent out with instructions to buy a 2/6 tube of toothpaste and then in addition to buy whatever else the salesman specifically suggested. Here was a no-top-limit opportunity for several hundred salesmen to boost their sales—and they all blew the chance without even knowing it. The average purchases at each store visited were less than 8/-! The shoppers encountered no serious efforts to develop additional sales—only routine phrases and pointless conversation. Most salesmen asked the same routine question. Can you surmise what it was? How would you improve on it? (Since this survey, retail selling in many drug stores has been changed into self-service, which has largely increased turnover.)
2 Throughout the world, gasoline stations have found that by

rewording the question 'How many gallons?' they can markedly increase their average sale. The same principle applies in selling razor blades, tobacco products, meals in restaurants, insurance, and many other things. What is the reworded form of the question?

3 Farrell Harrison sells building materials. He is above average intelligence and has many cultural interests, presents a well-cared-for appearance, knows his job, is a skilful talker, and reacts quickly. In his selling activities he is successful with big construction firms. Selling to small firms he finds very difficult, although he is by no means arrogant or patronising. What is the reason?

4 A group of chemical salesmen discuss the desirability of getting a good collection of information about the customer before visiting him. One of the men remarks that he formerly spent several hours before each call in advance investigation; thus he sometimes knew almost as much about his customers' personal tastes, needs, and hobbies as they knew themselves. The customers, it seems, did not appreciate his knowledge at all. He has therefore abandoned this method. Do you agree with his decision?

5 A sales manager noticed, and mentioned to him, one salesman's habit of hesitating before he stated the price to his customers. The sales manager regarded this habit as a serious fault, whereas the salesman felt that such a petty detail could have no effect on the sale.

Know what you say

'Have you ever systematically checked your selling points?'

'Do you know what selling points to present and how to present them?'

'Do you know which of your selling points are effective?'

'Our product has a dozen different strong selling points. Do you get them all into one sentence, or bring up each one by itself?'

'Do you—and how do you—meet competitive claims?'

'Do your customers usually believe what you tell them?' How can you check that?

'Do you speak longer than two minutes at a time?'

A sales manager put these questions to all his salesmen, and their answers confirmed his misgivings about the working methods of salesmen in general. Only a few salesmen know exactly what they are saying, how they are presenting their selling appeals, which appeals are effective and which are not. Most salesmen work in large part 'by guess and by gosh,' playing hunches and improvising.

Whatever your selling skill, thorough analysis of your methods is the first essential for any improvement. Questions of the kind just given are the beginning of such analysis.

Important details that seem petty

Always bear in mind—

—*that* even the smallest change in a sentence can decide the result of an interview.

—*that*, for instance, changing 'I think' to 'Don't you think' can help make a sale.

—*that* 'You can work out that answer yourself' is better than 'I can tell you the answer to that.'

—*that* 'you're probably aware of' will win more customers than 'you probably haven't thought of.'

—*that* 'you ought to stock a dozen of these; we're coming out with a big ad campaign' creates an unpleasant feeling in a dealer, whereas 'you can make a nice profit from a dozen of these during our ad campaign' will raise his desire to buy.

—*that* too much talk and too many selling points can strangle a sale.

—*that* one or two properly emphasised 'headlines' in a sales talk can impress a customer more than a dozen average selling points.

—*that* a selling point is more effective if it is presented alone than if it is one of several crammed into a single sentence.

—*that* active verbs are more effective than passive verbs or nouns.

—*that* a display of overwhelming enthusiasm will defeat its object.

—*that* selling normally does not mean comparing your product with other products.

—*that* only an acknowledged argument is a valuable contribution.

—*that* customers don't listen as well as they seem to.

—*that* correctly used pauses can be more effective than too many words.

—*that* a sales talk should not be a set speech or a monologue.

A salesman who lacks the feeling for the effect of small language differences will find it difficult to make a living in competitive selling.

Have you counted the number of these warnings to bear in mind? There are 15. Stop reading—give a minute and a half of thought to each of them; refer it to your own selling activity. In twenty-three minutes of thinking you can start on the way towards improved sales methods.

Sentences that sell

A wholesaler got a forthright refusal when he asked for a 'price reduction' on a big order. But he was successful in obtaining a 'bonus on the yearly turn-over'!

An insurance salesman might ask a customer, 'Suppose you were to die tomorrow—what would happen to your family?' Instead, he might ask, 'Suppose you had died yesterday? What would have happened to your family?' Can you sense the difference between these questions? The change of two expressions is enough to transform a disagreeable question into a highly effective selling appeal.

Your choice of language can decide whether you sell at all, and it can decide how much you sell.

At gasoline stations, the motorist is no longer asked 'How much?' or 'How many gallons?' The question is 'Fill it up?' and the average sale has been markedly increased.

In drug stores, good sales clerks suggest 'The large tube?' to the customer who asks for tooth paste or shaving cream. When a man says 'Razor blades,' they do not merely hand him a package of five or ten in the brand he names; they ask, before turning to the shelf, 'Twenty?' or 'Fifty?'—sometimes, 'Twenty or fifty?' This form of inquiry brings in more big-package sales than 'Do you want the small tube or the large tube?' or 'How many?'

When a lady asks to see 'a set of dishes,' the good salesman does not ask her 'For how many?' He proposes, instead, 'For eight places?' or 'For serving twelve?'

The insurance broker, approached for fire insurance, suggests 'Extended coverage?' instead of writing the fire policy and then proposing separate windstorm, burglary, or other policies.

These are examples of how well-chosen language increases the size of a sale where a sale of some quantity is assured. The right kind of question in a slightly different kind of situation leads people to buy where no purchase was contemplated.

The lunch-counter waiter offers a customer 'Soup? Or juice?' and the customer rarely says 'Neither.' Her next-on-station uses a different speaking tempo and tone, asking 'Souperjuice?' and it is easy for her customer to say 'No.' The waiter in a plush restaurant reminds the diner with 'For your salad?' instead of asking 'Will you take a salad?' The person who can't choose his breakfast responds more readily to 'Would you care for a boiled egg—or a poached egg?' than to 'An egg, maybe?'

Sales trainers and marketing people make much of 'related selling,' and rightly—as the offer of shaving cream to a razor-blade buyers, shoe trees with shoes, slip covers with furniture. The language in which the offer is made is important in this field also. Will the woman who has bought a dozen bath towels respond better to 'Do you want wash cloths?' or to 'These wash cloths match your towels'? When you can offer the customer something that naturally supplements or combines with an article already sold, concrete proposals are necessary but no complicated procedure is demanded. Simply showing the customer the related article may be enough to bring sales. Little or nothing need be said; a questioning or expectant expression in the salesman's demeanour invites the customer to buy.

Ideas from advertising

Salesmen can find many ideas for selling language in the advertising of the things they sell, and buy. They can scarcely use the words of an advertisement, but they can fit the idea into the face-to-face selling situation. How would you, perhaps work in the thought behind the slogan that sold many enlarging-developing kits: 'As easy as snapping the picture'? Can you get your customers to think of your product in terms of 'Cheaper by the dozen'? Although you probably avoid the ridiculed phrase 'Large economy size,' can you use the thought in a better wording? Can you learn from the fact that 'shampoo tones' are sold to women who would never buy 'hair dyes'? Do you remember the fancy-fruit gift sales that picked up the magazine-subscription slogan, 'You give this gift twelve times'? And, 'For people who can't brush after every meal'?

Sentences that never sell

Routine questions, murmured perfunctorily by weak or indifferent salesmen, almost never sell anything. 'Anything else?' almost automatically brings the answer 'No.' An automatic 'Yes' follows 'Is that all?' Concrete proposals, however low-pressure, are needed to get a customer to make additional purchases. There is no necessity for complicated methods. You can look at the customer with a questioning and expectant expression on your face and this is a silent but effective invitation to him to consider what else he should buy. Even just showing him a new product without a word can lead to an order.

'No' can become 'yes'

In certain cases the spontaneous 'no'—answer of many clients can be taken into consideration and the sales talk worded in such a manner that even a 'no' can lead to a positive situation. For instance, 'Is your display material protected against sunbeams?'—'Does your cooling system work fully automatic?'—'Are your tyres checked every three months?'—'Do you have unlimited storage space?' A negative answer is the avowal of a deficiency which should be corrected.

Pauses and stress in speaking

Actors influence their audiences, directly and skilfully, by pausing in their speech, by speaking rapidly or slowly, by stressing a word or phrase. Salesmen influence their customers—for good or ill, by intention or by chance—through the same qualities of speech. Many investigations have verified this fact. These 'small' things are highly important in the success or failure of a sales effort. They work against you or for you.

Pauses have the effect of imparting emphasis to the words they follow and the words that follow them. They are useful, therefore, for emphasising important points. They are dangerous, ordinarily, if they emphasise the price.

Stress obviously emphasises the words it falls on, and should not be permitted to emphasise the words that influence a sale adversely.

By the skilful use of stress and pauses, a basically low-pressure statement can be made more effective than any flood of superlatives. Pauses and stress enable a salesman to express personal conviction through his own voice and its inflections rather than through the overcharged words than anybody can use.

Stresses and pauses, as well as the other qualities of individual speech, make sales talks different. If two salesmen offer the same article, in similar circumstances, using the same basic sales talk, two different talks come out because the salesmen speak in two different ways. Voice and speech habits make the difference.

How does your voice sound?

It seems obvious that anything so important to salesmen as their voices should be under their control. Listen to your own voice from a tape recorder, or record. You may be horrified to find that it is unclear, indistinct, thin, or otherwise unattractive. If you discover such faults, be glad—you can correct them. You can deliver your whole sales talk to a tape, then hear it and improve it. You can cultivate your voice by listening to your own words, to what you say and to the way you say it. Your voice may be pleasant—mildly or extremely. Even a pleasant voice can be dangerous, for a customer can listen to it comfortably and almost go to sleep. To avoid this danger, the voice should be varied from time to time, irregularly, in rhythm, speed, and tone. It must, above all, penetrate.

Try to keep boredom out of your voice. You have heard your sales talk often, perhaps often enough to get tired of it. If the repetition bores you, it need not bore your customers unless you suggest boredom; they haven't heard the talk so often. Moreover, they can listen to a strong sales appeal more than once.

Pace your talk to fit your customer

The speed of your presentation must be to the perceptive faculty of your customer and the importance of your arguments.

Watch your customer as you speak, therefore, to see whether he is keeping up with you. Take care to proceed slowly with important points and with information that is difficult to comprehend. Don't waste your best selling points by rushing through them and away from them before they can have their effect.

Watch your customer, also, to see whether he is growing impatient with your talk. You may be belabouring the obvious, or trying to explain something he doesn't care about, or dwelling on things he already understands.

Two almost opposite kinds of customer behaviour may both indicate that you are going too fast. If a man's attention flags, if he begins looking out the window, he may have given up hope of following your reasoning and may be pretending to listen so he can avoid confessing ignorance. An equally confused customer, of slightly different temperament or in different circumstances, may interpose a great many objections to the points you are presenting. When you run into these symptoms, swing your talk back to an earlier stage, and slow down. Talking too fast for his customers—both words too fast and ideas too fast—was the difficulty that made the brilliant Mr Harrison unsuccessful with slow-thinking small construction contractors (Problem Three).

Public speaking and selling

Most salesmen will benefit from public-speaking lessons. Skill in public speaking carries over as skill in personal speaking, and enables the salesman to carry conviction quickly and to express ideas freely, fluently, and economically. Note well the word 'economically.' Skilful speaking is the ability to get the greatest possible meaning into the fewest possible words. This ability is the criterion of a good speaker, public or private.

The good speaker is also a good listener. Too many salesmen talk too much and cannot listen. Such streams of selling talks are abuses of the selling process, always have been, and always will be. It is the customer who should do the talking not the salesman. It is not difficult to get him to talk. If you keep resolutely quiet he will simply have to break the silence.

Since so many salesmen talk too much, it is quite possible that you are one of those who does. It is deadly easy to talk too much and too long without being conscious of the fact. Numerous experiments have proved that we all underestimate the amount of time that passes while we are speaking. Those who must listen—customers for example—are quite likely to overestimate it.

A few sales managers insist that their salesmen speak no longer than two minutes without giving the customer a chance to reply, comment, or ask a question. (Even two minutes is too long a time —try listening to someone for two minutes.) If you want to shorten up on long speeches, try laying your watch on the table at the start of a sales conversation. The reminder about time can keep you from becoming loquacious, and the gesture can suggest to your customer that you know the value of his time.

The argument analysis contained in the following pages can also help you in dividing time better between arguments of varying importance.

Language to avoid

Avoid meaningless phrases and language habits. There is no limit to the number of these, but some common ones are:

'As a matter of fact...'
'...so to speak.'
'You can believe me when I tell you...'
'It may or may not surprise you to know...'
'Between you and me...'
'Let's put it this way...'
'...more or less...'
'...Right?'
'In other words...'
'In any case...'

We all use fill-ups of this kind. We rarely realise how often we use them. Ask your friends to·point out such expressions when you fall into the habit of using them.

Avoid egocentric language. However modestly meant, it gives the effect of arrogance. Keep your language free from such expressions as:

'I think...'
'...in my opinion...'
'According to my experience...'
'If I were in your place...'
'I can tell you...'
'Take my advice...'
'Remember what I said...'
'I must say this:...'
'I'm telling you...'

Every one of those, and every expression like it, is poison in your sales talk. Ask your friends, your family, your boss, to help you get rid of them.

You must keep *your* personality in the background. Make the customer the centre and reference to your talk. Whenever you could say 'I', try to say 'you' instead.

Questions

The sales talk built on questions is the mark of genuine skill in creative selling.

The sales talk built on questions starts out with uncontroversial almost rhetorical inquiries. They are aimed at obtaining as many 'yes' answers as possible, charging the atmosphere with them. The man who has replied 'yes' to five or six successive questions has a tendency to keep on answering 'yes.' (And the man who has come back at you with 'no' to several questions will probably keep on saying 'no.')

An established negative attitude is difficult to change. A skilful salesman takes care at the beginning of a conversation to avoid asking questions or otherwise bringing up matters that may suggest even slight differences òf outlook and thus predispose the customer towards negative responses. Later in the conversation, if he must risk bringing up such a point, the disagreement it evokes is much less harmful.

The consistent use of questions to develop selling points is not an easy method, but can be highly successful to the salesman who uses it well.

'So what?'

Remember to test your selling points by asking 'So what?' Some will turn out not to be selling points. Some will become selling points when you reword them. Use only the selling points and the language that make sense to the customer and stimulate his interest or buying desire. Don't risk his saying 'So what?' You ask it, and don't use the selling point unless you know 'what.'

Are you in touch?

Applying the 'So what?' test is a way of asking in advance, 'Will I make myself clear? Will my talk make sense?' In the course of your talk, you maintain the same attitude of critically testing your talk. You watch the customer to see whether he is keeping up with you, whether he understands and accepts the points you are making. A good method is to ask, 'Have I made myself clear?' Give your customer every opportunity to talk and make his attitude clear to you.

You should only ask if you can leave his query till later on if his has interrupted a very important sales point.

Be careful about the sales points you use. There are some expressions which will actively promote a sale, and others which actively reduce your chances of making a sale—pro- and anti-sales terms like value and price, possess and buy. You will find further points to go by in check list 5 (p 252). Moreover you will find that in every enterprise there are certain terms floating around that are peculiar to the firm or branch, and they will be either incomprehensible to the customer or strange variations of familiar terms to him. Give these a particularly careful examination. It was found that in two important companies at any given time there were more than 40 of these anti-sales expressions being used by the salesman in their daily vocabulary.

You realise that a customer cannot pay attention to you or any salesman for ever. In fact, his willingness and his ability to absorb your presentation are limited—if only by the time he can give to the interview. If the interview is to bring a sale, therefore, you must present your most striking appeals and do so without losing time. You must find them (not more than three or four), phrase them, and use them to best advantage. An analysis of your sales talk and of your product's selling points is necessary, and is the object of the systematic method presented in the remainder of this chapter.

It consists of an analysis of (*a*) the *possible*, (*b*) the *used*, and (*c*) the most *appropriate* arguments.

Sales analysis

1 Make a list of all *possible* arguments for your offer.
2 Check off the arguments which you *normally use*.
3 When you have done this, you prepare a sales evaluation. With other words, you grade the advantages of your offer. Give each argument a mark, e.g. between 0 and 10. You will certainly discover that only few of the arguments reach a high mark, most of them being graded between 3 and 6. Except in special cases, the latter are too weak to be used. Probably, you will also find that some of the arguments (under point 2) only deserve a low mark and therefore should be dropped.
4 *Customer's Needs Analysis.*
Then prepare a buying analysis, as a check-up. Until now you graded *sales* points. Now measure the advantages of your proposal from the customer's point of view. Make a list of all *buying* motives

and grade them in the same manner as you did the sales points. In a good offer, the buying arguments must coincide at least with the most important sales arguments. If possible, they should also be graded similarly. E.g. you may sell a machine which needs only very little space, and you give the sales argument mark 9, but from the customer's point of view this may not be so important and would only deserve mark 5. On the contrary: Your machine makes a lot of noise and can only be graded 4 for the sales argument 'quiet operation'. But the customer thinks that a quiet operation is very important, let's say corresponding to mark 8. Obviously, the argument is negative.

The customer will certainly grade price higher than your offer, with other words, you as a salesman cannot meet the customer's desire in this respect. Your price argument may be worth 7, the customer's expectation 9. Price is usually, as explained in Chapter 7, a negative argument.

You get a positive difference in marks if your offer exceeds the customer's needs in a point which he will welcome. You may call this an 'over-value,' which will be particularly valuable, possibly as a 'compensating factor', as we shall see under 7.

5 *Strong Points*

This control-evaluation, which shows the differences between sales and buying arguments, gives you the possibility to obtain the most suitable combination of arguments and to build your sales talk around the much more effective buying motives. Remember, the customer is not interested in the overall quality of your proposal, but only in the points which are of pertinent value to him. It is obvious that the best arguments are the ones which get a high mark both as sales and as buying motives. In the example used earlier it would be dangerous for the salesman to talk about 'quiet operation', as the customer's needs are much higher than what he can offer. The 'space' argument can be used, but will certainly not create the impression it would logically deserve. If it happens to you that 'sure' arguments are disregarded or call forth objections, this is probably due to the fact that the customer does not grade this point as highly as you expected.

6 *Your Weak Points.*

This phase in the argument analysis follows the others logically in measuring the disadvantages. Every offer has disadvantages for the customer, which have to be offset in some way by valuable advantages. Your analysis will show you such weaknesses. If the sales argument is graded 4 and the customer's need 9, the disadvantage can be established at 5.

7 *Compensating Arguments.*

To offset these disadvantages, you will have to find corresponding compensating arguments. Theoretically, these advantages must reach at least the same number of plus-points. They are obtained from sales arguments grading higher than the customer's expectations (the 'over-value' mentioned before) or from the arguments where your offer equals the customer's high demands.

8 *Competitive Selling.*

In certain cases there is an eighth phase: the competitive sales technique. It is only used if the readiness to buy exists and the customer does not decide *if* he wants to buy, but *from whom* he is going to buy, in which case he will compare the offers of various competitors. Consequently, it will be good if you check your points in column 3 against the ones which could be obtained by the competitor (column 4—the customer's needs—remains unchanged). In most cases, the advantages of both offers will be about equivalent, but there will be one or a few points where you differ. It can be easily understood that if a salesman emphasises an argument which is equally true for his competitor's offer, he does not sell his own proposal but his competitor's. The stronger the argument—the better help goes to the competitor! Of course you should only stress the arguments which grade much higher in your offer than in your competitor's. But now even arguments with relatively low marks are favourable and can be used. In a competitive situation a normally fairly unimportant argument can make the sale if it is the only difference between the two offers.

The skill of a good salesman is often demonstrated if in such a competitive situation with two almost identical offers he can discover his small hidden advantages and present them so well that the sale is decided in his favour.

9 and 10 *Plus and Minus.*

Now you have filled in column 9—your own *plus* marks—and 10—your *minus* marks in comparison to your competitor. You are going to make use of your advantages; but you do not violate the everlasting sales rule that forbids you to speak disparagingly of competitors. If you emphasise the points where you have the advantage, the customer will notice that competition lacks them.

The sales talk analysis is not something done once and used for ever. You have to keep it up-to-date and revise it as many things change: the description of your offer; the relative importance of items in the description of your offer, in your competitor's offer, and the customer's needs. The sales analysis used systematically in your sales calls, is a valuable tool for self-control and forces you to make a clear plan of your presentation. Very often, this will lead to new knowledge about your customer and his problems. Either you gather the necessary information before the call, or you can use the first visit to ascertain the most important sales arguments. Such an analysis also gives you a good picture of the market position of your product. It should be prepared with or for each salesman.

Knowing your customer

A small warning: it is always very important that you know as much as possible about your customer's needs, interests, problems, views, position, way of life, etc. before you visit. But you will be wise not to use your knowledge in ways that would allow him to think you know too much (see Problem Four). The following specimen of a Sales Talk Analysis contains none of the primary appeals and basic human wishes mentioned in Chapters 1 and 2, which have been left out to keep the description as simple as possible. Industrial goods have been chosen for the example. The analysis is theoretical. The results are meant to be guideposts for the salesman's self-control.

SALES-TALK   ANALYSIS   (ILLUSTRATIVE   SPECIMEN)

The List is an itemised description of the offer.

Column 1 is the *possible-points column*. This column contains a check at all items that could be used as sales-talk points.

Column 2 is the *usual-points column*. This column contains a check mark at all items that the salesman normally uses as sales-talk points.

Column 3 is the *seller's-offer column*. This column contains a rating of the various points of the offer, on a scale of 1 to 10 for the range from poor to perfect.

Column 4 is the *customer's-needs column*. This column contains a rating of the various points of the customers needs on the same scale used to grade the offer in column 3.

Column 5 is the *strong-points column*.

Column 6 is the *weak-points column*.

Column 7 is the *compensating-advantages column*.

Column 8 is the *competitor's-offer column*. It is analogous to column 3.

Column   9 is the *competitive-advantage column.*
Column 10 is the *competitive-disadvantage column.*
These points are all explained on the previous pages.

Conclusion

What does this Sales Talk Analysis show? There are twenty possible arguments, and the salesman usually uses nine (columns 1 and 2). The sales arguments total 107 points and the buying arguments (showing the customer's needs) 105 points (columns 3 and 4). Therefore, the offer on the whole corresponds quite well to the customer's needs and should lead to a sale. An important negative difference between the sales and buying arguments would make a sale impossible or would certainly make the argumentation very difficult. The competitor's offer (column 8) with 97 points should prove rather difficult to sell. Rating 7 has been chosen as a minimum for usable arguments. In your practical sales activity, this can be lowered or lifted. The number of suitable arguments (column 5) is five, i.e. only one fourth of all possible arguments and four less than the salesman normally uses. Out of these five arguments, he uses only three (he avoids argument 25). Argument 25 is obviously difficult to explain.

The offer has three disadvantages (column 6) as can be seen from the higher grades in column 4 than column 3—among these one is very important (delivery, number 18). The total of disadvantages is −10, and compensating elements of at least equal importance have to be found. Column 7 shows that this is possible: the five real advantages total 11 points, i.e. one 'over-value'.

Calculating the compensating arguments

Each argument which rates plus 1 (difference between columns 3 and 4) over and above seven is a compensating argument worth one point. Also, all sales arguments (column 3) which rate 7 are compensating arguments, providing the customer's needs (column 4) also grade seven (i.e. the minimum we have established for this analysis. The following points are given these arguments: 7=1 point, 8=2 points, 9=3 points, 10=4 points. The first argument therefore gets one point 'over-value' due to the positive difference between columns 3 and 4 plus 2 points according to the above rule (8=2). Column 8 shows the salesman's analysis of a competitive

The List	The Columns									
	1	2	3	4	5	6	7	8	9	10
1 *Quality*: (*a*) of the article; (*b*) of the production; (*c*) of the workmanship; (*d*) of the finished product (in the case of manufactured goods when the article concerned is the main part); (*e*) with respect to construction — conformity with measurements, tolerances, specifications and special requirements.	√	√	8	7	√		+1 +2	8		
2. *Utility*: suitability for purpose.	√		7	9		−2		8		−1
3. *Design* of the article: shape, appearance, modernity, prestige value.	√		2	2				4		−2
4 *Price of the article*: (*a*) regarded as an expense; in relation to (*b*) offers of competitors; (*c*) earning capacity; (*d*) what the customer is prepared to pay; (*e*) what the customer can afford; (*f*) other considerations.	√	√	5	8		−3		4	+1	
5 (*a*) *Discount*; (*b*) *Payment conditions* (credit, instalment terms).	√		2	4				2		
6 *Trade-in or exchange* possibilities (for instance in the case of machinery).										
7 *Prestige* and reputation (of the firm, the salesman, the goods).										
8 (*a*) *Timeliness* of the offer of the article (seasonableness, unlimited supply); (*b*) special attraction.										
9 *Effectiveness*: (*a*) performance; (*b*) practical advantages (possibilty of new or extended production, increased manufacturing efficiency, etc.).	√	√	8	8	√		+2	8		

The List	The Columns									
	1	2	3	4	5	6	7	8	9	10
10 *Economy*: (*a*) money; (*b*) in consumption; (*c*) time; (*d*) energy; (*e*) upkeep; (*f*) labor; (*g*) inspection.	√	√	6	5				6		
11 *Increase of profit*: clear profit on buying.	√		5	3				3	+2	
12 *Greater* and better *selling possibilities* for the customer's goods: (*a*) higher selling value (better value for money, lower price); (*b*) new selling arguments; (*c*) sales to new categories of customers; (*d*) increased sales per customer or per sale; (*e*) new possibilities of use or adoption; (*f*) supporting advertising or other means of sales promotion.	√		6	6				6		
13 *Simplicity in use*: (*a*) easier (automatic running of the machine); (*b*) easily understood instructions for use; (*c*) more easily handled.	√		3	4				2	+1	
14 *Strength*: (*a*) robustness; (*b*) resistance to vibration; (*c*) resistance to shock; (*d*) stability; (*e*) resistance to heat, etc.	√		4	1				4		
15 *Durability*: length of life.	√	√	7	5				6	+1	
16 *Lightness*.										
17 *Space saving*: (*a*) ease of storage; (*b*) elasticity, bendability or collapsibility; (*c*) portability.										
18 *Delivery*: (*a*) quick delivery; (*b*) accessibility (geographical position, means of communica-	√		2	7		−5		3		−1

The List	The Columns									
	1	2	3	4	5	6	7	8	9	10
tion); (c) capacity, large stocks, articles in stock; (d) large selection.										
19 *Modernisation of customer's (mechanical) equipment*: (a) need for improvement; (b) need for replacement; (c) need for supplementation (greater number).	√		5	3				5		
20 *Reliability — safety*: (reduced risk) (a) for the purchaser; (b) for the purchaser's employees; (c) for the customers of the purchaser; (d) prevention of claims; (e) lower insurance premiums; (f) reduced risk of accident; (g) reliability of the supplier.	√	√	9	9	√		+3	7	+2	
21 *Quite running*: (reduction of noise and vibration).										
22 *Greater cleanliness* for the customer, the employees of the customer, the customer's factory and his product.										
23 (easier, cheaper, quicker) *Serice* (possibility of obtaining replacements, supervision, upkeep, inspection, repairs, technical information, training, instructions for use and maintenance etc.) — sales support — technical or other kind of collaboration over the solution of problems (research).	√	√	4	3				2	+2	
24 *Exchange business* or other forms of reciprocal selling.										

| | | The Columns | | | | | | | | |
The List	1	2	3	4	5	6	7	8	9	10
25 *Monopoly* (*a*) natural (source of materials); (*b*) temporary; (*c*) by patent; (*d*) exclusive agency rights; (*e*) selling cartels etc.; (*f*) pioneer position; (*g*) other unique characteristics — dependence of the customer on the deliverer.	√		7	7	√		+1	4	+3	
26 *Guarantees*—right of return.										
27 *Range of use and adaptability* (makes other purchases unnecessary—two articles in one).	√	√	5	5				5		
28 *Possibilities of resale* (possibility of disposing of the article without loss) —*investment* (the article is stable or increases in value).	√		7	7	√		+1	5	+2	
29 *Simplicity of purchase.* The order is facilitated through old association and tried and tested routine of order and despatch. Can be ordered by 'phone; salesman looks after all details, licences and so on.	√	√	5	2				5		
30 Other advantages.										
Total	20	9	107	105	5	−10	+10	97	+14	−4
									+10	

offer. He should only use this and the competitive sales technique (columns 8—10) if he is in direct competition. The analysis proves that the competitor's offer is worth much less than his own and does not suit the customer's needs.

In the analysis of a competitive offer, always be careful not to overestimate your own and underestimate the competitor's proposal.

You use the whole list, i.e. even less important arguments can play an important role if the customer has to choose between the advantages and disadvantages of two offers (therefore, in this case, include argument 23).

Column 10 shows the disadvantages of your own offer compared with your competitor's.

Once more, let me remind you that it is not the salesman's job to compare his proposal with another one (except if he is asked to). But he must know which arguments to use and which to avoid.

Study this analysis carefully. It may seem a bit difficult at first, but it is worth your trouble. In your actual sales activity, the use of this analysis requires something more than arithmetic. Advantages and disadvantages may concern more or less important matters. It may be difficult to use some of the arguments, and others may be hard to grade. The values can differ from one client to another, which would make it necessary to establish a new analysis.

This Sales Talk Analysis should be combined with a similar analysis of primary appeals (Chapters 1 and 2). Selling also to the (personal) primary appeals is certainly more effective than using secondary appeals only. Once you understand the method of this analysis, you should not encounter any great difficulty in extending it in such a way.

Maybe you will object that it is difficult in the daily sales activity to remember exactly which arguments to use in each conversation. But there is good help against forgetfulness: make notes! Put your notes on the desk during your sales call and explain to your customer that you have noted some points of interest to him. This will even increase the effect of your arguments. In this connection, study once more the Sales Plan in Chapter 11 and the check list on page 215.

What and how?

Now you have discovered the 'what'—decide on the 'how'. The right argument must also be well presented. The recommendations contained in this chapter ought to give you a good starting point.

Creative selling is planned selling. It demands minute analysis of what to say and how to say it. What seem to be petty details of choosing one selling point or dropping another, changing a few words in a sentence, altering the tone of a sales talk slightly, may mean a successful sale instead of a failure. Understanding these psychological facts saves you from becoming another hungry salesman.

The appeal area is the fourteenth area of creative selling, where sales are made and sales are lost.

NINETEEN

The conference selling area: How to sell to groups and committees

Can you answer these four questions?

1 Where lie the advantages and disadvantages of meeting with several people simultaneously?
2 What is 'role expectations'?
3 Is it of particular use to the salesman to know something about the technique of Conference leadership?
4 What advantages are there in a 'shirt-sleeve' get-together compared with a more formal meeting?

Can you solve the following five problems?

1 'The idea of group discussions may be quite interesting' admits one experienced salesman. 'But my case is different. My customers are buyers of big industrial companies. To try and contact other gentlemen in their enterprise already annoys them. As long as it is possible, I'd rather talk to one person at a time, which ought to be much easier than meeting a group.' In which respect is he right? Where is he wrong? What are the advantages of a group discussion?
2 Engineer Kohler has successfully worked his way through to the two foremen of a textile company, to whom he is trying to sell a new dye. Usually, this is where the resistance to the introduction of a novelty lies. After some tests he has been able to convince the two

men of the advantages of a change. The buyer, who takes a benevolent neutral position, calls a meeting to make the decision and invites, apart from the two foremen, the two Technical Managers and the laboratory supervisor. The salesman discussed their role with the foremen, and they promised to show a favourable attitude. But to his surprise they are extremely reserved, almost intimidated, and of no help. Can you explain why?

3 'How about a little break?' suggests Mr Moon, Manager of the Technical Department of a Chemical industry, who accompanied the salesman to a customer. The client's Commercial and Technical Managers, each with two assistants, take part in the meeting. Mr Moon and the salesman are seated at the head of the table. Everybody is grateful for Mr Moon's suggestion. The latter, a skilled negotiator, takes the two assistants by the arm and leads them to the salesman. He starts a general conversation and then retires to smoke a cigar in the Technical Manager's company. When the meeting is resumed, he takes a seat between the Technical Manager and his assistants and leaves the salesman alone at the head of the table. What is he trying to do? And what would you have done if you were the salesman?

4 'I'll call the gentlemen to the meeting room' the Sales Manager suggests. 'Then you try to convince them to take your tools along when they make sales calls in repair shops!' — 'How many salesmen are there?' asks salesman Brown. 'Eight.' — Couldn't we meet here? Would be easier, wouldn't it?' The Sales Manager shrugs his shoulders. 'If you like… But the meeting room is freshly decorated and very comfortable, with lots of space and a big table.' Mr Brown insists tactfully. After the successful meeting, the Sales Manager asks Brown for the reason of his choice of the locale. He is impressed by Brown's argument: 'There you're right. I hadn't thought of that!' How about you?

5 Salesman Coin is nervous. He is to give a sales talk for the personnel of a big retail store. He has prepared his speech for weeks, but he feels uneasy about it. Yet, it goes well. At the end, he asks participants for their comments or questions. Nobody says a word, and so the store owner closes the meeting with a word of thanks. Mr Coin tells his friend, another salesman, of this experience. 'I'd never have given a speech. You don't get any feed-back. You can do that much simpler, with less effort.' — 'What is feed-back? And how can you do it?'

Could you have answered these questions? Which method do you prefer?

The problem

Why Conference Selling? The classical dialogue sales procedure of one salesman facing one customer at a time, is becoming more and more obsolete in many fields. Increasingly more common is the situation where the salesman has to approach several people in one company who all assume a direct or indirect buying function. Parallel to this development, also the sales side is being more frequently represented by more than one salesman, whose efforts are backed up by technicians or executives.

Thus the salesman finds himself quite often in a situation where he has to meet with a group of buyers at one and the same occasion — although he may prefer to ignore this sales situation and meet his prospective buyers one by one or even restrict his contacts to just one of the group (for instance the official purchasing agent or the shop owner). This is quite understandable, though not pardonable. It is so much easier to deal with one person, or at least one person at a time, but if his results are meagre, this is not much of a consolation.

The salesman's dilemma

The psychological reason for the weak position the salesman himself fears to become involved in when facing several buyers, is of course the isolation (one against several), the lack of feed-back (there is little response from the group when he speaks), and the constant risk of becoming subjected to a cross-examination with complete loss of initiative (he either makes a speech and nobody says a word or the group will just ask questions and expect him to stick to answering these). This wholly unfavourable psychological setting must be changed by the salesman, if he wants to control the meeting and sell actively.

Strategy

His strategy must be to do everything to change the formal meeting atmosphere (with symbols such as formal seating, a chairman, parliamentary procedure, directive approach, speeches, etc).

In order to do that, he must seek every means to integrate himself with the group, so as to annihilate the picture of one salesman against a group of buyers. The outsider must become one of the insiders, and as far as possible their leader.

It is necessary to analyse the types of meetings that a salesman has to face or may have to bring about intentionally. Psychologically speaking there are four main ones:

Four types of meetings

1 The *sales meeting* in its most obvious form, where the salesman sells. Everybody expects the salesman to present his case and do his best to convince the buyers. They will accept their 'role' and do their best not to be influenced. This is the meeting which allows you least of all to integrate the group.

2 The *investigation meeting*. The salesman does not sell, but endeavours to join the group in searching, finding and presenting problems, needs, facts, conditions. There are no solutions offered (as yet), no selling effort felt and therefore group resistance is greatly reduced. This situation arises currently for instance in technical selling.

3 The *problem-solving meeting*. A problem, need or desire has been recognised and requires a solution. Various alternatives for a solution are discussed with the help of the salesman (or his technical team-mate for that matter), or the salesman offers himself a solution through directive or non-directive approach. Here, too, you are not noted a 'salesman.'

4 The *co-ordination meeting*. Either after having found a general solution as a consequence of the type 2 and 3 meetings, or quite independently, the salesman helps to work out integrating details of the solution, to eliminate conflicts (for instance between various departments), or to find a common denominator that takes into account the interests of those concerned. When internal discussions have reached a blind alley, the salesman becomes more of a saviour than a persuader.

It stands to reason that type 2, 3 and 4 are meetings which much more readily provide for the strategical objective recommended previously. The salesman will not be felt as a salesman, buying resistance will consequently be reduced, and the real influence of the salesman on the group considerably increased.

Therefore, do everything to avoid the type 1 meeting. This is done by developing it into the other types, which offer the strategical objective aimed for.

Tactics preparation

How should you proceed: 1, in the *planning* and *preparation*; 2, in the *execution* phase?

1 *The planning phase* (the importance of which is paramount for a successful outcome) :

(a) the *objective* part. The first step is a *realistic* appraisal of what result you want to reach by means of the meeting and what result you can reach. What are the arguments and appeals that will help you reach this goal, and how are they to be used?

What are the *key questions* to be prepared in advance that will be your main 'arms' to influence and change the type of the meeting, to integrate yourself into the group and to some extent become its leader?

What display material should be prepared and used?

(b) The *subjective* part of the preparation is just as important as it deals with analysing the participants of the meeting.

Who will take part?
And—not to be ignored—who could be influenced to participate or to stay away?
What do these men think?
What do they know?
What do they expect?
Who is likely to be an ally of the salesman?
Who an opponent?
Who neutral or indifferent?
How can these men be influenced or guided?

Remember that if you use visual or audio-visual aids, other participants can be influenced to take part who do not want to miss the 'show'.

Role expectation

In short, the salesman must analyse the *attitude(s)*, *knowledge* and *role expectations* he will meet. Every participant expects by virtue of status, position, personality etc. to play a certain part at the meeting, and it is most important to be aware of these role expectations and use the information accordingly.

Pre-meeting contacts

(c) In between the preparation and execution stages lies the important creation of *individual contacts* before the meeting. Much of the influencing attitudes that can be achieved is only possible by creating individual contacts before the meeting. It often decides the entire success of the sale to be made. Many situations in a meeting, which could not be foreseen, can only be controlled to a certain degree through these individual personal contacts. Tactics to be decided are:

Who is to be influenced?

How?

By whom (not necessarily by the salesman)?

Who can help?

What investigations, research or just conversations can lay the basis of a successful conference selling method?

Other questions in this connection concern the highly important choice and arrangement of the *meeting place.*

Where will it be?

Who is most at home in that setting?

Who won't open his mouth in that room, friend or fiend?

Can it be transferred to some other place?

Is there a reason to use the selling company?

What seating order will be applied?

How can that be influenced?

What requisites can be introduced to transform the meeting into an informal, 'shirt-sleeve' gathering, making it easier for the salesman to integrate?

Execution

2 *The Execution of the Conference.*

(a) 'Taking in' the Participants.

The execution of the salesman's role at the conference will largely follow the tactics established by the preparation. There is however one additional factor to be taken into consideration:

The relative importance of each participant. This aspect should be left neither to guesswork nor to improvisation. The following will help in getting a more exact appraisal of this factor and establish the *Importance* as reflected by the person's *prestige, knowledge of the subject matter, meeting personality* (a combination of general personality, meeting routine, normal meeting behaviour), *role expectation, authority* (formal position, competence, power of decision).

Participation

(b) Directing the meeting.
You will become accepted as an insider if you act as an *investigator, problem-solver* and *co-ordinator,* and stick to the various techniques explained before.

During the meeting itself your main method to gain and keep the initiative is *questions.* There are at least two dozen question techniques familiar to sales trainers that will help to direct the meeting, distribute roles, dose reactions, active participation, exclude and include members of the group, stress a sales point, bring out or disarm objections, neutralise conflicts, demonstrate empathy and knowledge, etc.

Apart from that the salesman will have to learn common conference techniques to forestall objections, summarise and stress part decisions reached, push forward for action, plan for follow-up steps to ensure results gained, break up proceedings, introduce new material, stimulate interest and gain acceptance.

In many fields of selling, the progressive salesman has to learn how to sell in a conference. He must overcome his natural reluctance of facing, often single-handed, a group of people, where he cannot use the traditional dialogue technique. Some of the methods to do this successfully have been explained here. He should no longer passively accept the frustrating role of an outsider subjected to questioning and examination by the inside group, but actively change the psychological setting of the conference so as to provide a fertile basis for a successful persuasion and selling.

The principles explained here will apply to an ever-increasing range of selling (don't forget their application in selling to dealers and their sales staff). To make them work effectively, however, the salesman must additionally get some training in public speaking and conference techniques, and acquire basic knowledge in communications and group psychology.

Learn all you can about selling to groups. It will become increasingly important.

The Conference selling area is the fifteenth area of creative selling, where sales are made and sales are lost.

TWENTY

The customer relations area : The customer is not always right, but complaints can offer sales opportunities

Can you answer these four questions?

1 When dealing with complaints, is there a better principle than the proposition that 'the customer is always right'?
2 To what extent can prestige motives influence complaints?
3 What dangers are inherent in complaints that are not asserted, and what can be done to combat them?
4 What is meant by the advice that salesmen should regard claims from the customer's viewpoint?

Can you solve the following five problems?

1 'We regret that our supplier has rejected your claim,' a jobber writes to a retailer. 'We presented the matter as you reported it to us, but we are told that the facts as reported offer no evidence that the difficulties are the consequence of defective material or faulty manufacture. Please be sure we understand your views in this matter, and we hope you feel that we have done all that we can do.' 'But the retailer does not feel anything of the sort and insists that the wholesaler owes him an adjustment of his claim without regard for the manufacturer's responsibility. Is he right?
2 'If we begin paying off on unjustified faulty-goods claims just to keep our customers,' a comptroller insists, 'we would be in the

position of acknowledging that a high proportion of our products are defective. I just don't see how we can do that.' Comptrollers and treasurers feel deep conviction in such matters, and object to urgings from the sales departments that their firms should be more ready to concede on complaints. The opposing views are seldom reconciled, though one or the other usually prevails. Which is right?

3 'You're a lousy outfit to do business with,' a customer protests over the telephone. 'You're two months late on that order, and on top of that you short-shipped. If I don't get the rest of it by tomorrow, don't send it—and get ready to take back the stuff I got today, because it will go back, collect. I'll do business with somebody else! And keep your alibis to yourselves—I've heard too many of them!' Lawrence Simpson, the salesman who has to sit and take this tirade, feels certain that these are empty threats. He knows the customer would not get delivery from another supplier for weeks and that he would have to pay higher prices for anything ordered now. As much in the customer's interest as to save the order, Simpson tries to explain tactfully how seriously the customer would injure himself by cancelling and returning. To Simpson's horror the customer blows up completely, carries out his threat, and cancels the order. After a little mild self-criticism, Simpson tries to shrug it off on the theory that nothing could have pleased the customer, that 'the guy was just plain crazy.' But the theory isn't entirely satisfying, and the order is lost.

4 Sherman Priddy handles all the customer complaints that come into his firm. Some come to him through channels in the firm; some are made by customers in person. Since he must refer them to other people, Priddy saves himself work by making several copies of the in-person complaints as they are made to him. The printed form he devises contains a great deal of detail, and Priddy must ask his complainants to proceed slowly, to supply a great deal of information, sometimes to repeat an entire series of statements. He has weeks of persistent uneasiness for fear this procedure will irritate the complainants still further—instead, however, he finds that it facilitates quiet settlements. How can this unexpected result be explained? Would you recommend a similar approach to your customer's complaints?

5 Priddy, in pursuing complaints to their sources, finds that some people in his firm question the value of his work. 'Everybody learns sooner or later that we've got one man giving his whole time to complaints—so they complain to him, and too much altogether. And

a lot of them have the idea that we're sloppy operators if we need one man's whole time to handle complaints. We'd have a lot fewer complaints if we didn't have a specialist to handle them.' Is this view-point correct?

Is the customer always right?

For the salesman caught in the middle, however, no slogan has a more painful sound than 'The customer is always right.' Salesmen know, and know well, that customers are often wrong. They don't like to tell a man submissively that of course he's right when they know he is wrong. Should they do so? In their own interests as salesmen, they often should, because complaints can open up many immediate and future chances to make new sales. But salesmen get fed up every once in a while, turn on a complaining customer, and gleefully prove that he is wrong, wrong, *wrong*! They are acting on a natural enough impulse. But the salesman who acts on it too often wrecks himself and his company.

Why feel yourself accused?

A salesman is often antagonistic towards claims because the complaints seem to reflect on the salesman. When a man feels personally reproached, when he interprets a complaint as a criticism of himself and his work, he wants to defend himself. If he can choke off the complaint immediately, it may never get to his boss. If he can prove the complaint is groundless, he hopes, it will deliver him from the imputation of having made a mistake or worse.

Since all salesmen tend to feel this way, smart sales managers and top managements make affirmative efforts to change their feeling. They try to establish the viewpoint that complaints, properly handled, are not major tragedies. When this viewpoint is established, the climate is 'unloaded' and salesmen get a new perspective. They get over their resentment at 'The customer is always right' and pay attention to the question, 'Is it worth while to let this customer be right?' Sometimes, they will admit, the customer obviously *is* right; then there is no question of 'letting.' In practice, however, the matter is rarely so simple—the problem is, 'Is he more right or less right?'

Letting the customer be right

But the problem is simplified when the emotion arousing question is replaced by two questions: (1) 'What do we *do* about the complaint?' and (2) 'Is it worth while to let this customer be right?'

The answer to the first question comes from the answer to the second. The salesman considers what advantage will come to the firm if he treats the complaint as correct. He can surmise with some confidence what will be the consequences of (*a*) accepting the complaint, or (*b*) rejecting it. If he rejects it, the firm may lose the customer, and other customers with him—his friends, and even prospects who get his view of the firm that rejected his complaint. Customers who feel insulted over unfair treatment display their disappointment publicly and love to tell their stories (the injured prestige, the hurt ego). They seldom credit the rejecting company with any good intentions.

When anyone takes away his business in protest about a rejected complaint, your company is hurt. It is really hurt if the customer is a large-scale buyer and the claim represents only a fraction of his year's purchases. Does it make sense in such a situation to stand on some abstract view and lose the customer? 'Is it worth while to let the customer be right?' Probably it is.

If the claimant is a big new customer, the firm has probably invested much time, money, and attention to make a customer of him. 'Is it worth while to let this customer be right?' Again, probably it is. If you keep the customers you have a chance to recover the cost of adjusting the complaint. Perhaps the customer is at fault—perhaps, being a new customer, he has misused the unfamiliar article he bought from you. If you reject the complaint, then as far as he is concerned, your article is no good; if you adjust it, you gain the chance to help him use the article correctly and understand its merits. Which, then, is the better decision?

Is it good business for a company to get itself the reputation of being stingy, or not standing behind its merchandise and its offers in the only way that means anything to a customer? To a customer, standing behind your offers means : adjusting complaints without quibbling; taking the customer's word without long, searching, and insulting investigations. Following this practice brings a company prestige among its customers and also discharges the obligation to serve the customers.

Generosity pays

As a general rule, a company serves its own interest by being generous about claims. People like to talk about those who have treated them well; countless records of difficult complaints confirm this point (ánd the opposite one stated a few paragraphs above). Generosity about claims is like a good glue—the customer gets stuck in it, and the glued piece is stronger after the repair than before the break. The contact between customer and supplier has a better and firmer basis after a complaint has been skilfully and generously handled. The generosity, moreover, is rarely so costly as might at first be feared. You seldom have to credit a customer with more than a part of the money involved in a transaction. And the customer is to give a credit memorandum to apply against future orders, not to take cash 'out of the till' and hand it over. The future orders run to far more dollars than the credit memorandum.

The complaint from the customer's viewpoint

Salesmen suspect many of their customers of using fault-finding as a tactic to gain unwarranted concessions. They suspect other customers of becoming agitated about minor incidentals. An umpire looking at the matter objectively, might agree with the salesman. But umpires place no orders; it is customers who give a salesman orders. And the customer looks at complaint matters subjectively—from his own viewpoint.

A customer, as the salesman should know, can experience a vast quantity of trouble and difficulty as the consequence of small causes. A faulty lot of parts, even a single faulty part, can stop a whole assembly line. A delivery a half day late can make a shop shut down for the shift at lunch time (often paying a full shift's wages for a half shift's production). An impure chemical can ruin a batch of expensive products. When one of these things has played the devil with a customer's operation, he can really blow his top at you if you respond to his complaint with an injured, 'We've never had this complaint before.' So what? He can get worse than excited if you ask him, 'Why get excited over a little thing like that?' He *could* tell you why, but you have made him too mad to tell it coherently. So he tells you off—fervently.

The time when trouble happens can make a big and understandable difference in your customer's subjective attitude. If a screw

shears and stops a machine at eleven-thirty in the morning, he calls
your emergency man, the machine is running again before twelve-
thirty, and he knows he got quick service. If it shears at eleven-
thirty at night while your plant is closed and you don't answer your
home phone, he is likely to feel very unhappy when he finally gets
you at eight-thirty next morning.

Auto dealers and garage men know this last situation intimately.
They get a floor of bitter complaints on Monday mornings. People
blame the garage man when their cars don't run at any time of the
week—they get good and sore at him when the car breaks down in
the country on a Sunday afternoon and they can't get even an
emergency repair.

To handle a complaint skilfully and with any satisfaction to the
customer, a salesman must see the matter as his customer sees it.
Being a salesman, he should know his customer's point of view in
any case. Seeing a complaint from the customer's point of view, the
salesman can readily comprehend its significance and importance to
him, can understand the emotional attitude of the customer, and
can make the customer more comfortable. Often the chief reason for
a customer's truculence is his fear that people will pay no attention
to him unless he is truculent. When he gets honest and understanding attention, knows that a serious matter is being taken seriously,
he is likely to calm down immediately. If, on the contrary, you
answer him with some 'soothing' words like 'It can't be that bad,'
you may discover that it can be worse—for you and for your firm.

The unjustified complainant

Some complaints are touched off by accumulated bad temper,
depression, nervous irritation, and other emotional tensions—they
have very little to do with the article on which they alight. Dealing
with this kind of complaint requires emotional stability of the salesman, the strength to help the customer regain his inner balance.
When the customer has been made comfortable, as by a friendly
answer to a nasty remark, the complaint sometimes vanishes into
nothing, entirely forgotten. When you hear a complaint, therefore,
that seems unduly bitter with little ground, you cannot lose by
assuming that the trouble is in the customer's emotions; if you relax
his emotions, even a valid complaint will be easier to handle.

Sometimes a complaint seems unjustified by facts and unexplain-
able as a mere emotional symptom. The cause of such a complaint

is hard to trace. You may find, in these cases, that the customer's dissatisfaction is not with the merits of the article but with the fact that he should not have bought it. Perhaps it does not fit his needs : perhaps he simply does not like it. Men close to a product often cannot believe that a customer 'just doesn't like it.' He may have bought the article under high-pressure selling, and regret it. He may have been given faulty instruction in how to use it. The salesman may have sold him an article that isn't quite right. In any event, you can be sure that the customer won't be satisfied with the article he 'just doesn't like,' no matter how good it may be. So the test question again is, 'Is it worth while to let his customer be right?' a liberal policy in connection with these complaints helps the salesman sell, increases buying desires and stimulates impulsive purchases. These impulsive purchases are likely to be so profitable that a seller can afford to be generous in adjusting complaints about them.

Exorbitant claims

When a complaining customer asserts a claim for an unreasonable amount of money, it is easy and natural to suspect that the whole claim is a fraud and reject the complaint without much consideration. However, even when the amount is exorbitant the complaint may be justified. Experienced people in business and industry know that such exorbitant claims can be reduced to a reasonable level by patient negotiation. They resist the temptation either to deny the basic validity of the complaint or to challenge the amount of the claim immediately and arbitrarily.

The seller's suspicion about the motive behind a complaint may grow out of an innately distrustful personality, or a tendency to hurry to conclusions before the evidence is complete. Experienced business people find again and again that complaints turn out to be justified, or at least made in good faith, which at the beginning appeared to be calculated swindles. Sometimes the unfounded complaint or the exorbitant claim arises out of ignorance rather than dishonesty. You should never, therefore, jump to conclusions. Think first of the occasion when your own motives have been unjustly questioned. Remember that a combination of improbabilities, the very combination that gives rise to a complaint, can also make it sound incredible (it is *improbable* that your article has a defect that passed inspectors; it is *improbable* that it could be damaged in shipment; it is *improbable* that the order was taken with the wrong specifications; and yet the customer may be right!) *Give the customer the benefit of the doubt.* Trust him rather than suspect him, agree with him rather than insult him.

Customers do, often, claim more than is justified. They find one detail wrong and feel such disappointment and displeasure that they say the whole proposition is no good. This one-wrong-all-wrong process is a rule, not an exception, a natural psychological tendency and not a crafty approach to fraud. It is one of the reasons why manufacturers and dealers try so hard to keep small defects out of their merchandise. In dealing with the one-wrong-all-wrong attitude you direct your efforts towards bringing the complaint to the actual point at issue and towards reducing enlargements and digression. Most people will co-operate.

Chronic grumblers do exist, people who deserve the answer 'No' when you ask, 'Is it worth while to let this customer be right?' But these are not numerous. Most people find it so embarrassing to make any complaint that they tend instead to be silent in unsatisfactory situations. They fear wrangles, they dislike being doubted, they don't want to get drawn into time-taking negotiations or into discussions of trivialities—the consequences of complaints in so many cases. If such people feel they must complain, they do so in anticipation of such disagreeable experience that they are oversensitive to the slightest sign of distrust or resistance. Since many complaints arise from this kind of person, you need to display restraint and the utmost care when dealing with claims and complaints.

Do you put yourself in a bad light by recognising complaints?

People who are responsible for seeing that a product is sound and free from defects feel, sometimes, that they are unfairly criticised when an unjustified complaint is not rejected. They may feel that a policy of accepting complaints without protest is equivalent to a policy of acknowledging that the produce is generally faulty (Problem Two). They need not feel so. Accepting a customer's complaint without an argument does not mean agreeing with him on the facts at issue. It means simply not contesting the issue, neither denying nor agreeing there is any fault. All concerned should feel simply that the company wants to make the customer satisfied, that the company takes seriously its obligation to serve its customers. This philosophy should be clearly presented both to the complaining customer and to the conscientious employees. It relieves the employees of resentment and intimates to the customer, in a tactful way, that the concession is not a confession and not a precedent for the future.

When settling complaints which are not wholly justified, it is always recommended to emphasise that the action does not indicate that future complaints of the same kind will be accepted without challenge.

Situations do occur where a claim cannot be accepted without undue loss to the seller, where generosity cannot be the policy, where an invalid complaint must be rejected. These situations can be perceived by putting the test question, 'Is it worth while to let this customer be right?'

But the acceptance of a claim later shown to be unjustified (either the customer's fault or nobody's fault) often brings out the best side of a customer, makes him grateful, leads him to respond by being generous. He may withdraw his claim, or may offer to share the loss.

Prestige complaints

Sometimes a customer feels his standing is at stake with respect to a complaint, that he will be humiliated if the complaint is disallowed. To some temperaments and in some societies, getting one's rights even in small matters is almost a commanding moral duty. Complaint situations of this sort are 'loaded,' and it may be advisable to offer at least a nominal adjustment however unjustified the claim.

Loosely worded guarantees give rise to such situations. The customer and the supplier understand them differently, each feels he has right on his side, and the issue becomes hot. The customer thinks he has been high-pressured, even swindled. Hence the salesman should never let a customer expect more from a guarantee than the guarantee is expected to offer. If the customer does not understand the guarantee, if the salesman suspects that he does not understand it, then the guarantee should be discussed and made clear to the customer before he buys.

A kind of guarantee that causes a great deal of unhappiness is the undertaking to exchange faulty parts for new ones but not to pay for the labour of replacing them. It looks like a bad joke to a customer when he has to pay a labour charge for £10 to get the 'free' replacement of a £1 spring.

A customer feels that he can look to his supplier for satisfaction of complaints: the consumer to the retailer, the retailer to the wholesaler, and so on. A conscientious supplier will share this attitude— the jobber will then take responsibility for the retailer's claim and reimburse himself by presenting it as a claim to the manufacturer. If the buyer must look to a third party for adjustment of claims, he should be given to understand the fact clearly when he buys. Otherwise he has both his original complaint and a secondary complaint of buck passing.

The excited complaint

You can't talk to a man when he's angry.

If only salesmen remembered this rule, many business differences would not amount to anything. Salesman Simpson of Problem Three could well have remembered it. Simpson was right—of course the customer was injuring himself. But because he was angry, it did worse than no good to tell him the truth. He blew up and cancelled the order. He 'taught that—salesman a lesson!' Did the salesman learn it? If he had avoided prolonging the telephone discussion, had asked for permission to call at the customer's office as soon as he could to look into the trouble, he might have achieved several things:

1 He would have conveyed to the customer that he was seeing the complaint as a serious matter and personally doing something about it.

2 He would have paved the way for face-to-face conversation, in which it is always easier to be reasonable than on the telephone.

3 He would have delayed definitive action for a day, with the probability that the customer would have calmed down—time always dilutes fury!—and given himself a chance to work out a possible solution; plus—

4 He would have made a cancellation on the next day impossible, even if the merchandise had not been delivered.

Rejecting complaints

When you must reject a complaint (and sometimes you must) what do you do?

You give your customer a complete and detailed explanation.
You show him documents—original or photostat.

You report your investigation, to show that you have given his complaint full attention—that the rejection is not the outcome of perfunctoriness or haste or ignorance or lack of appreciation of his importance.

You review the investigation with him if he wishes, helping him to get possible insight into what you have done and learned.

You establish as clearly as possible—and that means unchallengeably—the fact that the fault cannot have occurred in your province. You do *not* labour or even state, if you can avoid it, the fault must be his or his employees'; you let him come to this point himself. There may be no *logical* difference between telling him and letting him deduce this conclusion; but there is an important *psychological* difference.

Remember, the human being does not react logically, but psychologically. Show the customer that many important people in your own Company have thoroughly studied his case.

Try to avoid correspondence concerning complaints—particularly if you have to reject them. A personal interview will bring better results—and leave less ill feelings behind. If technical reports have to be forwarded, have them checked by a 'censor'—they often contain dynamite for hurt feelings.

The abusive complainant

Treat an abusive customer with friendliness!

It takes two to make a quarrel, and if your abusive customer can't get an antagonist he can't quarrel. His fire may sputter out, but it is out.

What do you say to the enraged customer? If you take the advice of the claim adjuster for a large automobile firm, the best thing you can say is 'I understand'—putting all the feeling and sympathy you can express into your voice, your attitude, and your facial expression. You can *understand* him on any point. If in addition you can *agree* with him on some partial points, he will quiet down in a little while and you can get on to investigating the facts in the matter, or at least to hearing his version of them in a coherent statement.

If you feel helpless with an angry customer, if you feel you are in danger of losing your own self-control and becoming angry, or if the customer is too excited for any objective conversation, promise him that you will carry out an inquiry and return next day. Then get out—quickly. Above all, do *not* try to calm a man by telling him to be calm. No angry man has ever accepted that advice.

Most angry customers do calm down after they have had a night's sleep. But before your visit, be sure that you do make the inquiry and have something to report, or at least that you have prepared some questions that will show you are trying to deal with the problem. Procrastination is a sure method for fixing the grievance permanently in the customer's mind. You don't have to settle a complaint at the first discussion, but you do want to get some action started. It is important to have the customer know, immediately, that his claim is being studied and not just being shoved aside.

Make notes

A very useful procedure in dealing with complaints, especially those of an irritated or excited customer, is to put his complaint in writing. Take precise notes of his statements. Tell him (and of course, mean it) that these are preliminary and necessary to a thorough inquiry. You create a natural situation for asking the customer many questions that might offend him in any other than a record-taking situation. He sees you writing, and pours out the details that may clarify the matter. As he talks, he may even talk himself out of his anger, either because the talking is a relief or because reciting the facts helps him to realise his complaint is weak. Having to talk slowly as you write, the customer thinks seriously of his statements because he realises you are taking them seriously. And he quietens down—no one can scold at a slow pace. Such was the experience of Sherman Priddy, the complaint specialist, in Problem Four.

Act swiftly

Time may be the most important thing in rectifying a complaint—sometimes every minute of delay hurts the customer and runs up the claim. In such cases, you rectify the harm done as quickly as you can, not waiting to finish an investigation of cause or responsibility.

Even in less urgent situations, delays in attending to a complaint are dangerous. They give rise to additional bad feeling that may remain after the original claim is settled as the customer asked. If you can do nothing more, you can acknowledge receipt of the complaint (it is good to give an in-person complainant a copy of your notes), promise to investigate and report by a certain date, and keep the promise by reporting something specific.

Legal responsibility

If the customer can enforce his claim on you as a legal responsibility, don't wait for him to go to law. If the law is on your side, you may want to use its protection, or may have to. But being legally secure is poor consolation for losing a customer.

You may want to know where you stand under the law. When complaints involve large amounts it is wise to have legal advice. But it may be well to keep legal resources in reserve and deal with the complaints on a mutual-advantage business basis.

Make complaints easy for the customer

Yes! Make it easy for the customer to lodge complaints!

The object of this policy is not to encourage complaining but to avoid the most dangerous kind of complaint—the one never asserted, the one you never get a chance to rectify. You really suffer when a customer does not approach you with his complaint, looks for a new supplier, and tells his friends of his unsatisfactory experience.

If your customer wishes to complain, it is best for you and for him that he should complain to you and not to others. They can't remedy his complaint; you can. If you know of the complaint, you can clear the matter up if you think the claim is justified or a concession is expedient. Thus an arrangement of the kind described in Problem Five creates a feeling in customers that they can get attention to complaints, that someone has the duty to help them with their difficulties. Then they are less likely to grumble to outsiders. The company reduces the danger of unexpressed dissatisfactions. In this climate, complaints do not arise so readily as they would otherwise, and the complaints that do arise are not loaded with resentment.

The same line of thinking should guide you in dealing with a customer who has for some reason turned from you to another supplier. If he did this because he felt neglected, felt that you had not given him the proper treatment over a (perhaps unexpressed) complaint. You should give it attention as a complaint, not just let an old customer go. Write him a letter, phone him, or call at his office, and make it easy for him to give you his complaint in a form that you can deal with and perhaps adjust to his satisfaction. Such a step shows the customer that you value his business and want to remedy his complaint. Amazingly, salesmen and suppliers often do not take this step.

The customer in such a situation usually does not mind telling you what the trouble is. It may come out easier because it is in a sense past and over. If you can't use the information to win him back you can still use it to trace troubles in your organisation and prevent another customer from having the same trouble. In this way, as in many others, you make a complaint the channel towards increased sales.

Prevent future complaints

You should always regard a complaint as a general problem in addition to seeing it as a specific difficulty to be remedied. When you have dealt with the individual complaint, apply what you have learned to the general relation between your firm and other customers—prevent them from having the same complaint. Settling complaints one at a time and only one at a time is like taking aspirins for every headache and not seeking the reason why you have so many headaches.

Justified complaints

Little has been said in this discussion about justified *claims*—quite simply because there is nothing much to be said about them. You remedy them cordially and without delay, you apologise, and you take care that they do not arise again. And since you deal tactfully, generously, and sympathetically with complaints that may be or are unjustified, you surely deal tactfully, generously and sympathetically with the clearly justified complaints. Give assurance that there will be no recurrence of the fact, and offer to pay for direct or indirect costs connected with the error.

Eighteen rules for dealing with complaints

Here is a summary of the most important principles on the treatment of claims and complaints.

1 The customer is *not* always right but it is often worth while to let him be right.

2 Generosity usually pays for itself; it can lead immediately to further business.

3 Complaints are, within certain limits, a natural business phenomena and are not tragic or disgraceful. The salesman should not, therefore, feel personally guilty, or feel required to defend himself.

4 To be able to judge a complaint and the customer's reaction, the salesman must endeavour to see the claim as the customer sees it, subjectively, from the customer's point of view. It does not matter that the objective source of the complaint may be a petty detail.

5 Customers are rarely in emotional equilibrium when they are presenting complaints—they are likely to be supersensitive to questions and to any uncordial attitudes.

6 Complaints based on prestige feelings and the need for self-assertion demand special care.

7 Complaints need not always be concerned with the quantity or quality of the goods but may be based on their use and application.

8 Don't jump to conclusions against the honesty of a complaining customer. Until or unless you can prove he has spoken untruthfully, give him the benefit of the doubt. He can be acting in entire good faith even when he is entirely wrong.

9 Your generosity in doubtful claims need not mean that you accept the blame or agree to a precedent.

10 You can sometimes satisfy customers by paying part of a claim or by sharing the costs of remedying a complaint.

11 Before resisting a claim, find out how much it amounts to. This may be less than you thought at first.

12 If you reject a claim, give good and plentiful reasons, and give them tactfully.

13 Don't set up complaints by giving loosely worded or evasive guarantees.

14 Don't try to talk to an angry customer.

15 Always let the customer feel that his complaint is being taken seriously and is being honestly investigated. Keep him informed and avoid delays.

16 Avoid handling complaints by correspondence. You get further and faster in face-to-face contact.

17 Facilitate the lodging of complaints. Try to locate unexpressed dissatisfaction.

18 Obviously justified claims do not demand any special rules. Deal with them quickly and let the customer feel that you are genuinely sorry.

Complaints can lead to increased sales if the causes are properly analysed and if the customers are treated properly with a view to future business. The customer is not always right, but it must pay to let him be right.

The customer relations area is the sixteenth area of creative selling, where sales are made and sales are lost.

Check List 1
20 points for your sales arguments

Do you put forward the right arguments? Here is a list of 20 check
questions. Are you being honest with yourself in the sales points
arising out of the following questions? Test yourself as severely and
critically as you can before answering every question.

This check list, and those following will be a very suitable basis
for you to test whether the most important elements are present in
your sales-talks, and are logically organised. See to it that you yourself make a critical examination and check each point; especially
before important visits to customers (see Chapter 18). Above all,
test your arguments one month after you have read this book.
Unless the book has totally failed to make its point you will have
corrected some part of your work method already.

		Yes	No
1	*Do you use the right facts?* Does your sales talk give the customer just the facts he needs—no more and no fewer?		
2	*Do you support what you say in your sales talk?* Do you offer convincing evidence, in your sales talk, to back up any claims you make for your proposition?		
3	*Is your sales talk the kind your customer can understand?* Are your language and your choice of material fitted to his capacities as to his knowledge? (The words you use, the things you talk about, the way you talk about them, and how fast you talk?)		

		Yes	*No*
4	*Is your sales talk based on sound knowledge of your customer's needs?*		
5	*Do your sales points refer to the customer's needs and to the benefits he will receive from your offer?* Do you sell in terms of what he needs rather than what you have to sell, in terms of benefits to him rather than benefits in general?		
6	*Do you concentrate your sales talk on your few best sales points?* Do you emphasise the strong and convincing features of your offer as the centre of your sales talk?		
7	*Do you draw your customer into your sales talk?* Are your sales points presented as questions and do they guide your customer to the answers you want?		
8	*Do you keep your sales points in order?* Do they follow a clear and logical line from the beginning to the end of your sales talk?		
9	*Are your sales points truthful and believable?* Do you not only hold yourself to true statements but also make them appear true?		
10	*Do you stick to low-pressure methods?* In the things you say and the way you say them, do you take care to avoid generating sales resistance and stubbornness?		
11	*Does your sales talk bring you into real contact with your customer?* Does he reply to your questions? Does he ask any questions or otherwise get into the conversation? Do you fit your talk to him and avoid controversial statements? Do you give him a chance to offer his opinion—and does he offer it?		
12	*Is your sales talk convincing?* Does it display your own conviction? Do you know and show that you know your offer is good for the customer? Does your customer feel your conviction?		
13	*Is your sales talk specific?* Do you avoid superlatives and the kind of statement that can't be proved or disproved?		
14	*Do you present your sales points at the right time in in the sales talk?* Do you know what is the right time for stressing quality, for example?		
15	*Do you keep objections from spoiling your sales talk?*		

		Yes	No
	Do you deal with them in such a manner that you keep the buying process moving smoothly towards the closing stage?		
16	*Does your sales talk get your customer's immediate attention?*		
17	*Does your sales talk arouse the customer's personal interest?* Does it make him aware of how he will benefit from accepting your offer?		
18	*Does your sales talk arouse your customer's desire to buy?* Do you present your points so that he wants to have your product and is convinced that he needs it and should buy it?		
19	*Do you create conviction?* Do you convince the customer that he needs and desires your proposition?		
20	*Does your sales talk end with buying action?* Does it build up to the moment for the buying decison, and is your closing technique effective?		

Use this and the following check lists as a basis to ensure that the most important points are included in your sales talk and that it is well constructed. Judge and check yourself, particularly before visits to important customers.

6   How to Win Customers

The work of the professional salesman demands this attitude to a far greater extent. At the same time he naturally needs to absorb the principle of selling ideas or else he will be unable to produce consistently successful results.

Now, can you answer the four introductory questions and solve the five sales problems?

You don't sell an article—you sell an idea. Every salesman must understand this principle and act accordingly.

The idea area is the first area of creative selling, where sales are made and sales are lost.

Check List 2
30 situations that can undermine your sales success

Put a mark against the most important items, think them through (why is this so?), look for solutions, establish a plan of action and, if suitable, request the assistance of others.

	Correct	Partly Correct	Not Correct
1 My preparation is inefficient—due to lack of either time, concentration, patience or lack of interest			
2 I do not organise my selling activity well enough—I improvise too much			
3 I find all desk-work distasteful—this is probably why I do not have enough notes, documents, data at disposal for first and repeat visits			
4 My day-form changes—sometimes I am in shape—sometimes I feel in advance failures which usually follow			
5 I prefer to do things my own way—I do not like to learn from others and feel restless and bored at sales instructions, training conferences			
6 I am over-sensitive against rulings from above and resist them consciously or unconsciously			

	Correct	Partly Correct	Not Correct
7 I feel that my work is not much appreciated by others. This frustrates me—also the feeling of not getting ahead			
8 Maybe I make too few or too 'easy' visits, especially at times when I am not too successful			
9 I am not too good at obtaining interviews by telephone or by making 'cold' visits, when approaching difficult customers (through receptionists)			
10 I find it awkward to overcome the first difficult minutes of a sales talk and create a proper climate—especially at: (a) first visits (b) repeat visits (c) with negative customers (a) or (b)			
11 During many sales visits I notice that I am lacking a proper plan and consequently the necessary assurance			
12 I do know that the sale only starts when the customer says 'No', but in practical life it suffocates my drive			
13 I find it difficult to start with the admittedly excellent opening to talk about 'problems, needs, desires, goals and interests' of the customer or start with a catch-appeal			
14 I appreciate the value of the so-called 'question technique', but find it much easier to use statements and assumptions—which on the other hand deprives me of the necessary feedback from the customer			
15 'Selling the idea' is more than a slogan to me, but in real life I use probably much too little			
16 I have no problems in overcoming the resistances and objectives, but it often leads to irritation or impatience, either with the customer or with myself			
17 My product knowledge (our own and competitive) leaves considerable room for improvement—also my market knowledge			

	Correct	Partly Correct	Not Correct
18 Probably I talk too much and the customer too little			
19 I make frequent errors when judging customer reactions—I overestimate his interest and approval, rely on half-promises, judge too logically instead of psychologically			
20 Compact price resistance gives me much trouble—I admittedly do not feel at ease when dealing with price in general			
21 Negotiating simultaneously with several people is a heavy handicap to me			
22 My ability to express myself (arguments rhetoric) is open for improvement			
23 It often happens that inside me I find myself agreeing with the customer (and disagreeing with my Company); I do not like to be unpopular or hurt anybody's feelings. Probably this takes away some of my enthusiasm and dynamism			
24 The sales promotion material of my Company (samples, folders, models, advertising, etc.) does not always correspond to my taste; I probably use it too little, as well as all other means of audio-visual presentation (paper and pencil, etc.)			
25 During the closing phase I feel insecure and nervous—my closing technique is certainly open for improvement			
26 There are customers whom I dislike and with whom I just can't get along			
27 Sometimes I am fed up with selling—especially these last weeks			
28 At failures I find too easily plausible explanations that justify my own behaviour			
29 I could certainly make two or three more sales visits a week, perhaps more			
30 Another important mistake I often make is:			

These 30 attitudes can be 30 reasons to restrict your sales success.

Check List 3
Why did I miss the business?

1 Was the offer right? If not, why?
2 What would the customer have gained in giving me the business?
3 Was I able to explain this point early enough, and well enough?
4 Which were his decisive buying resistances and buying motives?
5 Did my sales points match these?
6 Did they follow the principle of 'selling the idea'? Were they supported by proof?
7 Was I properly prepared? With a real plan?
8 Was my opening right?
9 Did I use audio-visual methods?
10 Was there a real conversation with genuine participation of the customer?
11 Did I use intelligent closing appeals and a proper closing approach?
12 Was my behaviour and attitude right? Was the climate good?
13 Did I deal with the proper, competent persons?
14 Did I give up too soon?
15 Which mistakes did I make during the negotiation? What did I, for instance, forget?
16 If I had to do it all over again, what would I do differently?
17 Did I find the real reasons for the refusal?
18 Is there still a chance to change the decision?
19 What does this experience teach me for my future work?
20 What am I going to do about it?

Only a fool believes that he makes no mistakes. The professional salesman recognises them, learns from them, and thus turns failures of the past into successes of the future.

Check List 4
The business that means the most to me

1 Why?
2 Who is your customer? Description of his business, the buyer, his competence to make the sale.
3 What does he want really? Problems, needs (=motives) mentality:
    (a) of the firm
    (b) the buyer
4 Why have things gone wrong up till now? (Obstacles, objections)
    (a) method used up to now
    (b) others not used, why?
5 What can I do? Alternative solutions.
6 Which have been rejected as unsuitable?
7 What support do I need? Who can help me?
8 How do I proceed step by step?
9 Most important sales points for the different phases of the negotiation.
10 Other remarks (observations for personal improvement).

Check List 5
Can you distinguish pro- and anti-sales terms?

Mark the pro-sales terms with a +, the anti-sales terms with — ! There are 16 of each in either column. Can you find them?

capital, investment	expenditure	tested	well-known
costs	economy	weigh up	delay
dispose over a long period	buy over a long period	you will get	we are giving you
change	development	approximately	exactly
duty	capability	produce	show
as a result	as a characteristic quality	needs	desires
burden	responsibility	cheap	reasonable
tomorrow	by return	of great value	expensive
security	no risk involved	agreement	contract
we serve our customers	we attend to our customers	suggest a solution	suggest an improvement
value of product	advantages	training	instruction

guarantee	insurance	favourable	optimal
I	you	conversation	negotiation
delivery time	final delivery date	in our opinion	in our experience
competitors	rivals	because of difficulties with delivery	because of increased demand
you can	you must	demonstrate pay	show settle
		you question the matter	you wonder

Check List 6
25 examples of key phases or deciding factors in sales in several areas

Comments for my work

1 Number of visits
2 Frequency of visits
3 Number of demonstrations
4 Personal relationships
5 Right time to make the visit
6 Level of visit. Contact with top people
7 Visits to customers, together with interested parties
8 Tests, leaving on appro', taking back goods, guarantees
9 Invitations by key people to visit works
10 Sales promotion and putting through deal for the customer
11 References and testimonials
12 Acquiring worthwhile customers
13 Assessment of sales tips
14 Placing the product with the retailer
15 Attitude of sales staff
16 Support by sales managers
17 Number and distribution of follow-ups
18 Delightful customers
19 Exact information about customers' projects and budgets
20 Speed of offer
21 Special offers

22 Adaptability and having solutions
    'made-to-measure'
23 Special selling campaigns
24 Toughness of salesman
25 Working as a group (in pairs, with
    technicians, specialists etc.)

This list is incomplete. It is designed to make you examine the decisive factors for *your* sales and ensure *your* profits. You cannot do everything, so concentrate on the courses which seem to be most successful.

A final word

This book has pursued, above all else, the *one* objective of showing you how to win customers and improve your sales technique in the nineteen essential areas of creative selling. It has attempted to break up the sales process into its component parts. It has tried to lead you to examine your working methods, to be critical of them, and to change some of them.

You yourself can check some of the results with the aid of the various check-lists. Has your selling technique improved in any of the nineteen points?

In addition to this list, the book contains questions, examples, hints, problems and solutions, and other check-lists throughout.

To finish what it has undertaken, this book now puts, in the emphatic final place, a few further points that greatly affect the work of selling.

1 *You must devote a maximum of time to planned selling.* In spheres where sales results depend almost entirely on the number of real contacts (not perfunctory calls) made with customers, this is a compelling necessity. You should plan the week's work in advance and follow your time-table. To avoid wasting time, take into account your customers' geographical distribution, their practices as to interviewing salesmen, and the importance of their business. By doing so you concentrate your time on the most valuable customers, you cut down on your visits to customers who buy very little or who buy in any case, and you can learn through systematic records how much time you spend and should spend with your various customers.

2 *Free yourself from generalisations and wisecracks* that cater to your comfort and not to your sales efficiency. For instance:

Don't be so sure that some days are no good for selling.

Don't be so sure that Monday mornings and Friday afternoons produce no business.

Don't be so sure that seeing too many customers in a day wears you down.

Don't be so sure that you cannot and should not do anything about customers who have once said 'no'.

Don't be so sure that there are hopeless customers who can't and won't understand what is good for them.

Don't be so sure that chance or extraordinary ideas have more to do with making a sale than careful planning.

Don't be so sure that you should avoid selling on rainy days because customers are in a bad humour.

Don't be so sure that the market is saturated and people don't want to buy (the oldest alibi?).

Don't be so sure that your territory is sold up or played out.

Don't be so sure that you are just a hard-luck Joe.

Don't be so sure that customers are becoming more and more sales-resistant.

Don't be so sure that selling is a matter of inspiration.

Don't be so sure that dirty competitors make decent selling impossible.

Don't be so sure that other salesmen have an easier set-up.

Don't be sure you are working too hard.

Don't be so sure that just now times are particularly bad.

Don't be so sure that your business is spoilt by 'dirty' competition.

Don't be so sure that we are always too expensive.

Don't be so sure that competition is more ruthless and more skilful than we are.

Don't be so sure that is not worth planning and preparing, because everything will be different anyhow.

Don't be so sure that our business policy is obsolete.

Don't be so sure that you only get in trouble if you talk to various people in the same enterprise.

Don't be so sure that you cannot learn much from your colleagues, because everybody has to work his own way.

Don't be so sure that it is easier for other salesmen.

Don't be so sure you knew everything all along.

Don't be so sure you should not try harder.

The last *don't* is an important one. The more contacts and the better contacts you make, the better are your chances of selling. Every salesman thinks he is working as hard and as well as he possibly can, whether he is making three bad visits a day or seven good ones, even though other salesmen with the same line and in the same firm are making more good calls and selling more.

3 *Work energetically.* Freeing yourself from comfortable self-deceptions leads you to the next point: Most of us could work harder. We can all visit one more customer every day. We can get up a half-hour earlier. We can see more customers earlier (they may prefer it). We can get in one or two or three visits before the usual calling hours. We can make quick calls on a customer who can't make up his mind, rather than phone him only. Abundant experience has proved that salesmen can do all these things. They have done it when they got bonuses for making more calls per day. They have done it when they could take Friday afternoons off after completing the week's quota (these men made *more* calls in the short week!) There are innumerable ways of stimulating salesmen (and stimulating yourself) to get better results.

Do not consider these remarks as an admonition merely to work harder. Working harder does little good unless you work better. When you work with a plan, you work better. When you look for new ways to simplify your work, you can work with less effort. When you analyse your methods, they will improve.

Set yourself a specific target; enter into competition with yourself and others; learn to find more joy in your work (you do so by increasing your knowledge and thus increasing your success); and learn to find more pleasure in contacts with your customers (they give you your living). Start improving by agreeing that you are not yet perfectly efficient and that you can become more efficient. Learn, and you are bound to improve. This attitude, for which no knowledge or talent can substitute, is the true essential of self-preservation—in the profession of salesmanship more than in any other.

The author wishes you every possible success in your sales career.